Gerard & Kelly

Carré d'Art-Musée d'art contemporain de Nîmes
Mousse Publishing

RUINS

Foreword

Jean-Marc Prevost

1.
Claire Bishop, "Black Box, White Cube, Gray Zone: Dance Exhibitions and Audience Attention," in *Performance Works* (Milan: Mousse Publishing, 2019): 66.

For several years, Carré d'Art has opened its programming and collection to performance and contemporary dance, including exhibitions by Anne Imhof, Emmanuelle Huynh and Jocelyn Cottencin, and Tarik Kiswanson. *A Different Way to Move: Minimalisms, New York, 1960–1980*, evoked the complex relationship between postmodern dance and Minimalism. At first the ephemeral nature of dance promised an escape from the commodification and reification of art. With time things have radically changed; performance has legitimately entered the space of the museum and its collections. It is nonetheless certain that this subject matter, by its presence in the museum, retains a critical stance toward representation. The shifting nature of gesture, continually bound to its context and the time in which it occurs, demands a new way of reading. By bringing performing bodies into the exhibition space, the museum questions its limits, positioning itself as an institution dedicated to the memory of gestures and their transmission. The presence of performance in the museum "reveals a genuine desire—on the part of performers and audiences alike—for experiences that stand as a counterpoint to our lives online: embodied immediacy, shared collective presence, physical proximity, a sense of place, and an internal meditation in the company of others."[1] It is as if, paradoxically, the "white cube" of the museum, long considered a neutral and cold device, has allowed us to reconnect with a certain form of intimacy.

Gerard & Kelly—artists originating in the field of choreography—enter the museum in a manner that is manifestly consistent with the visual arts. *Ruins* is a presentation of video installations, sculptures, site-specific interventions, performance, and works on paper. In a way the exhibition tracks the artists' movement from live body-based experimentations to their representation, which one could already find in Gerard & Kelly's shift from performances to films. The installations throughout the galleries of the museum can be viewed as a *mise en abyme*, where the body of the spectator emerges into the frame of the exhibition space.

For several years, Gerard & Kelly have developed their work around the project *Modern Living*, a series of performances and films in which the artists examine architectural projects that thwart traditional bourgeois and patriarchal usage. They have performed in the Schindler House in West Hollywood, California, and in Philip Johnson's Glass House in Connecticut—homes the architects designed for themselves and their loved ones to house relationships as experimental as their designs. The house becomes the setting for performances in which dancers and spectators learn to live together. In a sense, it is a way of rethinking notions of gender, the couple, and shared intimate space. Schindler designed his house in 1922 for two couples in a sketch of communal living. Johnson designed his, built in 1949 in a forest setting, to shelter life with his partner David Whitney.

A recent production, *Panorama* (2021), was filmed at the Bourse de Commerce, which now houses the Pinault Collection. This building, originally a grain market, was transformed in the nineteenth century into an architecture glorifying commerce and finance. Dating from 1889, the paintings of the rotunda idealize the exchanges between European and American nations as well as with the French colonies of Africa and the East. Three performers—each of different origins, cultures, and training—inhabit Tadao Ando's purified space, one still charged with the history of European imperialism. Their fragile forms manifest as multiple identities to confront the colonial discourse represented in the monumental frieze.

In *Bright Hours* (2022), Gerard & Kelly engage Le Corbusier's Cité Radieuse and the architect's relationship with Josephine Baker, with whom he had an affair in 1929 on a transatlantic crossing from São Paulo to Bordeaux. The film considers how this encounter between a white European architect and a Black American dancer transformed modern architecture.

Gerard & Kelly's *Ruins* makes visible the unknown stories and situations of the architectural icons that surround us. Another little-known history features, fortuitously, in the exhibition project. Thomas Jefferson, ambassador to France from 1785 to 1789 before becoming the third president of the United States, visited Nîmes. He fell in love with the Maison Carrée, a first-century Roman temple still standing today across from the museum. Jefferson took the Maison Carrée as his model for the Capitol building in Richmond, Virginia. Ironically, the Capitol was appropriated by slave-holding states as the seat of the Confederacy from 1861 to 1865. Toward the end of the exhibition the Maison Carrée becomes the background for *State of* (2019), a performance in which three dancers use the American flag, the national anthem, and a pole dance to question symbols of nationalism.

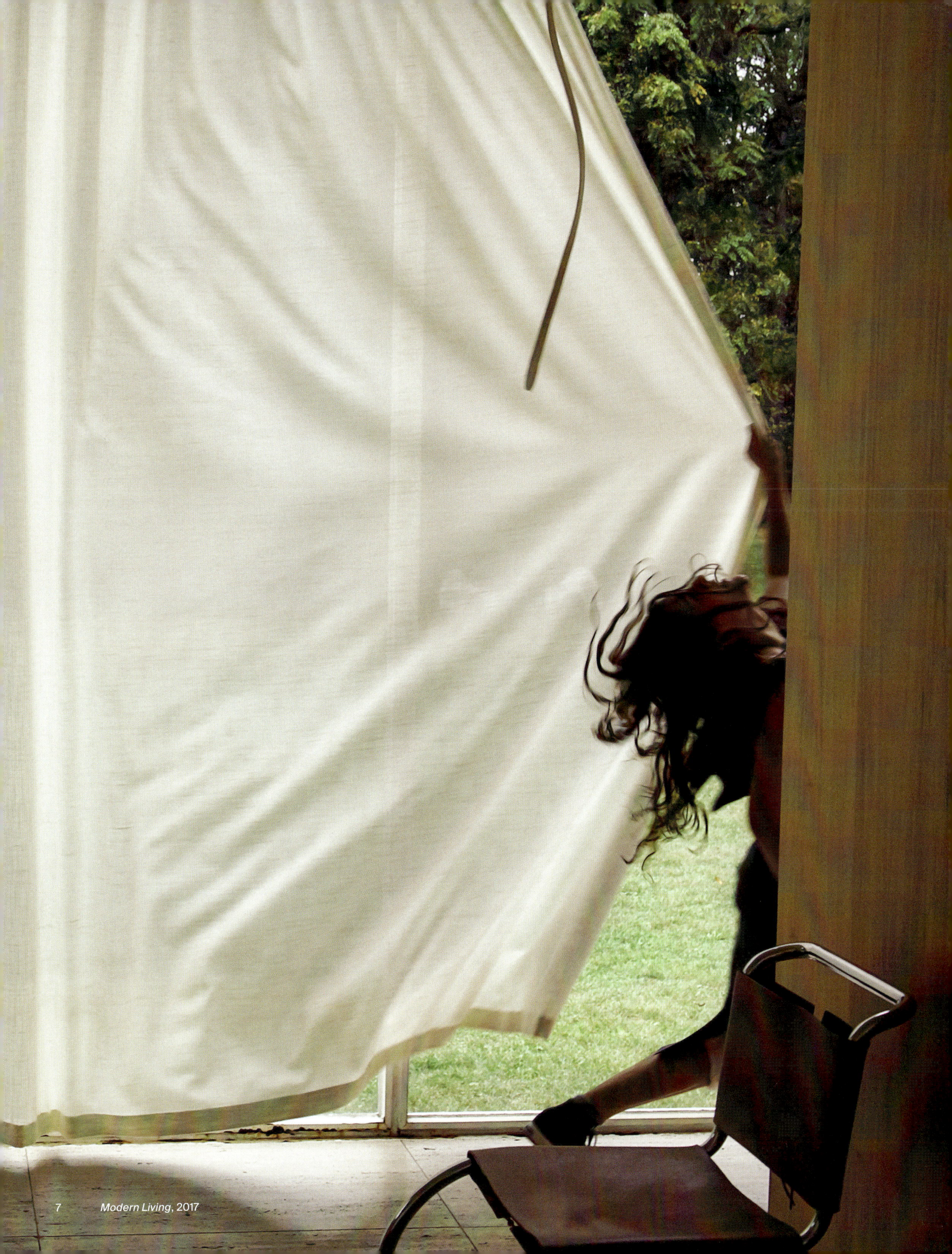

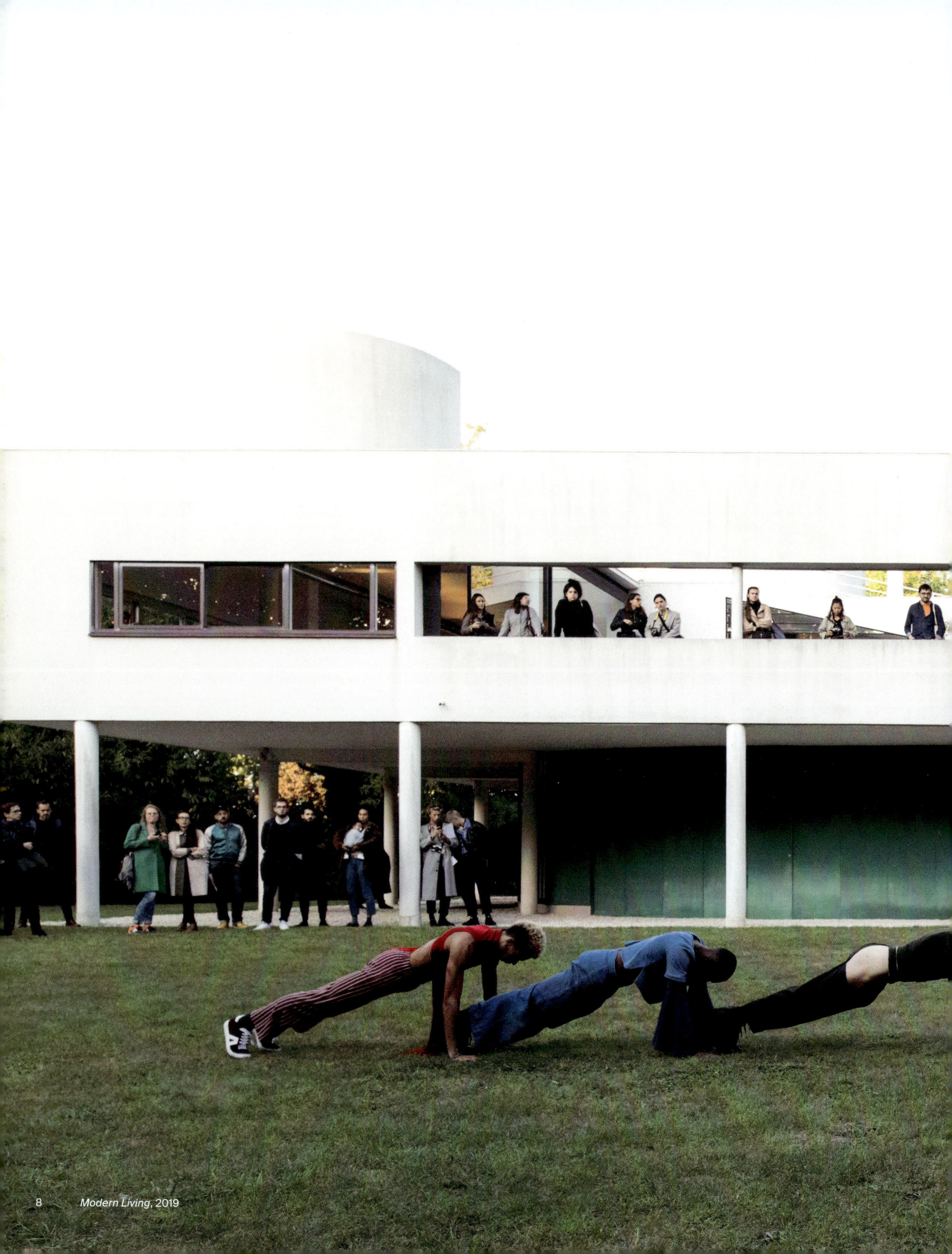

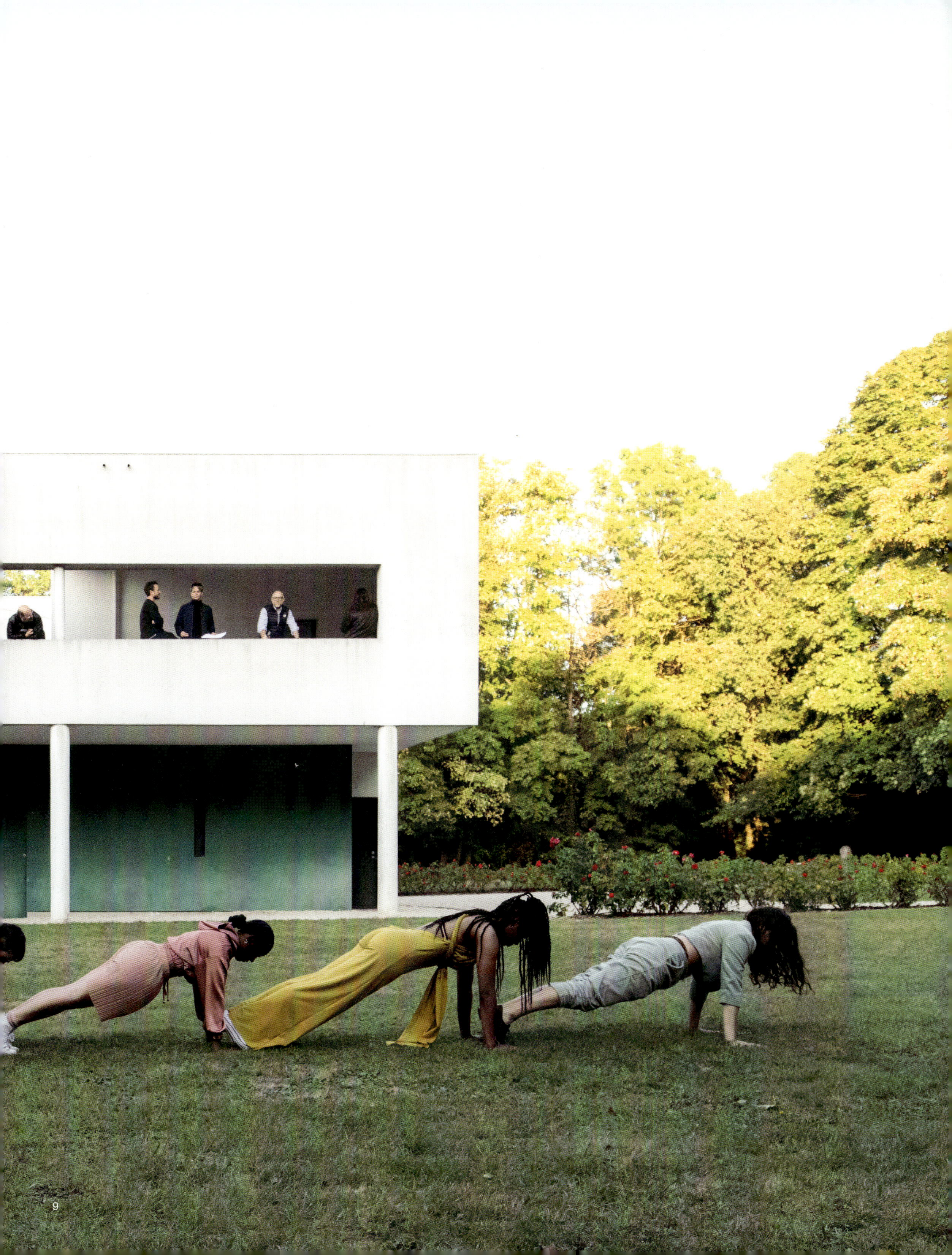

Through the Remains of Future Dreaming:

Gerard & Kelly's Art of Allegorical Constellations

Miwon Kwon

1.
Craig Owens, "The Allegorical Impulse: Toward a Theory of Postmodernism," *October* 102 (Spring 1980): 84. Owens makes this claim in relation to Walter Benjamin's theory of allegory as presented in the latter's *The Origin of German Tragic Drama* (1928). Owens writes: "The book on baroque tragedy thus throws into relief the essentially allegorical nature of all of Benjamin's work—the 'Paris Arcades' project, for example, where the urban landscape was to be treated as a sedimentation in depth of layers of meaning which would gradually be unearthed. For Benjamin, *inter*pretation is dis*intern*ment." The critic's emphasis on "inter" in both words indicates his desire to underscore the prefix's meaning of "between" as central to understanding Benjamin's work in general and his theory of allegory in particular. Owens' theorization of allegory will be addressed in depth in relation to Gerard & Kelly's work in this essay.
2.
Gerard & Kelly, "Notes on *Panorama*" (unpublished artist dossier, October 23, 2021), 3.
3.
The roles of Memory, Avenir ("Future"), and Allegory are performed by Soa de Muse, Guillaume Diop, and Germain Louvet respectively.
4.
First constructed as the Hotel de Soisson for Catherine de Médicis in the sixteenth century, the most recent form, purpose, and name is dated to 1889, the year of the Universal Exposition in which the Bourse de Commerce was featured alongside the Eiffel Tower to exemplify the advancement of French modernity. https://www.architecturaldigest.com/story/architect-tadao-ando-transformed-paris-bourse-de-commerce.
5.
Bourse de Commerce is the fourth major architectural renovation/redesign project to be commissioned by Francois Pinault and completed by Tadao Ando. The three prior projects are all located in Venice, Italy: the renovation of the Palazzo Grassi (2006), the transformation of the fifteenth century customs building Punta della Dogana into a contemporary art museum (2009); and the rehabilitation of Teatrino del Palazzo Grassi (2013). All considered highly successful transformations, these large-scale urban projects resuscitating old buildings and reanimating defunct spaces reflect the highly productive partnership of Pinault-Ando and evidence Pinault's long-term and deep engagement with both contemporary art and architecture.

... *inter*pretation is dis*inter*nment.[1]
—Craig Owens, 1980

Times lived, and times yet to come, are joined by art of ambivalent and unsettled meaning in *Panorama*, a 22-minute film by American artists Brennan Gerard and Ryan Kelly (working collaboratively as Gerard & Kelly since 2003 and based in Paris since 2018). Described by the artists as "a hybrid between a dance film and a cinematographic essay,"[2] *Panorama* convenes three muse-like figures—Memory, Avenir, and Allegory[3]—at the historic site of the Bourse de Commerce in central Paris.[4] Filmed in late 2020 following the completion of Tadao Ando's redesign and renovation of the building and before it opened to the public, *Panorama* marks a very precise moment in the transformation of the centuries-old commodities exchange into a museum of contemporary art dedicated to the housing and presentation of businessman François Pinault's extensive private collection.[5] As such, *Panorama* can be seen as the informal, unofficial inauguration of a new French art institution to be henceforth called "Bourse de Commerce - Pinault Collection." Conceptually occupying the hyphenated gap in the name that bridges the building's longstanding past identity as a site of commercial trade and its new identity as an exhibition space devoted to the "art of our time,"[6] *Panorama* simultaneously witnesses and instantiates art's displacement of commerce at this neoclassical monument whose original architecture, especially its iron and glass dome, was once hailed as the epitome of the most advanced art of its time.[7]

While the exact timing of the staging and filming of *Panorama* was not in Gerard & Kelly's total control (admittedly the timing of the project's realization was somewhat serendipitous),[8] the gathering of Memory, Avenir, and Allegory for what could be interpreted as a ritualistic cleansing of the building prior to its opening to the public was most precisely designed. Reminiscent of the trope of goddess trios of classical mythology and other sisterly threesomes of fate from ancient times and literature who could see or determine human destinies, the three muses of *Panorama* dance, sing, and speak as they confront the histories and possible futures embedded in the old and new architecture of the Bourse de Commerce.

Firstly, *Panorama* calls forth and responds to the vision of the greatness of France as captured in the central decorative program of the building, the grand allegorical mural "Panorama du Commerce," also known as "Triumphal France," which was originally completed in 1889 for the Universal Exposition and painstakingly restored for the reopening of the building as a contemporary art museum.[9] Wrapping 360 degrees around the entire rotunda as a frieze below the enormous dome, the panorama measures 10 meters high and 140 meters long (approximately 32 feet high and 460 feet long) and depicts the horizon of French progress that was to be realized through global trade and commerce as it was projected at the end of the nineteenth century.[10] Painted by five different artists, each assigned different regions of the earth, this panorama is essentially a collage, a construction made of discrete and partial sections that are sutured together in order to create a seemingly continuous and fantastical whole. While some experts have remarked on the lack of pictorial coherence in the work

6.
The hyphenated name of the institution declares a marriage between the state and a private citizen as the basis of this new enterprise. The "Welcome" page of Bourse de Commerce - Pinault Collection website clearly states the purpose of the space, however, as a showcase for "displaying the collections of a passionate and committed collector." Significantly, the graphic identity of the new institution as presented on its website and presumably in other media materials treats the "Pinault Collection" in bold type face against the comparatively fainter "Bourse de Commerce," emphasizing the greater importance of the former in the present, with the latter fading into history. See https://www.pinaultcollection.com/en/boursedecommerce/publics/welcome.

7.
The current metal structure of the dome dates back to 1811 when François-Joseph Bélanger and François Brunet replaced the wooden cupola with an iron and copper one. The existing dome of the Bourse de Commerce was classified as a historic landmark in 1986. See https://www.pop.culture.gouv.fr/notice/merimee/PA00085784.

8.
Gerard & Kelly, "Notes on *Panorama*," 4. On the delayed opening of Bourse de Commerce - Pinault Collection due to the second "confinement" enforced in France during the Covid pandemic, see https://www.connaissancedesarts.com/arts-expositions/report-de-louverture-de-la-bourse-de-commerce-pinault-collection-11137591/.

9.
The mural was restored for the first time in 1995 with certain sections receiving a second restoration treatment in 2010–13 following a fire. For a more detailed account of the restoration work on the panorama, see https://www.pinaultcollection.com/en/boursedecommerce/restoration-panorama-du-commerce.

10.
Often associated with motion pictures today, the term "panorama," which comes from Greek for "all" + "view," was coined by Robert Barker, an English/Irish painter who in 1787 patented a 360-degree visual medium under the title "Apparatus for Exhibiting Pictures." His paintings of London and Edinburgh drew large audiences as mass entertainment in the eighteenth century. Providing an immersive panoptic experience of a vista, the all-encompassing view that panoramas offer is comparable to the view once available from the top of the World Trade Center in downtown Manhattan, which Michel de Certeau analyzed in his *The Practice of Everyday Life* (1980). Such a view, de Certeau argued, fortifies the viewer's sense of power and dominion over the landscape, topography, historical incidents, and even people contained in the image/view. As such, the panorama is a type of visuality that is consistent with a colonial or imperial gaze. Interestingly, an American inventor named Robert Fulton introduced the panorama to the French. For a deep study on the history of the panorama, especially in England, France, and Germany, see Stephan Oettermann, *The Panorama: History of a Mass Medium*, trans. Deborah Lucas Schneider (New York: Zone Books, 1997).

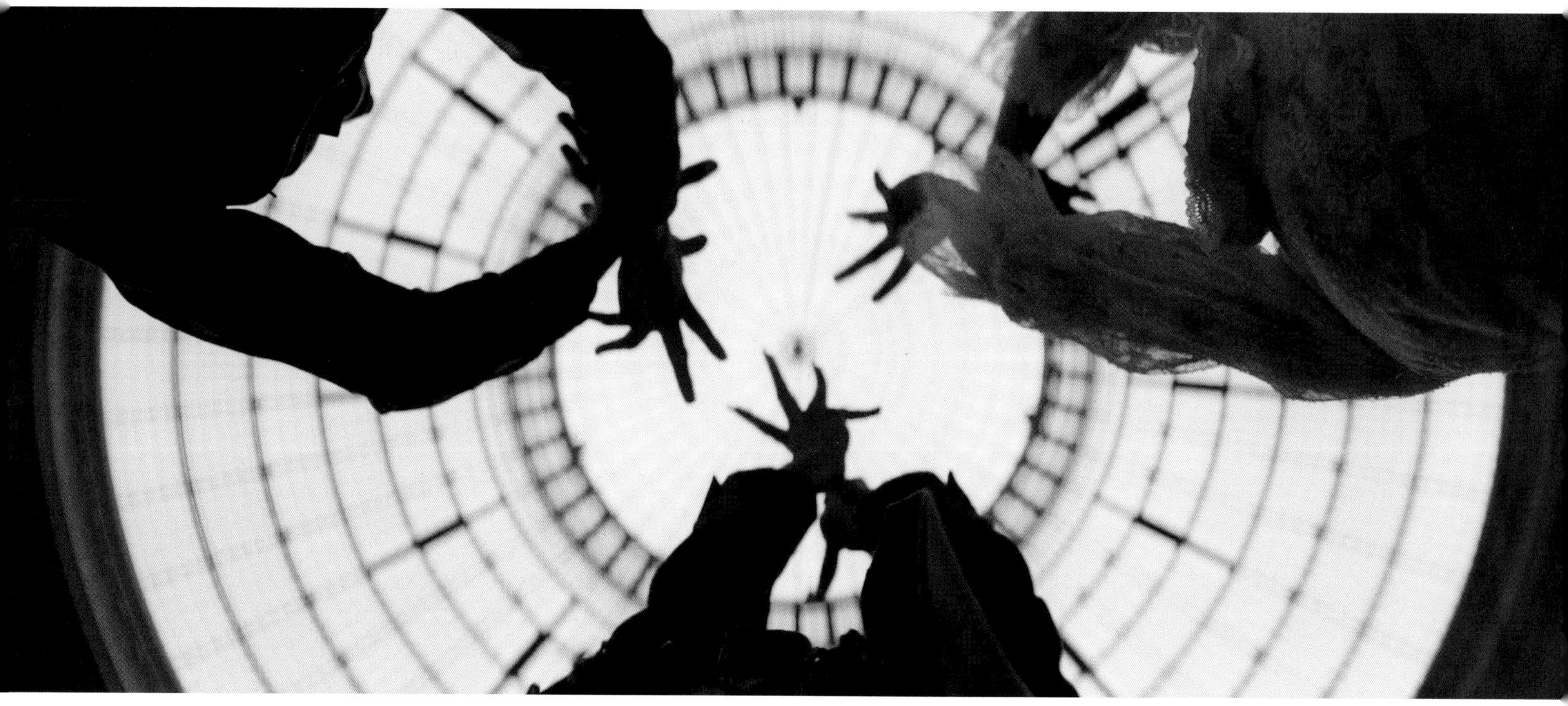

(partly due to the involvement of too many artists), "Panorama du Commerce" nonetheless presents an ideologically unified world view reflecting the aspirational vision if not the triumphalist reach of France in the modern era.[11]

Following a brief prelude comprised of gently degraded archival clips of the exterior and interior views of Bourse de Commerce, which establishes the film's setting and the building's advanced age, *Panorama* soon takes the viewers to the clearing inside the middle of the rotunda as Ando has prepared it. Memory is found there, a lone figure against the sweeping minimalist backdrop of the concrete cylinder—9 meters high and 30 meters in diameter (approximately 30 feet high and 95 feet in diameter)—that the Japanese architect has fitted into the central void of the building. Dressed in a smart magenta suit, perfectly groomed in long strands of braids and impeccably manicured nails, Memory is seated on the ground barefooted with knees folded under her like a supplicant. She is singing softly, her voice gently rising in volume, while wiping (or more like caressing) the floor with a water-soaked sponge. Avenir is looking on, through refracted reflections of his own face. Allegory is seen next, also "cleaning" Ando's architecture. Standing on an upper floor overlooking Memory's presence in the rotunda below, he is drawing a line across the top ledge of the concrete cylinder with a wet sponge that is plugged into his mouth.[12] Then the fugitive presence of Avenir speaks, seemingly from a distance or maybe from another time, with a question for Memory: "What do you remember?"

Memory's response is a recitation of things found in the panorama: objects, persons, buildings, landscapes, activities, interactions. She cries out, her gaze scanning and darting across the various scenes in the mural:

A leopard
A quarry

11.
According to Alix Laveau, curator with the Direction des Musées de France, "The panorama is the work of not one, but five artists, which explains the lack of coherence mentioned in some newspaper articles. Four of them represented commerce in a given part of the world: Évariste-Vital Luminais was assigned America; Désiré-François Laugée, Russia and the North; Georges-Victor Clairin, Asia and Africa; and finally, Hippolyte Lucas, Europe. In between these scenes, Alexis Mazerolle, who supervised the project, added allegories of the continents and regions depicted by the individual artists, in each of the four cardinal directions: Europe is represented by the arts and architecture; Africa by a lion and the hunt; Asia and the Orient by a hookah and elephants; and the North by a polar bear. This large, detailed composition takes viewers on a visual journey across the world." Although the mural is sometimes referred to as a fresco, it is important to correct this misattribution in order to fully understand the significance of this work in formal, material, and art historical terms. The panorama, in fact, was composed of separate canvases painted by the different artists off site, then recut and (re) arranged before being attached to the wall in-situ by the artists using the technique of marouflage, which utilizes white lead as an adhesive. See Guillaume Picon, interview with Alix Laveau, "Restoration of the 'panorama du commerce,'" *Pinault Collection*, January 11, 2021, see https://www.pinaultcollection.com/en/boursedecommerce/restoration-panorama-du-commerce.
12.
This brief choreographic sequence recalls LaMonte Young's *Composition 1960 #10 (for Bob Morris),* a text-based score, which reads: "draw a straight line and follow it." The most well-known enactment of the score is Nam June Paik's at the 1962 Fluxus concert in Wiesbaden, Germany, in which the artist dunked different part of his body, including his head, in a bowl of ink and drew lines across long sheets of paper.

13.
Gerard & Kelly, *Panorama*, 2021, 4K video, color, sound, 22', 04:45–06:28. Memory speaks in French and Creole throughout the film, with occasional English words thrown in strategically here and there.

An Indian chief protecting his face
Two indigenous children holding hands
Mother. . .
Mother? [breaks from French into English]

Two slaves carrying a tree
The train
The spear
Tons of cotton
Hectares of wheat
A bow and arrow
A ship in the clouds [in English]
Columbus in the cumulus castellanus
Columbus up my anus [in English]
Damn. . .
Cows, cowboys, a bull
A bearded white man at his desk [then as if correcting herself. . .]
Um. A Caucasian accountant. . . I guess.

Moss covers stones
A steamboat
A light house
A factory in the distance. . . spitting out yellow
A bridge
Horses, horses
A monkey, two monkeys
Napoleon's hat

French flag
Wicker basket
A Chinese man sells yellow silk
Geisha, geisha, geisha
Two tattooed Michaelangelos tug a canoe
American flag. . . [starts singing "God Bless America"]
A cherub's ass

And the name of the painter engraved in stone
E. Luminais[13]

Memory's recollection here covers a wild array, from emblems of modern industrial production (quarry, factories with their yellow "spit") and new means of transportation (steamboats, bridges, ships, trains), to various commodity goods (hectares of wheat, tons of cotton, wicker baskets, yellow silk) as well as exotic and working animals (leopard, monkeys, bull, horses, cows), and merchants and laborers of foreign origins (Indian chief, indigenous children, slaves, geisha girls, a Chinese man, cowboys). Intermixed into this eclectic inventory, Memory further recalls with biting irreverence a number of symbols of Western power in the panorama (Columbus on his ship, a bearded white man counting his money, Napoleon's hat, the ass of a cherub), adding on the French Tricolour and the American Stars and Stripes, which are further emphasized by Memory's short melodic tracings of "La Marseillaise" and "God Bless America." She ends her channeling of the past with an acknowledgment of Évariste-Vital Luminais, the painter responsible for the North America section of the panorama,

14.
In some ways, Memory resembles what Walter Benjamin saw in Paul Klee's *Angelus Novus* (1920), a small monoprint that the philosopher purchased in 1921. Benjamin wrote: "A Klee painting named *Angelus Novus* shows an angel looking as though he is about to move away from something he is fixedly contemplating. His eyes are staring, his mouth is open, his wings are spread. This is how one pictures the angel of history. His face is turned toward the past. Where we perceive a chain of events, he sees one single catastrophe which keeps piling wreckage upon wreckage and hurls it in front of his feet. The angel would like to stay, awaken the dead, and make whole what has been smashed. But a storm is blowing from Paradise; it has got caught in his wings with such violence that the angel can no longer close them. The storm irresistibly propels him into the future to which his back is turned, while the pile of debris before him grows skyward. This storm is what we call progress." Walter Benjamin, "Theses on the Philosophy of History" (1940), *Illuminations*, trans. Harry Zohn (New York: Schocken Books, 1969), 249.

15.
Leslie Camhi, "The Bourse de Commerce–Pinault Collection, a Museum 20 Years in the Making, Prepares for Its Grand Opening," *Vogue*, May 20, 2021, see https://www.vogue.com/article/bourse-de-commerce-pinault-collection-opens.

16.
Martin Bethenod, the former founding director of the Bourse de Commerce – Pinault Collection explained: "That moment of the Bourse's reopening [in 1889] corresponded to the beginnings of capitalism and globalization, and in a less positive light to a period of great colonialism." He concedes this historical fact is not something that the museum can hide. Quoted in Camhi, "The Bourse de Commerce–Pinault Collection."

whose name, she notes, is embedded in stone, confirming his status as an artist entombed in history. Then, following a brief pause to reset, Memory concludes quietly and portentously: "A storm is coming."

What Memory remembers, in fleeting and fragmentary bits like things glimpsed in a turbulent dream or found in a crowded collage, is a historical pile-up of remainders from (which are also reminders of) the projected plans of a global future that churned European modernism and industrial capitalism forward into the twentieth century, expanding toward and extracting from lands and peoples far and wide. Perhaps it is not a mystery that Memory foretells of a storm coming.[14] Standing in the future that the "Panorama du Commerce" projected, today's viewers know of the many failings that this vision brought to humanity. For even as the mural "depicts the triumph of trade across the continents, from snowy Russia to an emerging New World and the markets of the East,"[15] the twentieth century also experienced the ongoing perpetration of colonialist enterprises around the world in the very name of progress, enlightenment, and modernization (wherein certain human beings and territories were treated as commodities to be taken and sold and traded). The last century also saw technological advancements and tribalistic nationalisms that nurtured competition and will for domination more than mutuality or collaboration, achieving great catastrophes of world wars, unprecedented destruction, and unfathomable human atrocities and natural depravations.[16] But even with the warning of a coming storm—or perhaps because of it—Memory, Avenir, and Allegory converge in the rotunda. And they dance.

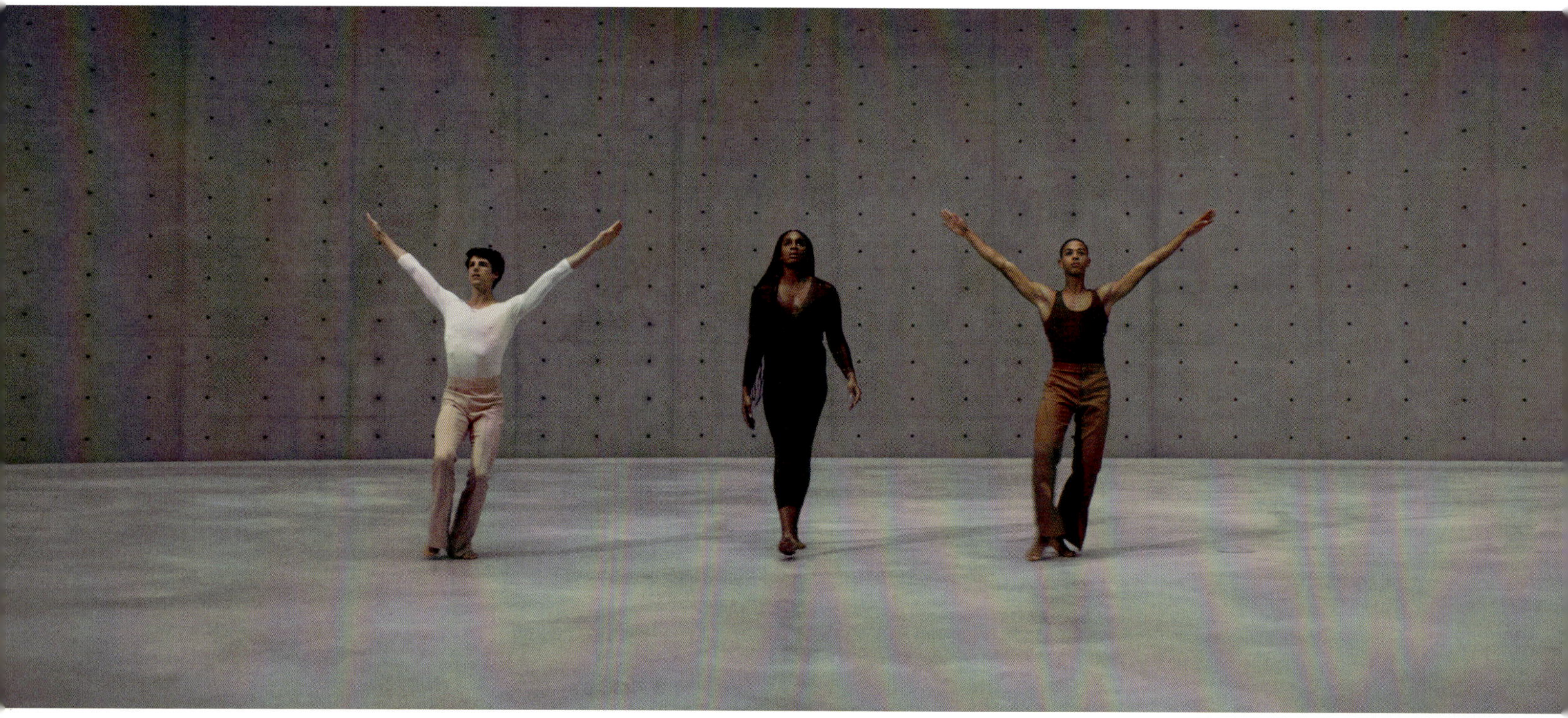

Of course, it is very common for art to serve as a palliative if not a redemptive mechanism. Like magic, art can transform the beastly into the beautiful and convert trash into gold. Art can not only elevate something from "low" to "high," it can also function to disguise, assuage, or excuse what might be unacceptable, even horrific and contemptible, in other contexts. Seen in this light, the opening sequence of *Panorama*, which seems to forward "cleansing" as a leitmotif—with Memory's wiping of the floor of the Bourse de Commerce and her exhortations serving as metaphors for an exorcism of all the historical sins that could have occurred within its confines and beyond, literally and symbolically—could be mistaken as a redemptive gesture on the part of Gerard & Kelly. But as the subsequent dance and performative sequences of the film reveal, the sins of the past cannot be washed away or covered over. What follows the "cleansing" gambit in *Panorama* is more a reckoning with the past and an apprehensive contemplation of the future. Memory, Avenir, and Allegory's dance in the face of a coming storm is neither a grieving nor a celebration. It is not an effort at transcendence or absolution. Instead, the trio makes demands—of history, of society, of the gods. They perform a defiant and playful overwriting of the inherited narratives and values from bygone eras that actually do not sleep or die but continue to live on in the present. So, as they dance, they collectively and repetitively assert:

> *I am an empty house*
> *A house without an interior*
> *I am a surface*
> *Who demands the right to be multiple*[17]

Here, the muses are declaring a model of identity and subjectivity that is not anchored to or motivated by a fixed and stable inner essence. The core of "I" is a vacancy. The self/identity as an empty vessel means it can only be known or "filled" as an effect of the inscriptions that are either forcibly imposed upon its surface—by language, cultural and societal codes, legal systems, historical inheritances, etc.—or performatively adopted and continually recoded (often in resistance to the enforced inscriptions). And as such a surface, "I" is impermanent, unfixed, forever shifting as a basic condition of being alive, contingent upon particular times, places, and desires. Thus, Memory, Avenir, and Allegory's declaration of being an empty house and their demand for the right to be multiple, posed in reaction to the myth of a unified national identity that is pictured as triumphant over otherness and difference in the panorama, must be understood as both politically and existentially charged. Their demand challenges the dominant belief of coherent and singular identities (of individuals as well as cultures and nations) that fears, refuses, or represses difference, internally and in the world. More locally, Memory, Avenir, and Allegory call for the house of Pinault to embrace multiplicity.

Which is to say, an empty house, without an interior, could also be a reference to the openness at the heart of the Bourse de Commerce building itself. According to Gerard & Kelly, the reckoning with history that unfolds in *Panorama* vis-à-vis a critical engagement with its nineteenth-century decorative mural was in large part inspired by Tadao Ando's "brutal poetics." The artists have described Ando's architectural nesting of an outsized concrete cylinder inside the existing rotunda as, on the one hand, a physical framing of the panorama that encircles the building's interior and, on the other hand, and perhaps more importantly, as a "radical proposition to face and reflect upon the past while re-inventing the world in the present tense."[18] Ando himself has characterized the coming together of the rotunda and the silo-like concrete cylinder as connecting the past with the

17.
Gerard & Kelly, *Panorama*, 07:05–08:15. At the beginning of this sequence, Memory and Allegory move and speak together with Avenir following like an echo and shadow, imitating theirs gestures and words a beat out of sync. Soon after Avenir comes into sync, with all three moving and speaking in unison, Memory departs, leaving Avenir to lead with Allegory by his side.

18.
Gerard & Kelly, "Notes on *Panorama*," 2. It is significant that the artists do not say "re-inventing the world in the present." Adding the word "tense" at the end—"re-inventing the world in the present *tense*"—avoids the sense of a full stop in the present and maintains the work of reinvention as an active ongoing, continuous effort, (re) imagining the present without stop.

present and the future. The architect has stated: "It is my hope that the layering of the rotunda and the cylinder and of old and new will give rise to a sequence of even more powerful, varied spaces and create a lively place appropriate for upholding the city's culture for the next generation."[19] While this statement sounds platitudinal as press statements typically do, it is nevertheless important to realize that Ando's redesign and renovation is not a standard rehabilitation of a building that generically "respects" the old and introduces the new.

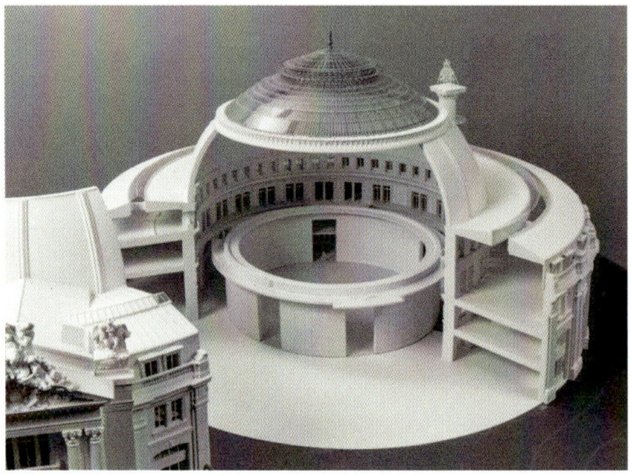

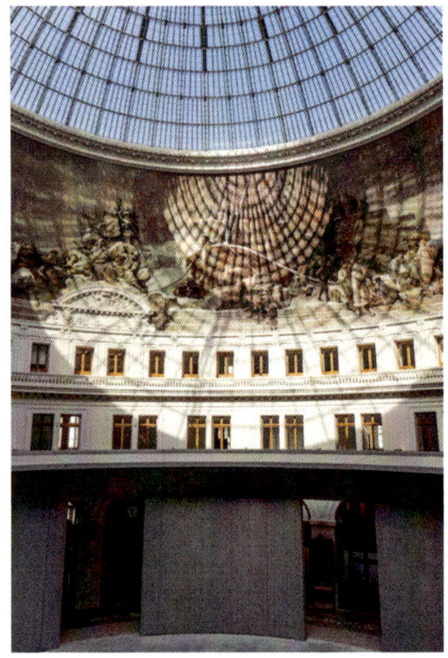

Left: Tadao Ando, cutaway model for the Bourse de Commerce – Pinault Collection, Paris / Right: Tadao Ando, view of the rotunda of Bourse de Commerce – Pinault Collection, Paris, 2021

Ando's work at the Bourse de Commerce, as in so many of his other projects, does not simply offer opposites in the same space, like the past and the present, for instance. Rather, his architecture achieves a rigorous *interpenetration* of qualities that are normally considered discrete *as* opposites—past and present, old and new, light and dark, nature and culture, abstraction and figuration, hard and soft, presence and absence, masculine and feminine, East and West, etc. More precisely, Ando's architecture reveals the mutually constitutive dynamic and movement, the *dialectic*, between opposites that *sustain their identities relationally*. In this sense, to say Ando's architecture achieves a miraculous harmony as is often said, or that it synthesizes or reconciles opposites, even if uttered by the architect himself,[20] would not be one-hundred percent accurate since dialectical movement does not end in a stasis that results from synthesis, reconciliation, or resolution. Ando's use of the term "layering" to describe his architectural gesture of inserting a concrete cylinder inside the existing rotunda may get us a little closer to the dialectics of his design, but it still falls short of what Gerard & Kelly have recognized as its "brutal poetics," the radicality of its proposition. For Ando's architecture at the Bourse de Commerce is not just the juxtaposition of past and present or their additive accumulation, like strata of time, one over the other. It realizes instead a superimposition, or interpenetration as said already, of opposites, of past and present. In this architecture, past is not so much a remote historical reference point distinct from the present (a different layer of time one could say) but is immediately *one with the now*, inseparable from the present and by extension the future. Ando's architectural "layering" thus allows for the experience of not only non-linear temporality but also the *multiplicity* of times *inside* the present. Yesterday is today is yesterday is tomorrow is today . . . Not unlike a palimpsest, his work materializes time as always already multiple.[21] Gerard & Kelly's interest in the co-articulation of the past,

19.
Tadao Ando, "To France, the Country of Culture and Art," *archilovers*, February 13, 2019, see https://www.archilovers.com/projects/245021/bourse-de-commerce-pinault-collection.html#info.

20.
See Tadao Ando, as quoted by Camhi, "The Bourse de Commerce."

21.
Sometimes this includes primordial sense of time before history. When Ando's project is a new construction rather than a renovation of a historical building as in this case, the sense of the past that come to the fore seem less bound to history and more to nature, something more primitive or primeval. His architecture at Naoshima, Japan, for example, falls into this category. See Miwon Kwon, "A Position of Elsewhere: Lessons from Naoshima," in *Naoshima: Nature, Art, Architecture*, ed., Kayo Tokuda (Naoshima, Japan and Ostfildern, Germany: Benesse Holdings Inc. and Naoshima Fukutake Art Museum Foundation and Hatje Cantz Verlag, 2010).

22.
By the time "Panorama du Commerce" is painted, slavery is legally abolished in France (1848) and the United States (1865) although not eradicated in practice. Given that the mural is not strictly a historical painting depicting specific incidents or personages, however, the figures in this scene, as in the rest of the panorama, are allegorical and function as emblems.

present, and future in *Panorama*, their conjuring of multiple identities and multiple times in the film, is deeply resonant with this dialectic of Ando's architecture.

Identity and time as multiple, and also performative, is explicitly demonstrated in a later sequence of *Panorama* in which Memory, Avenir, and Allegory imitate three figures that are depicted in a small scene in the North America section of the panorama. The hierarchy of power relations is unambiguous in the painted scene: a genteel white woman, seated on a green silk cushion on top of a stone plinth is accompanied by a younger black woman, her servant if not her slave,[22] who is attending to her by holding up a large parasol. Protected from the harsh sun, the mistress on her makeshift throne is looking upwards at the parasol toward the sky. She fails to notice a young Native American boy on the ground, kneeling at her feet, deferentially lifting towards her a two-handed offering of an exotic bird. This frozen organization of power relations across race and gender, between white and not, between master and slave, comes alive and simultaneously comes apart with Soa de Muse, Guillaume Diop, and Germain Louvet striking poses in the semblance of the scene. As they mimic or quote the triangulated interaction in the panorama vignette, they playfully switch roles and scramble the hierarchy of their positions in the process. As they do so, their identities as Memory, Avenir, and Allegory, the roles that each personified respectively in the film thus far (and will again), overlay onto their becoming and unbecoming a black girl, a white woman, a native boy, a colonizer, a gift giver, a servant, etc. At the same time, the three performers are, in fact, beautiful cosmopolitan Parisians of the twenty-first century, professional dancers and artists. Their identities of mixed race, gender, and sexuality as Soa, Guillaume, and Germain are perhaps more fluid and freer than what is pictured or allowed for with the characters in the nineteenth-century mural, but the three are nonetheless performing given roles and constructing their identities, too.

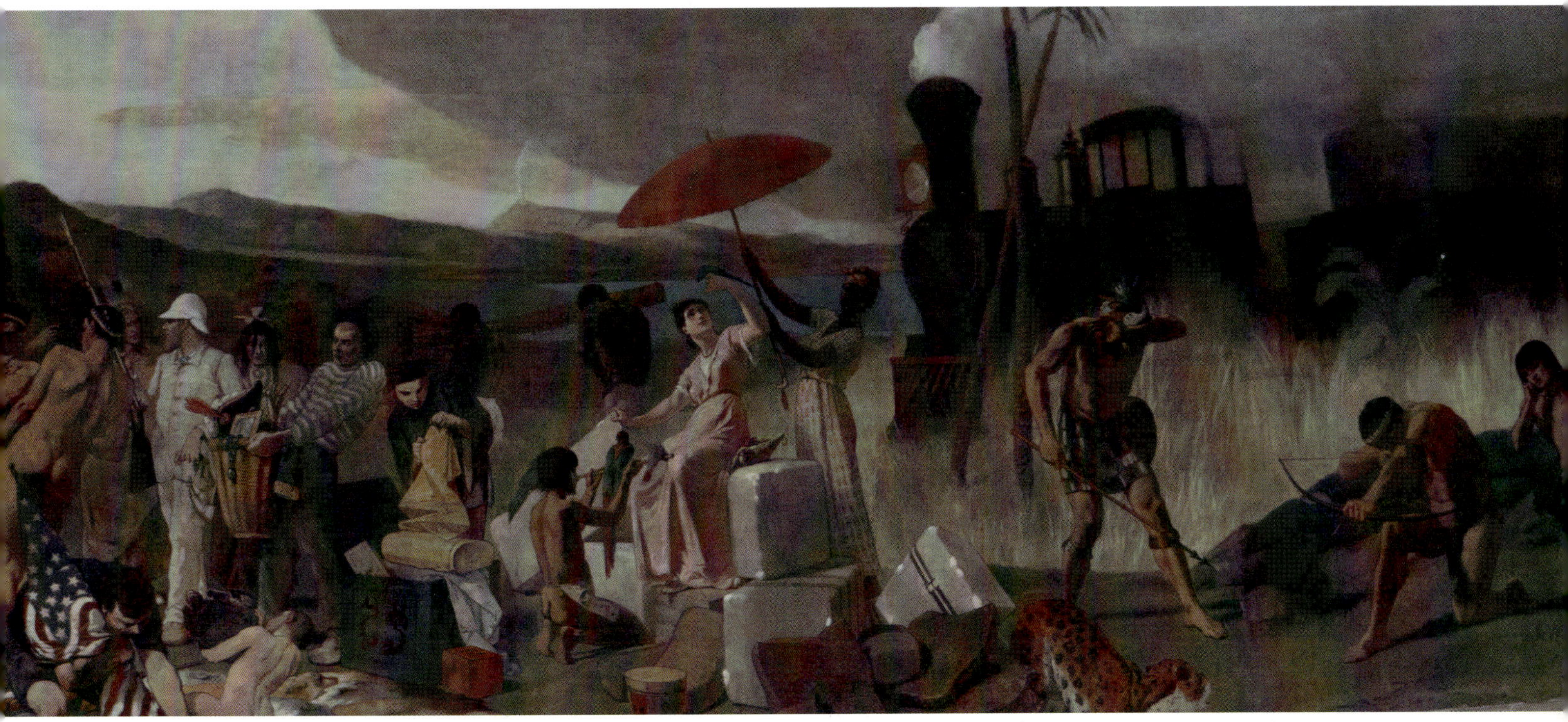

 Évariste-Vital Luminais, detail of North America section of "Panorama du Commerce," 1889

23.
The most obvious reference here is the work of feminist film theorist Laura Mulvey and in particular her highly influential essay "Visual Pleasure and Narrative Cinema" published in 1975 in the British journal *Screen*. Her analysis of cinematic construction of the gaze and its relationship to the organization of power along the lines of masculine-feminine, looker-looked at, with agency-without agency, subject-object, possessive-possessed, etc. had a profound and broad impact on the development of not only film theory but feminist studies, art history, and cultural studies in the 1980s and beyond.

24.
Google's English dictionary definitions are provided by Oxford Languages.

As the camera slowly pulls back from the three central performers, who embody multiple identities and occupy multiple times as described, the artificial theatricality of the situation is revealed with the coming and going of technical assistants, costumer, gaffer, prop manager, dresser, makeup artist, etc. entering the film's frame. The pull-back breaks the "fourth wall" to show a different organization of power and authority that is structuring *this* scene (which is in the midst of deconstructing the organization of power and authority depicted in a historical scene from over a century ago). The camera finally discloses Brennan Gerard and Ryan Kelly standing in the shadows behind their camera, huddled together and quietly directing the crew and performers and overseeing the entire staging as Gerard & Kelly, an author position that is internally split and multiple. This disclosure is also a self-reflexive acknowledgement of the artists' role as creators of *Panorama*'s representational construction and their position as the eye behind even the eye that sees *them*. Importantly, however, while this self-reflexive disclosure harkens back to postmodernist discourses on the politics of the gaze, Gerard & Kelly sidestep the oppositional binarism that structure its lessons.[23] This sequence does not end with Gerard & Kelly's critical revelation of their own authorial role. The camera continues its travel. Moving on past the artists, it retraces its path back to the three performers still in rehearsal or preparatory mode, each finetuning the task of vivifying the scene from the panorama. The camera, closer in on the reenactment now, sees that the correspondence between the nineteenth-century scene and its twenty-first-century doubling is close to being perfect, ready for its photographic or filmic capture for perpetuity. But wait. Soa, Guillaume, and Germain, before taking their final positions as native boy (Memory), white woman (Avenir), and slave girl (Allegory), insist on taking a group selfie to commemorate the moment for themselves, asserting their own "real" identities and posing for the camera that is in one of their smartphones (although this interlude of their self-fashioning is for Gerard & Kelly's camera, too). Following this cheeky "real life" interruption, which introduces yet another sense of time and only momentarily disrupts the artificial reality of the restaging, an invisible male voice asserts "CUT" to end the sequence.

The (re)presentation of multiple identities and their transposability in this segment of the film effects an interpenetration of past and present, not unlike Ando's architecture, as well as the blurring of representational time and space and "real" time and space (all further complexified in this case by the imbrication of the politics of the gaze). It becomes a space of multi-temporality and polyvocality that does not leave the past to rest in peace or to be lost in oblivion. As such, the palimpsest reappears as an appropriate metaphor for Gerard & Kelly's work, too, since a palimpsest is a text in which past inscriptions may get obscured through successive new inscriptions, but they remain inside the text as part of its present-day identity. The new inscription's meaning, therefore, is not independent of the past inscriptions; they share the same body. Or more plainly put according to Google, a palimpsest is "something reused or altered but still bearing visible traces of its earlier form,"[24] like, for example, Soa, Guillaume, and Germain simultaneously replicating and altering the positions of the threesome in the panorama scene, or Memory, Avenir, and Allegory radically overwriting the Three Fates (or Moirai) of

25.
Owens, "The Allegorical Impulse," 69. The emphasis on "read through" is in the original.
26.
Owens, "The Allegorical Impulse," 68.
27.
Owens, "The Allegorical Impulse," 69.

Greek mythology and all subsequent reworkings of them by countless other writers, artists, and filmmakers across time.

To say that *Panorama* is like a palimpsest, then, is to say that its structure as a work of art is like a text, a new inscription, that is acting upon prior texts (the "Panorama du Commerce," the Bourse de Commerce), attending to their traces and transforming them for the present. The artwork parasitically attaches to and emerges from the given/past inscriptions, re-rendering their meaning as a supplement. Which recalls the insights of American art critic and theorist Craig Owens, who, in his seminal 1980 essay "The Allegorical Impulse: Toward a Theory of Postmodernism," discerned the resurgence of allegory from its proscribed status in modernism and identified the palimpsest as allegory's premier paradigm. He stated: "In allegorical structure, [. . .] one text is *read through* another, however fragmentary, intermittent, or chaotic their relationship may be; the paradigm for the allegorical work is thus the palimpsest."[25] For Owens, allegory is "an attitude as well as a technique, a perception as well as a procedure," and it occurs "whenever one text is doubled by another."[26] He went on: the "allegorist does not invent images but confiscates them" and "lays claim to the culturally significant, poses as its interpreter. And in his hands the image becomes something other [. . .] He does not restore an original meaning that may have been lost or obscured; allegory is not hermeneutics. Rather he adds another meaning to the image. If he adds, however, he does so only to replace: the allegorical meaning supplants an antecedent one; it is a supplement."[27]

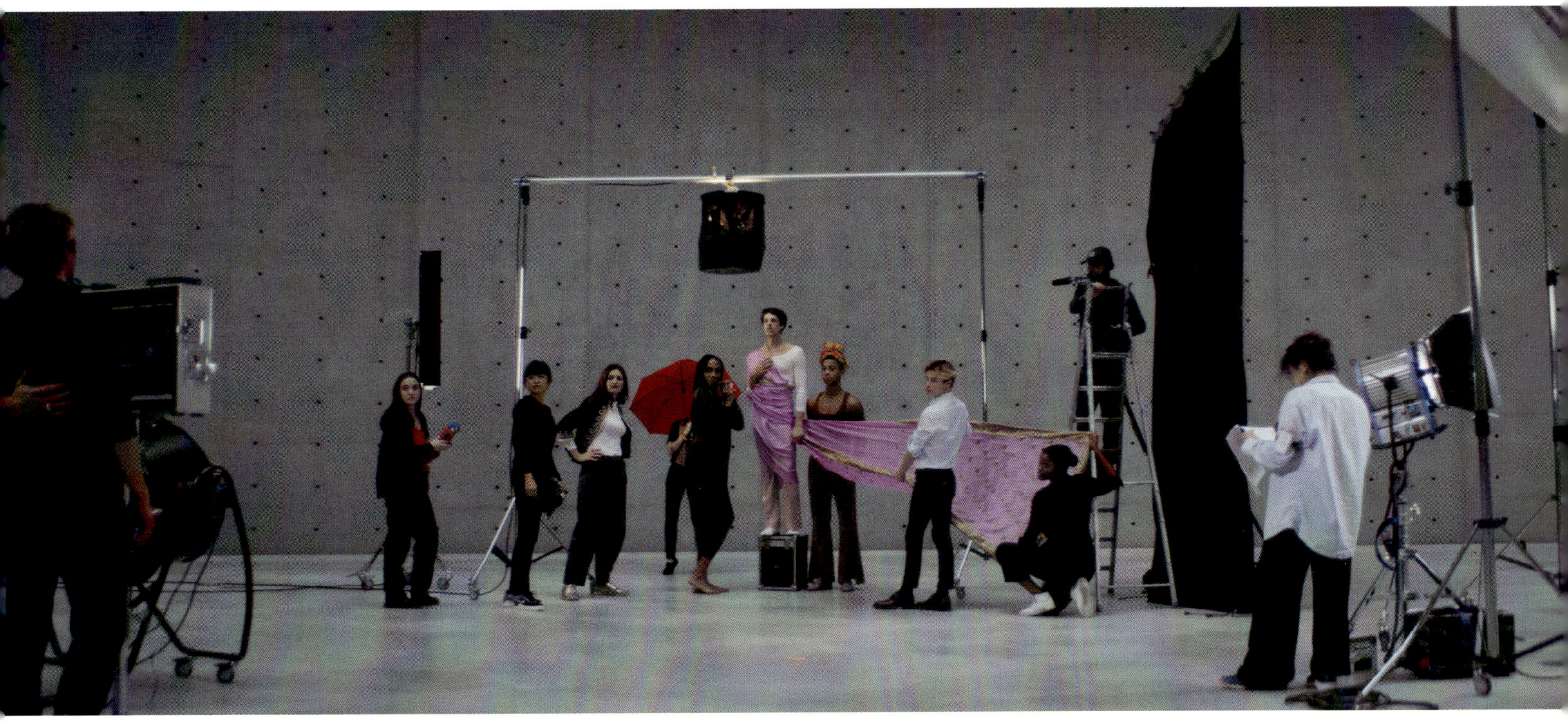

Pondering Owens' theorization could lead some to think that all forms of artistic interpretation, commentary, or production that involve some kind of appropriative rewriting of a primary or prior text could be deemed allegorical. But the critic was keen to specify allegorical relationships as something happening *within* the work of art, structuring its very logic. And he promoted this as a distinguishing characteristic, a generation-defining tendency, to be found in postmodernist art practices of his time. He outlined additional attributes of the allegorical impulse in his essay while simultaneously deconstructing the deep roots of its prohibition, suppression, and marginalization within modernist aesthetics and art history, reaching back to nineteenth-century French painting (the very moment of the making of "Panorama du Commerce" by coincidence) and the debates that surrounded it.[28] Although a comprehensive review or critique of Owens' complex thinking would not be appropriate to pursue in this essay, it is worth recalling some of his key points as a means to better understand the extent to which Gerard & Kelly's art practice, beyond what has already been accounted for in *Panorama*, further extends the allegorical attitude, technique, perception, and procedure that Owens theorized.

First, for Owens "allegorical work is synthetic; it crosses aesthetic boundaries." Rather than aspiring to achieve the purity of a medium or a genre as might have driven certain modernists, an allegorical work mixes and confuses them. "This confusion of genre," the critic added, "reappears today in hybridization, in eclectic works which ostentatiously combine previously distinct art mediums."[29] Gerard & Kelly's art, restlessly manifesting as a combinatory amalgam of dance, sculpture, choreography, drawing, installation, film, design, writing, and even architecture—in "real" spaces of homes and museums as well as representational spaces of the stage, screening rooms, and exhibition galleries—indeed engages many mediums and genres confusing established artistic categories. As the reader will recall from the beginning of this essay, the artists described *Panorama* as "a hybrid between a dance film and a cinematographic essay,"[30] a precise description of its indeterminate, multiply identifiable status. This kind of hybridization, which attends *all* of Gerard & Kelly's artistic production beyond *Panorama*, also aligns with Owens' claim of allegory's more general disrespect for the distinction between the visual and the verbal. Allegory proposes a reciprocity between words and images—"words are often treated as purely visual phenomena, while visual images are offered as script to be deciphered." In this regard, allegory is "pictogrammatical" according to Owens, like a hieroglyph or a rebus.[31] As already demonstrated, Gerard & Kelly's work also engages the language of hieroglyphs and rebuses. But with the integration of choreography and dance as central elements or the engine of their work, words and images and their reciprocity are conjugated into the register of motion and movement in their art, coalescing and dissolving in time.

This transient and ephemeral quality of Gerard & Kelly's art affirms another aspect of allegory that Owens highlighted: a penchant for a site-specific mode of practice wherein the works are calibrated as a response to the existing conditions of realization or presentation, and as such are "impermanent, installed in particular locations for a limited duration, their impermanence providing the measure of their circumstantiality."[32] Granted, at the time of Owens' writing in 1980, the notion of site specificity was not yet fully developed.[33] So it is not surprising that he foregrounded the *physical* embeddedness of a work into its site as a defining quality and saw the art of Robert Smithson, the *Spiral Jetty* (1970) in particular, as exemplary. The critic stated: "The site-specific work often aspires to a prehistoric

28.
According to Owens, "The history of modernist painting is begun with Manet and not Courbet, who persisted in painting 'real allegories.' Even the most supportive of Courbet's contemporaries (Prudhon and Champfleury) were perplexed by his allegorical bent; one was either a realist *or* an allegorist, they insisted, meaning that one was either modernist or historicist. [. . .] So that by the time Courbet attempted to rescue allegory for modernity, the line which separated them had been clearly drawn, and allegory, conceived as antithetical to the modernist credo *Il faut être de son temps*, was condemned, along with history painting, to a purely marginal historical existence." Owens, "The Allegorical Impulse," 76–77.
29.
Owens, "The Allegorical Impulse," 75.
30.
For this writer, the term "hybrid" does not sound entirely correct as a description for Gerard & Kelly's work since the artists seem to retain a sense of multiplicity (of categories) rather than achieving a new synthesis in their practice. *Panorama* is an accumulation of dance, *and* a film, *and* an essay, not necessarily their merging.
31.
Owens, "The Allegorical Impulse," 74–75.
32.
Owens, "The Allegorical Impulse," 71.
33.
Alongside Douglas Crimp, Owens is one of the key thinkers who early on established the terms for site specificity as a postmodern practice. Another important early text on site-specific art is Rosalind Krauss, "Sculpture in the Expanded Field," *October* 8 (Spring 1979): 30–44. On the development and elaboration of site-specific art into the 1990s, see Miwon Kwon, *One Place After Another: Site-specific Art and Locational Identity* (Cambridge, MA: MIT Press, 2002).

34.
Owens, "The Allegorical Impulse," 71.

35.
Owens, "The Allegorical Impulse," 71. Smithson's theorization of the site/non-site is of a piece with this understanding of the relationship between the work and site as dialectical. Owens concludes his essay with a return to Smithson and the artist's important text, "A Sedimentation of the Mind" (1968).

36.
The doubling operation in *Spiral Jetty* is actually multiple: as *Spiral Jetty* the earthwork replicates the site in a new sculptural form, it is replicated in a filmic double (also called *Spiral Jetty*) as well as a textual one (titled *The Spiral Jetty*). Indeed, visual and verbal worlds converge in Smithson's art.

37.
Owens, "The Allegorical Impulse," 71.

38.
Owens, "The Allegorical Impulse," 70.

39.
Owens, "The Allegorical Impulse," 78.

monumentality; Stonehenge and the Nazca lines are taken as prototypes. Its 'content' is frequently mythical." And the work "appears to have merged physically into its setting, to be embedded in the place where we encounter it."[34] Importantly, even in what reads as an outdated and limited conceptualization of site specificity, Owens still recognized that the relationship between the work and its site needed to be understood as *dialectical*. Smithson's work at the Great Salt Lake, Owens argued, engages in a "*reading* of the site, in terms not only of its topographical specifics but also of its psychological resonances. Work and site thus stand in a dialectical relationship."[35] Which is to say, the *Spiral Jetty* is also a palimpsest. For Owens, this canonic earthwork, as an allegorical reading of the site, an inscription upon its many layers of sedimented inscriptions, is, at the same time, the site's dialectical doubling.[36]

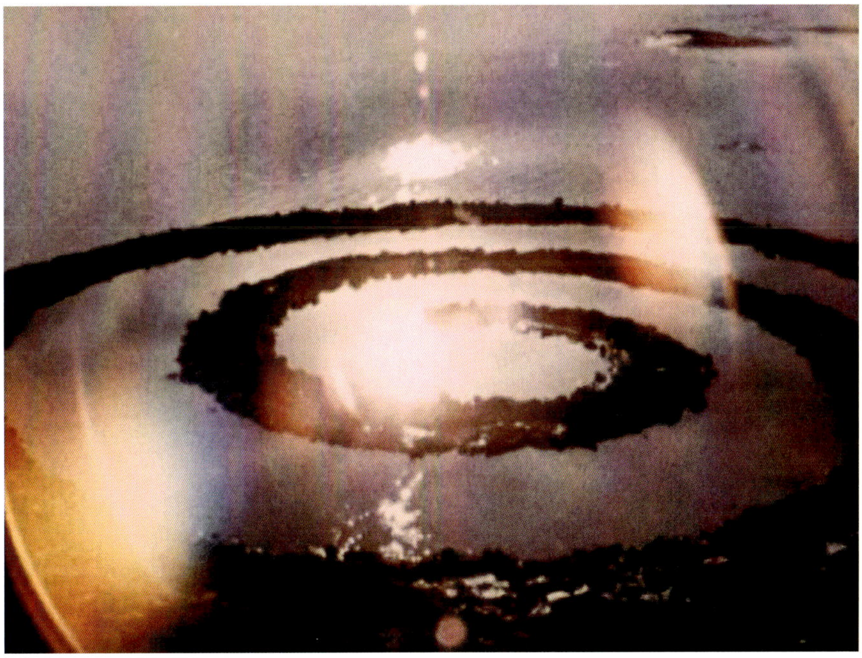

The interest in site specificity as an exemplary mode of contemporary allegorical work led Owens to a revelatory claim that site-specific art, in becoming an emblem of transience and the ephemerality of *all* phenomena, is the "memento mori of the twentieth century."[37] The claim follows an earlier statement: "Allegory is consistently attracted to the fragmentary, the imperfect, the incomplete—an affinity which finds its most comprehensive expression in the ruin, which [Walter] Benjamin identified as the allegorical emblem par excellence. Here the works of man are reabsorbed into the landscape; ruins thus stand for history as an irreversible process of dissolution and decay, a progressive distancing from origin."[38] Indeed, Owens posited that it is the interest in ruins, as reminders of not only the past but of the passing of all things (identified as entropy in Smithson's case), that fueled site specificity and not the other way around. The ruin is attractive to an allegorist not only because of its qualities of being an imperfect and incomplete fragment but also because these qualities bespeak a particular sense of time and history, both conceived as moving inevitably toward decay, disintegration, and loss. "Allegory emerges from the will to preserve the traces of something that was dead, or about to die."[39] To further elaborate on this sense of time that compels the allegorist (as evidenced in his fascination with ruins), Owens

 Robert Smithson, *Spiral Jetty*, 1970

highlighted Benjamin's analysis of Charles Baudelaire's writings on modernity, reclaiming the famed writer of modern life as a defender of allegory. While recognizing "the transient, the fleeting, the contingent" as salient characteristics of his modern present, Baudelaire also saw in the hustle and bustle of his Paris its future decline and disappearance and understood the future as a lost past, as a ruin of the present, just like the ancient cities of Greece and Rome that have disappeared and were no longer available to the poet.[40] Owens argued that for Baudelaire and others, the interest in ruins was inflected with an intense sensitivity to the demise and inaccessibility of the present in/for the future, reflecting allegory's peculiar temporal orientation of moving toward the future while facing the past.[41]

Given all that has been discussed so far, it is perhaps not a surprise to discover that the ruin is a critically generative concept for Gerard & Kelly as well, although their sense of the term may be differently nuanced than as found in the work of Baudelaire, Benjamin, Smithson, and Owens.[42] The artists have stated on more than one occasion the significance of the ruin as a heuristic through which they approach many of their projects. For instance, regarding *Panorama*, they have said:

> The ["Panorama du Commerce"] detaches from the rest of the building like a relic, an antagonism to Ando's simplicity, out of sync with the aspirations of our contemporary, multicultural and cosmopolitan society. It is a ruin that whispers from another world, across the gulf of time, to share a view of history whose violent effects are still present in the contemporary perceptions we have of ourselves and others.[43]

In characterizing "Panorama du Commerce" as a relic and a ruin, the artists mean to recognize both the outmodedness of the pictorial conventions of the mural's traditional academic composition and the pastness of what it represents, the underlying political-economic-nationalist ethos that drove Euro-Western industrial capitalism and its accompanying colonialist and imperialist enterprises across the world. Both seem to be out-of-date today, no longer viable for one reason or another so not of "our time," or in the artists' words, "out of sync with the aspirations of our contemporary, multicultural, and cosmopolitan society." But to say that the "Panorama du Commerce" and what it represents is a ruin is not to say that it is no longer relevant or significant in and for our time. To be sure, as the artists acknowledge, aspects of the future dreams registered in "Panorama du Commerce" are not completely dead. They live on as ruins. And to the extent that they literally provide an evidentiary connection to the past, albeit in an incomplete and fragmentary way, ruins also offer opportunities to reimagine past futures and future pasts, that is, our time. What Owens saw as the theoretical underpinning of Baudelaire's work–the "amalgamation of past and present"[44]–and as I described earlier as the interpenetration of past and present, is also congealed in ruins, and as such they allow what Gerard & Kelly have described as a chance to "reflect upon the past while re-inventing the world in the present tense."

• • •

40.
Following Walter Benjamin's lead, Owens argued that Baudelaire tried to protect or claim allegory for modernity. The critic pointed out that in the poet's key writings, there is a "theoretical underpinning of an amalgamation of the present and the past," an idea that has already been posited as central to the work of Gerard & Kelly. Owens went on to say that for Baudelaire modernity is defined as "the transient, the fleeting, the contingent" but this is "one half of [modern] art, the other being the eternal and the immovable.'" Owens continued: "If the modern artist was exhorted to concentrate on the ephemeral, however, it was *because* it was ephemeral, that is, it threatened to disappear without a trace. Baudelaire conceived modern art at least in part as the rescuing of modernity for eternity." According to Owens, Walter Benjamin recognized this allegorical dimension of Baudelaire's thinking and characterized it as being in affinity with Maxime Du Camp's immense study of the daily life of Paris, *Paris, ses organs, ses fonctions, sa vie dans la seconde moitie du XIXe siècle* (1869–1875). Perhaps not by accident, Du Camp is better known today for photographs from his travels in Africa, the Middle East, and the Orient, many of which are images of ruins. For more details on the intricacies of Owens' argument on Baudelaire, see Owens, "The Allegorical Impulse," 77–78.

41.
See footnote 14 on the figuration of this orientation in Paul Klee's *Angelus Novus* (1920) as interpreted by Walter Benjamin.

42.
The sensibility regarding ruins that Owens covers in his essay may not be 100% coincident with Gerard & Kelly's use of the ruin since the critic asserted that the will to preserve the traces of something dead or dying is a key characteristic of allegory. Gerard & Kelly's interest in ruins is not invested in preservation, for instance. It does not reflect any fetishistic desire to freeze the remnants of the past in order to have them exist as dead specimens for the present and into the future. Which is to say, their engagement with ruins is not motivated by the kind of ethos regarding the past that commonly define historic preservation or art conservation in which the past is conceptually maintained as a distant entity, separate and remote in relation to the present. It may also deviate from the kind of fascination of ruins that fuels the allegorical model posed by Owens.

43.
Gerard & Kelly, "Notes on *Panorama*," 4.

44.
Owens, "The Allegorical Impulse," 77.

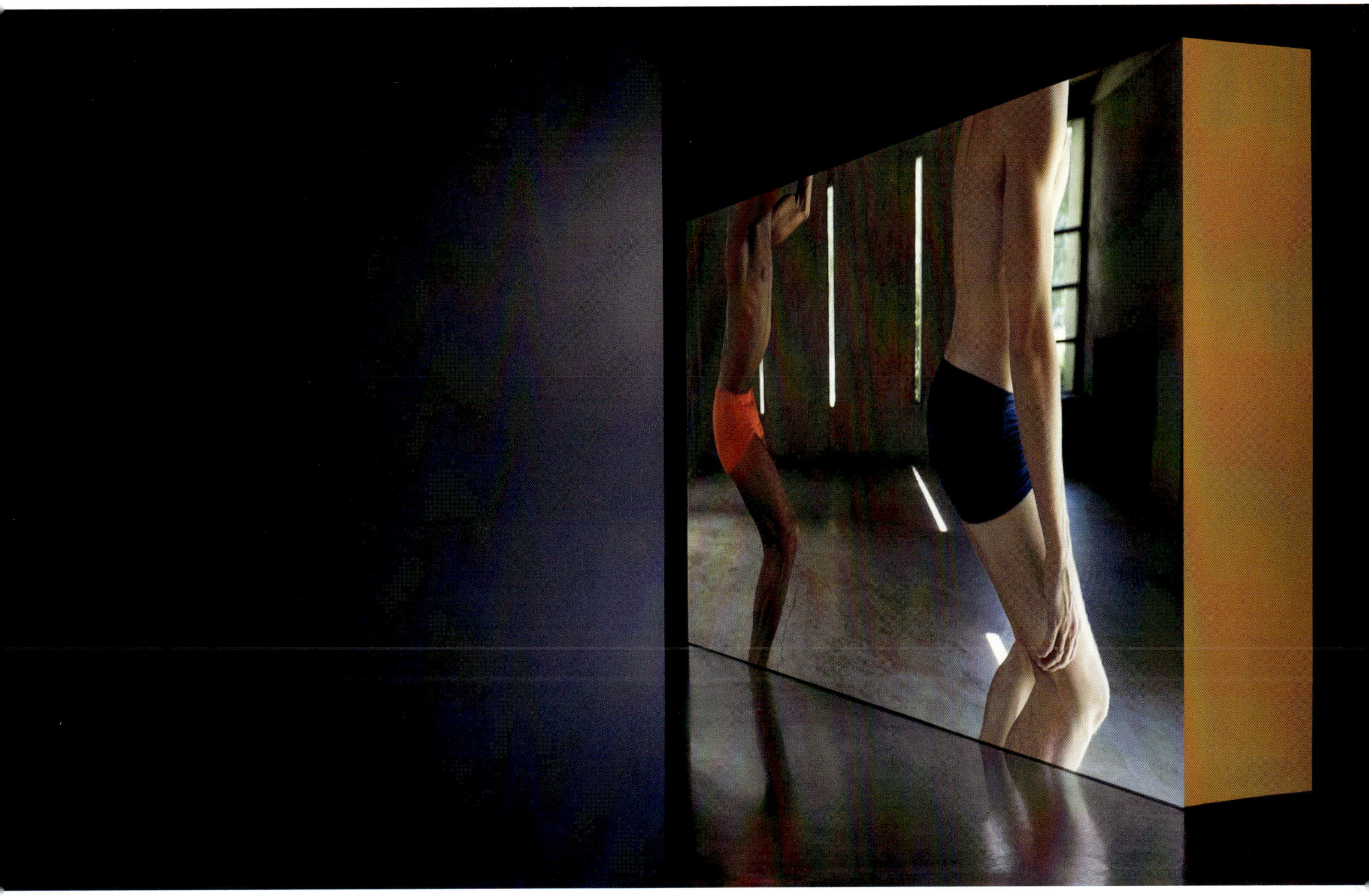

45.
The notion of "ruins of modernism" appears in several unpublished writings and program documents from Gerard & Kelly's archive. It also appears in a range of publicity materials on their *Modern Living* series. See, for example, https://pioneerworks.org/exhibitions/gerard-kelly and https://www.gsd.harvard.edu/event/gerard-and-kelly-on-modern-living/.

46.
The series, according to the artists, is structured in chapters and is ongoing. The completed projects at the four buildings mentioned constitute the first four chapters of *Modern Living*. A fifth chapter is planned for the E-1027 Villa designed by Eileen Gray in Roquebrune-Cap-Martin, France (1929).

Unexpectedly, the artists have declared modern buildings, much newer than the Bourse de Commerce, as ruins as well. Unlike the site of *Panorama*, these buildings are small structures, private homes, originally designed to be inhabited by a handful of people at the most. Although much smaller in scale and size than the Bourse de Commerce, each building is not any less monumental, however, in its stature as a canonic edifice of architectural modernism of the twentieth century. But these modern buildings, meant to shelter and support newly emancipated and liberated lives that would redefine domesticity, family, intimacy, and privacy, are all empty houses now, open to the public as historical relics, what the artists call "ruins of modernism."[45] The Schindler House designed by Rudolf M. Schindler in West Hollywood, California, USA (1922), the Villa Savoye designed by Le Corbusier in Poissy, France (1931), the Glass House designed by Philip Johnson in New Caanan, Connecticut, USA (1949), and the Farnsworth House designed by Mies van der Rohe in Plano, Illinois, USA (1951) have each served as the staging ground for site-specific dance performances written and choreographed by Gerard & Kelly that have evolved (and continue to do so) beyond the in-situ events into films/videos, sculptures, performances, installations, and exhibitions that collectively belong to the artists' *Modern Living* series begun in 2016.[46]

Like archeologists confronting the elusory remains of a bygone civilization, Gerard & Kelly have approached these famous houses to both retrieve aspects of their lost histories and to search for clues that may unlock possible paths to the "reinvention of the world in the present tense." Understanding architecture as another form of choreography, the artists have activated the carcass-like structures of these buildings with living bodies to excavate the memories and dreams, as well as identities and relationships, that the designers of these homes once realized or aspired to realize. At the Schindler House, with its pinwheel plan originally designed to house two newlywed couples, the artists mined its buried ambition of achieving a model of communal living that eschews the ideology of the heteronormative couple and family.[47] The house not only breaks down the division between interior and exterior with walls that slide away, it also rejects the convention of having fixed functions for spaces defined as rooms, exclusively dedicated to eating, cooking, sleeping, gathering, having sex, reading, playing, working, etc. With possibilities for open-ended, overlapping, and combinatory spaces, Schindler and his composer wife Pauline Gibling imagined open-ended, overlapping, and combinatory relationships between the inhabitants.[48] At the Glass House, Gerard & Kelly took a cue from Johnson's clever architectural play on the notion of an "open secret," exploring how the extreme visual exposure afforded by the complete transparency of the rectangular prism paradoxically functions to deflect and obscure views. The architecture here simultaneously reveals *and* "closets" the life within, manifesting both the desire to see and to be seen alongside the equally strong desire to remain undetected and invisible. The architectural treatment of this seemingly contradictory desire as a fundamental attribute of the Glass House is especially meaningful given that it protected Johnson's gay identity and his long-term relationship with his life partner, art collector and curator David Whitney. The house's purposeful confusion of transparency and opacity allowed for homosexual domesticity and intimacy to hide in plain sight at a time when they were considered deviant and criminal.[49]

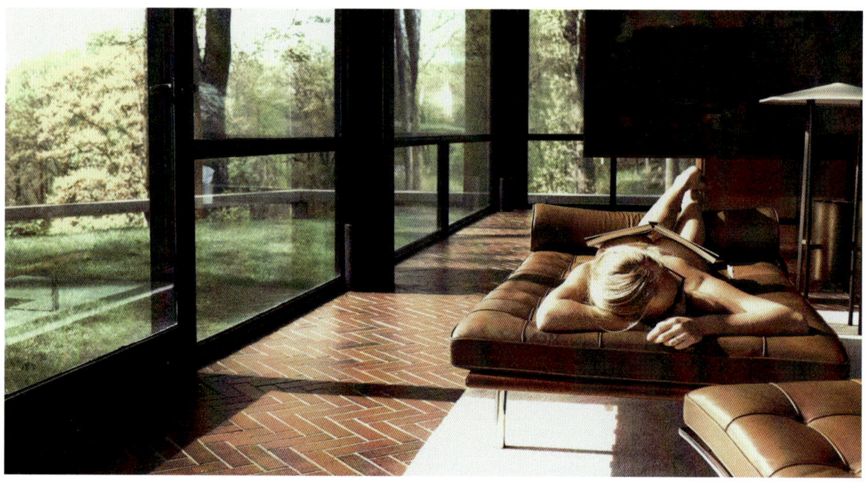

Gerard & Kelly's two-channel film installation entitled *Schindler/Glass* from 2017 constellates these two buildings as a pair, with film segments from the dance performances at the two houses presented on two free-standing walls that sometimes appear adjoined as one depending on the movement of the viewer through the exhibition space. The together-and-separate disposition of these two walls made for the film projection is a false diptych. It is a sculptural translation of the conceptual throughline in this work and the *Modern Living* series in general, carrying into the physical gallery space the interrogation of the notion of the "couple," the commonplace twosome, the

47.
Since 1994, the Schindler House has been the home of the MAK Center for Art and Architecture, functioning as a non-profit arts organization and a satellite of Museum of Applied Arts in Vienna. For general information on the center's history and programs, see https://www.makcenter.org/.

48.
For an incisive summary of the history of the Schindler house and Gerard & Kelly's 2016 performance there, see Mimi Cheng, "Modern Lives, Modern Loves: Gerard & Kelly's *Schindler/Glass*," in *Avery Review* 33 (September 2018), http://averyreview.com/issues/33/modern-lives-modern-loves.

49.
It should be remembered that the Glass House was designed and built twenty years before the Stonewall Rebellion and before a more public call for gay civil rights fomented at a large societal scale. The Glass House was also designed and constructed at the same time as the Brick House, the two structures conceived as one composition. The two buildings are not only sited near one another on the 50-acre property today but are linked by a grassy court. If the Glass House is all about light and transparency, so much so that it looks to disappear into the landscape at certain times, the Brick House is about enclosure and containment and is an obdurate presence. One could argue the two buildings function like a mirror reflection of the other, an experiment on the coordination of opposites as well as, perhaps, an architectural essay on the couple. On the relationship between Johnson's gay identity and the reading of the Glass House as a queer space, see, https://theglasshouse.org/whats-on/the-glass-house-as-queer-space/.

smallest unit of identity beyond the individual self. Which is to say, *Schindler/Glass* moves beyond the origin stories of the two houses as specific architect-designed homes for specific architect-arts couples. The work showcases, on the one hand, the two buildings' unique features that frame vision and movement, emphasizing how their architecture (re)orders interactions and relationships as well as fantasies and desires, ultimately mapping alternative models of private life, domesticity, and intimacy. On the other hand, *Schindler/Glass* extrapolates and brings to the fore the divergent models of collectivity and sociality—beyond the couple to the family, a community, to even possibly a society and a nation—that are also embedded in the form and history of these outdated structures.

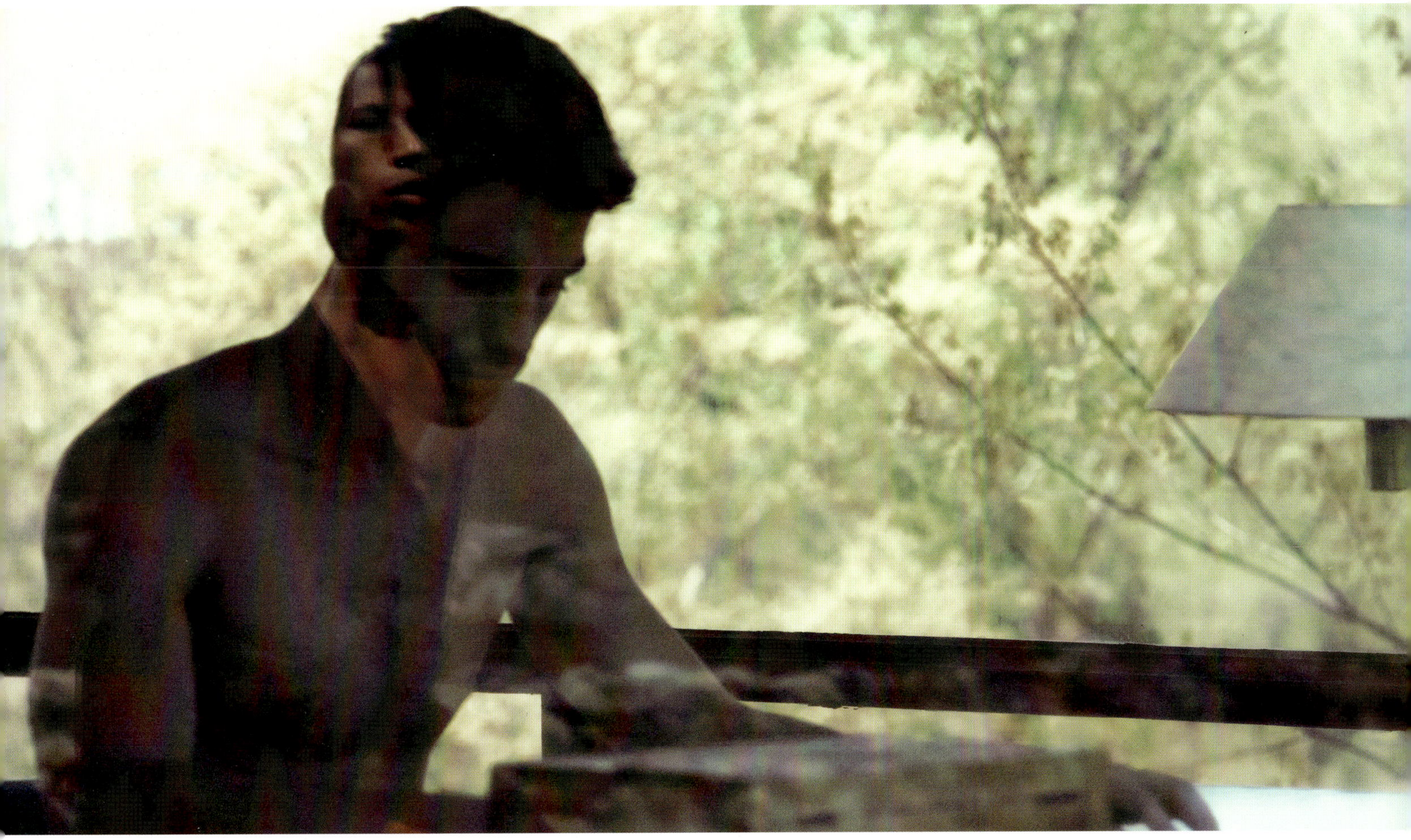

The Schindler House and the Glass House are both adaptations of European modernist ideals from the early twentieth century for a new way of building and living (and by extension shaping society), transplanted and realized on North American soil, one on the west coast in sunny Los Angeles, which in the early 1920s was far from the urban metropolis that it is now, and the other on the east coast in a well-established small town of white suburban affluence that remains so today. In these contrasting contexts, and built almost twenty years apart, the two houses offer contrasting (utopic) visions of human co-habitation and gathering. On the Glass House side of the *Schindler/Glass* coupling, which comes first and comprises about half of the film, Gerard & Kelly's choreography sequentially introduces three distinct couples—they could be siblings or lovers—each moving through choreographic duets while calling out a set of numbers. "*. . . three, four, three, four, five, five, five, five. . . ten, ten, eleven, eleven, eleven,*

25 *Schindler/Glass*, 2017

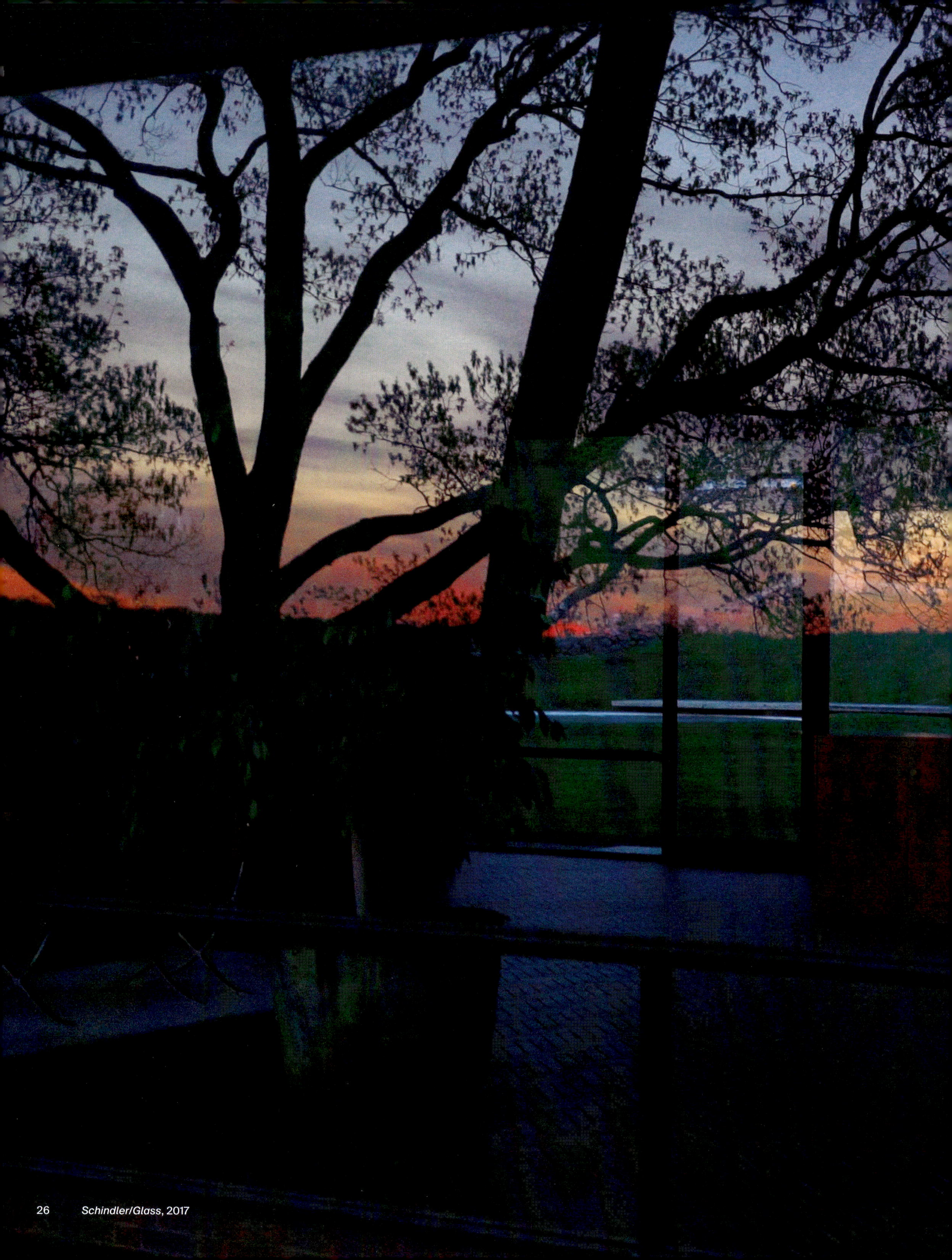

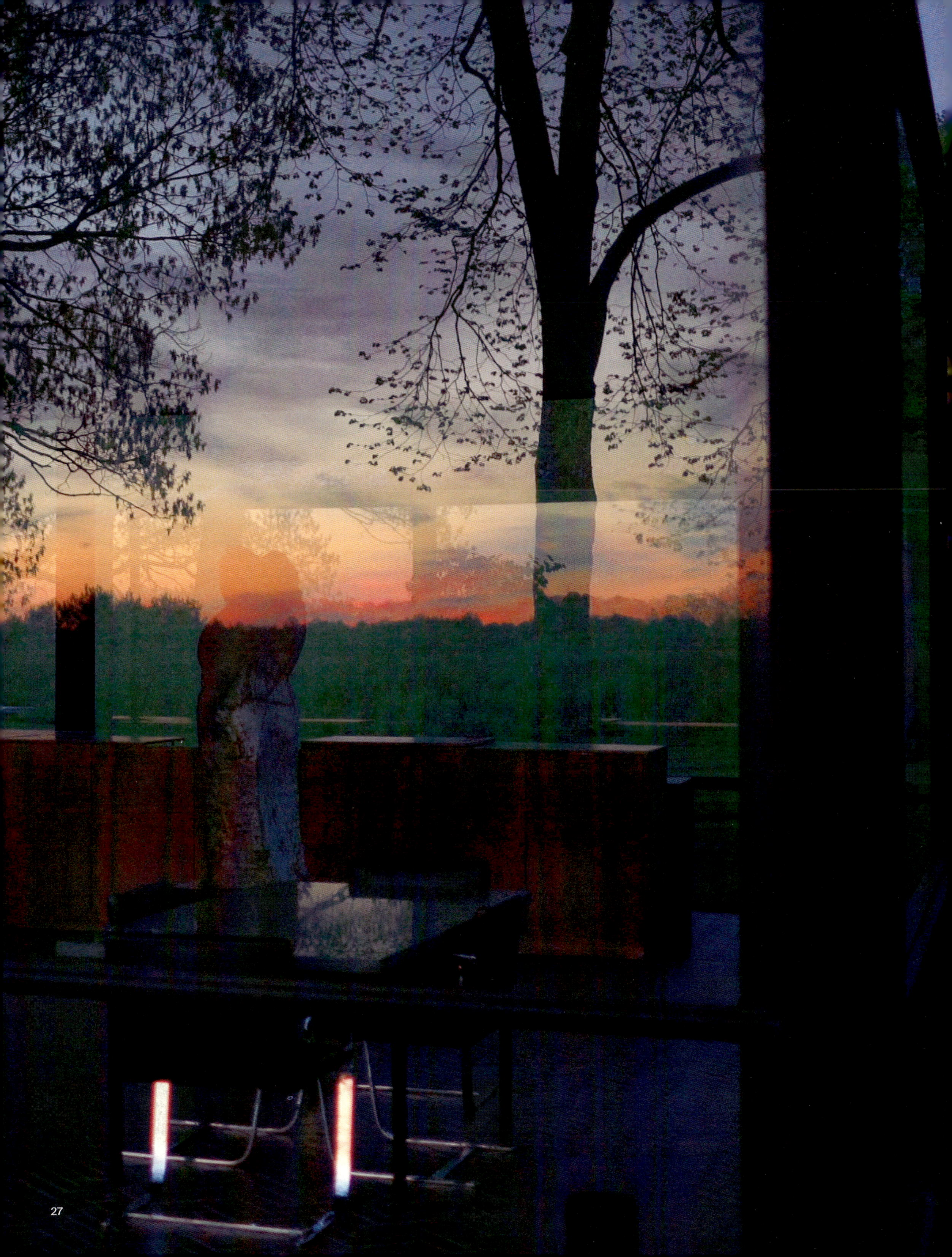

eleven, eleven, twelve,. . ."[50] This counting at the opening of the film could be part of a game, like kids following their own mysterious and idiosyncratic rules of play. But counting is also the sound of marking time and marking steps, a method of learning, repeating and remembering movements in relation to time, an activity especially familiar to dancers.[51] This vocalized accounting of time accompanies all three of the couples' internal interactions, underscoring their synchronicity (oneness) at certain moments and their disconnection (separateness) at others. Eventually, the counting comes to an end with the declaration of "Infinity," spoken by one of the dancers. Then, sound and image shifts dramatically to the presence of a new group of people inside the Glass House, men and women all dressed in same black suits and lined up in a grid formation, executing identical movements. Their singing of an anthem-like tune is soon overtaken by what could be sounds of heavy boots on the ground, the metronomic rhythms of marching feet echoing the rhythmic mathematics of Johnson's modular architecture. And as the camera pulls back from the scene of this quasi-militaristic gathering, the film delivers a darkening view of the Glass House, disappearing into its own reflections against a hot setting sun.[52]

Superimposed onto the fading image of the Glass House, the Schindler House gradually appears, specifically its outdoor fireplace burning brightly into the night. As the house soon awakens from its slumber, sounds of chimes and gongs vibrate through the air announcing an earthy and somewhat primitivistic morning call (in contrast to the electronic beats and soundscapes that enveloped the Glass House earlier).[53] Most of the dancers who were seen at the Glass House are here again, this time individually stationed at set positions throughout the house and across the luscious grounds that surround it. The camera is active, framing two or three dancers at a time to accentuate Schindler's architectural framing of them, while at the same time competing with the architecture, cutting across walls and windows to construct alternative cinematic visual-spatial coordinates between the performers. All the while, in this opening segment, Gerard & Kelly pays homage to Trisha Brown's *Roof Piece* (1971)[54] with their nine dancers each taking their turns mimicking short movement sequences performed by another dancer some distance away. The reactivation of Brown's simple choreography at the Schindler House, an allegorical doubling of a prior text in Owens' sense, demonstrates in a highly condensed and abstracted form the fundamental process of transmission of knowledge. Imitation is a basic

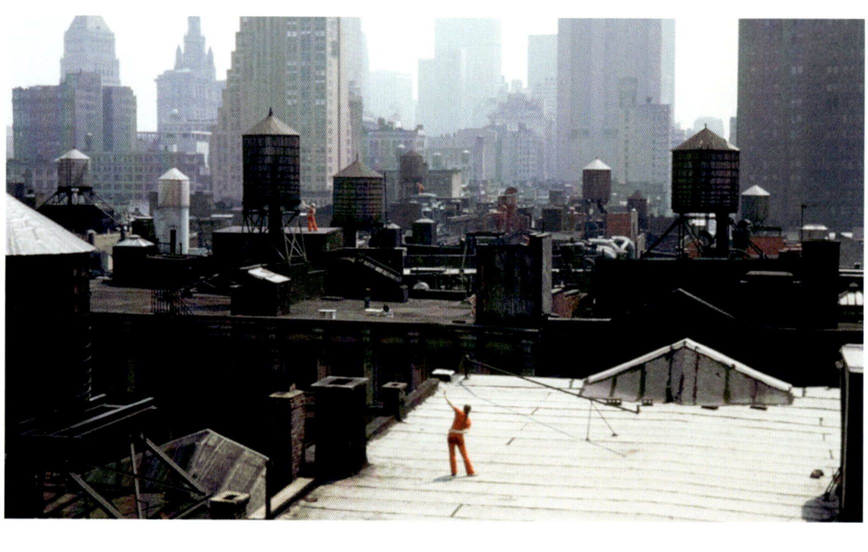

Trisha Brown, *Roof Piece*, 1973

50.
Gerard & Kelly, *Schindler/Glass*, 2017, HD video on two channels, color, sound, 35', 00:24–01:15.

51.
Other Gerard & Kelly performance works, such as *Timelining* (2014) and *Clockwork* (2018), also involve performers vocally marking time through counting as a structure for the generation and sequencing of movement. Dancers become their own clocks, integrating fragments of their own personal memories as part of the material basis of their performances. Some aspects of *Timelining* and *Clockwork* along these lines can be found in sequences within *Schindler/Glass*. Additionally, although not explicit, works by Félix González-Torres, especially those manifesting the concurrent passages of time and bodies, as well as his longstanding deliberations on the couple, both well captured in the twin dying clocks of *Untitled (Perfect Lovers)*, (1991), for example, are critical touchstones for Gerard & Kelly's practice. The richness of this connection will have to wait another opportunity for elaboration in an entirely separate essay.

52.
Some of the choreography in this final segment at the Glass House incorporates the ghost of a Nazi salute, invoking Philip Johnson's controversial involvement with Nazism in his early years, which haunted the architect's otherwise celebrated career. The anthem-like tune that the dancers hum in unison is also linked to this history. According to Gerard & Kelly, this hymn is their transcription for voice of the third movement of Igor Stravinsky's *Symphony in Three Movements* (completed in 1945 and first performed in 1946 by the New York Philharmonic Orchestra), which the composer described as being inspired by his recollection of German soldiers goose-stepping. Interestingly, George Balanchine choreographed a ballet set to the composition in 1972 for the New York City Ballet, whose home is another building designed by Johnson, the New York State Theater (renamed in 2008 as the David H. Koch Theater), where Ryan Kelly performed as a member of the dance company in the early 2000s. Buried in Gerard & Kelly's critical reflection on Johnson›s politics in *Schindler/Glass* is a subtle homage to the architect's design of the New York State Theater, which positions the Glass House in a related but different constellation of private and public histories. (Ryan Kelly, email message to author, August 30, 2022.)

53.
The composer for the Glass House part of *Schindler/Glass* is the late music producer SOPHIE. The composers for the Schindler House part of the film are the Los Angeles-based experimental music duo Lucky Dragons.

54.
Trisha Brown is rightly considered an exemplary figure in the multidisciplinary or intermedia artistic experimentations of the postwar era. In recent years, more scholars from the field of art history have begun to pay closer attention to her important contribution to the development of contemporary art (beyond dance). Taking dance off the proscenium stage and out of the theater setting into the urban terrain of downtown Manhattan, *Roof Piece* from 1971 placed dancers across several rooftops of loft buildings in and around Wooster and Lafayette Streets in SoHo, each performer mimicking the movement of another dancer on a different rooftop. The work has been reperformed in recent years on rooftops at various locales. For a consideration of the issues raised in the restaging of this site-specific work, see Amanda Jane Graham's essay "Out of Site: Trisha Brown's 'Roof Piece,'" *Dance Chronicle*, vol. 36, no. 1 (2013): 56–76. Importantly, while the recent re-presentations of this work attempt to confirm the authenticity and originality of the piece as a singular work of art created by Trisha Brown as author, Gerard & Kelly's homage/imitation at the Schindler House allegorically doubles and disperses the work instead.

55.
This relay and transmission process, including not just watching and imitating but listening and replicating, structures Gerard & Kelly's earlier work *Reusable Parts/Endless Love* (2011).
56.
Like Trisha Brown, Simone Forti is a central figure in the development of postwar art, Minimalism in particular, whose influence and contributions remain underacknowledged and understudied. Her position as a dancer and choreographer and her penchant for working against the grain of both dance and art as well as the marketplace has put her in the margins of art history (which continues to be allergic to what it deems to be "theatrical"). But fortunately, more scholarship is emerging from a younger generation. Of particular value is Megan Metcalf's work on Forti. See her "Making the Museum Dance: Simone Forti's *Huddle* (1961) and its Acquisition by the Museum of Modern Art," *Dance Chronicle*, vol 45 (2022): 30–56.

method of learning for children as well as dancers, and it is a form of connection and communication, too, literally a relay, from one person to another.[55] Watch-and-repeat is also, of course, a mode of reproduction, which, in the context of Gerard & Kelly's ongoing interrogation of the couple, is deeply resonant both biologically and ideologically.

Couples and counting, which we saw at the Glass House, recur at the Schindler House, although there is a greater variety of pairings and groupings of performers here, with more fluidity of movement between interior and exterior spaces. There is, in fact, a general breakdown of boundaries through the subsequent scenes, with multiplicity of relations enacted by the dancers—hugging, resisting, embracing, rejecting, slapping, mimicking, holding, pulling, reclining, following, jumping, and supporting one another in pairs or groups that continuously change. Their movements channel the open-ended multiplicity of possibilities of habitation that are offered by the various spaces of the house. Manifesting an exuberant sense of ludic play and even infantilism at times, the dancers ultimately turn into a feral brood on the lawn. From there, they confrontationally declare, "The family is a system of regeneration." The statement is ambiguous in how it can be understood as a critical calling out of conventional family structures (which is an apparatus of ideological reproduction of normative social values) and at the same time a calling for the regeneration of families of a different kind, like the one we see on the screen. But soon the brood falls apart and the dancers all fall down as if life was suddenly sucked out of their bodies. The scene conjures a collective death of innocents, resonant with the dark underbelly of the nursery rhyme "Ring Around the Rosie" (and "we all fall down") as well as the all-too-serious and frequently reported carnage from mass shootings or wars in the news. These references are not far away in the listless bodies of the dancers on the ground at the Schindler House. But this is not the end, and movement emerges anew. Slowly the camera follows the awakening of the dancers, capturing the regeneration of life. In the final sequence of the film, Gerard & Kelly pays homage to another dance pioneer, Simone Forti, and her extraordinary 1961 Dance Construction, *Huddle*.[56] Melting away the division

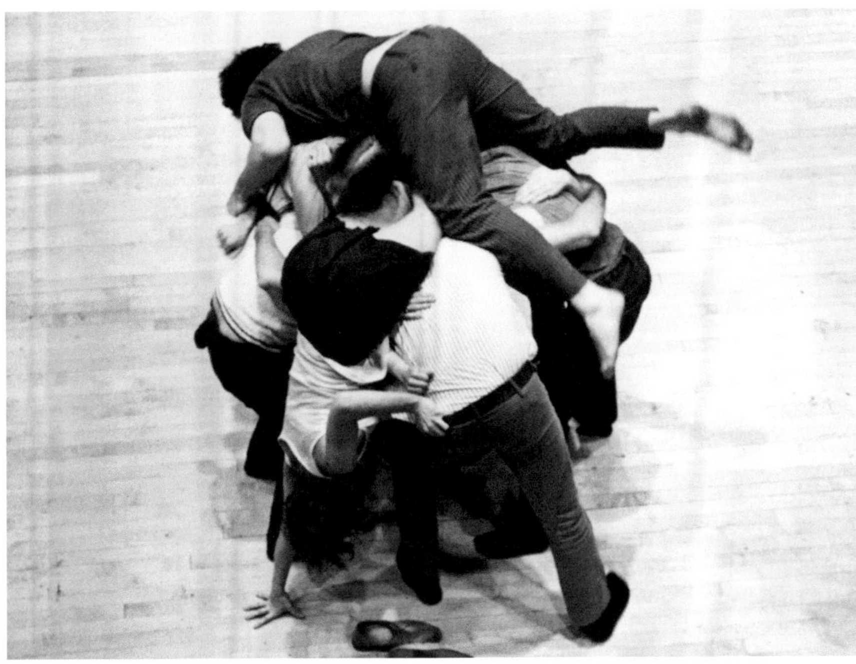

Simone Forti, *Huddle*, 1961

between self and other, the dancers languidly slide above, around, and below one another as the independence of their limbs and bodies become lost in the togetherness of the whole. This huddle's movement is like a molten flow, and the intimate closeup of its evolving formlessness makes even the camera seem like it is part of the process. Importantly, this regeneration does not rise up. Its energy does not reach for the sky. Instead, it moves laterally, keeping close to the earth, immersed in its own churning process of continuous becoming as the film fades to black.

In this way, *Schindler/Glass* offers two very different modern visions of a collective body, two different models of together-and-separate at a larger scale beyond the couple. If we ended with the specter of a fascist army at the Glass House, with individuals maintaining their singularity of self within a field of regularized sameness, we find an entangled pile up of bodies at the Schindler House, pushing toward the obliteration of the boundary between self and other. In the latter, there is an ecstatic overflowing of the self, almost an orgiastic and lawless convergence of bodies and desires that resonates with the hippie counterculture to come in the 1960s, stereotypically associated with California. In the former setting, in contrast, regimentation and disciplined bodies rule, offering an unnervingly satisfying aesthetic of hyper rationality and order that provides its own form of erotic pleasure. Whether or not reducible to the classic opposition of Apollonian vs. Dionysian impulses, Gerard & Kelly's dyadic constellation of the Glass House and the Schindler House in *Schindler/Glass* seems to pose the two sites as a dialectically bound couple, together-and-separate, reflecting the ruins of modernism's complex aesthetic-political legacies.

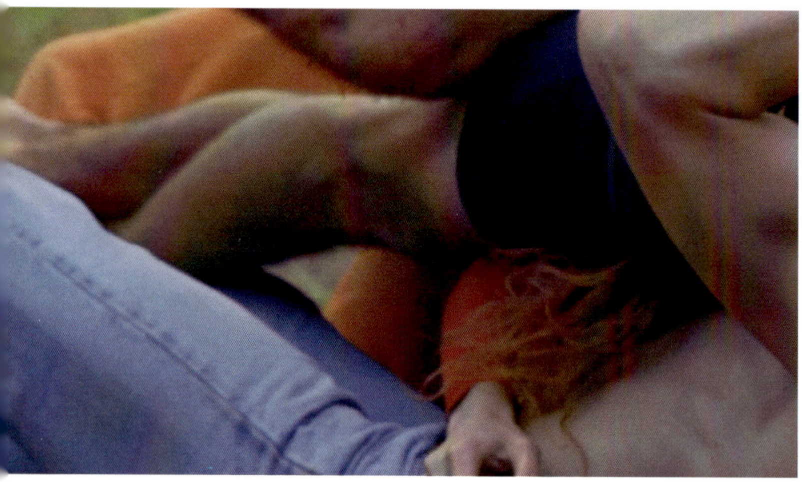

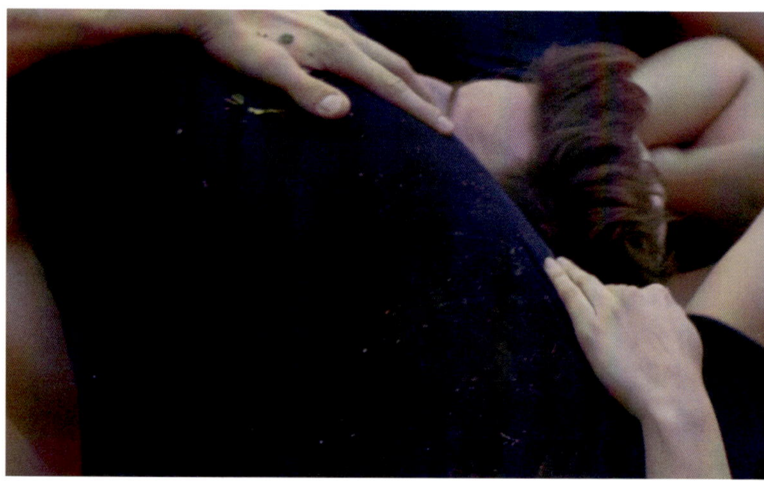

The exploration of the couple and allegory as a mode of inquiry have continued in Gerard & Kelly's performances at the Farnsworth House (2017) and the Villa Savoye (2019), both part of their *Modern Living* series. At the Farnsworth House, the architecture is interrogated through an examination of the couple relationship between the architect and client–Mies van der Rohe and Edith Farnsworth–uncovering how the immaculate perfection of the building's design and its liberatory rhetoric failed to support domestic needs and realities of even a very progressive client. Presence-ing Dr. Farnsworth through voice and movement, Gerard & Kelly reveal the entrenched and repressive gender politics informing the Farnsworth House and

Schindler/Glass, 2017

57.
For an in-depth description of this work in relation to the history and historiography of the Farnsworth House as well as Gerard & Kelly's working process in creating the piece, see Nora Wendl, "I remember: On *Modern Living*," in *Ventriloquism, Performance, and Contemporary Art*, eds. Jennie Hirsch and Isabelle Loring Wallace (Abingdon, England; New York, NY: Routledge, forthcoming).

58.
The performance at the Villa Savoye was part of the Festival d'Automne à Paris and was presented to the public September 28–29 and October 5–6, 2019. The program notes from the event reads: "The work channels the encounter between the architect [Le Corbusier] and American performer Josephine Baker, which took place on a transatlantic voyage in 1929 at the same time he was designing the house." See also https://www.festival-automne.com/en/edition-2019/gerard-kelly-modern-living.

its subsequent historicization as a monument of International Style architecture. Unlike *Schindler/Glass*, however, in which dance performances evolved into a film installation, the two-dancer program at the Farnsworth House has yielded large-scale sculptures instead. *Untitled (for Edith)* and *skin and bones*, both dated 2018, materially reinscribe aspects of the Farnsworth House and its history as palimpsestic constructions.[57] Likewise, the performance event at the Villa Savoye did not directly develop into a film. Here, at the site of another monument of International Style architecture, Gerard & Kelly orchestrate the coupling of the Swiss/French architect Le Corbusier and African-American singer/dancer Josephine Baker, allowing their performers to translate the architect's writings and concepts into movement and the singer's songs and dances into spatial relationships.[58] The historical fact of Le Corbusier and Baker's affair is carried forward beyond the in-situ performance at the Villa Savoye, functioning as the potent basis for Gerard & Kelly's most recently completed film *Bright Hours* (2022). Sited at the Cité Radieuse in Marseille, the most well-known and celebrated of Le Corbusier's Unité d'Habitation residential housing complexes, the artists reflect on the amorous meeting of a white European man and a Black American woman on a cruise ship in 1929 as it may have impacted not only the couple, each carrying his and her own historical burdens and desires, but also the innovative forms of the building and its utopian aspirations.

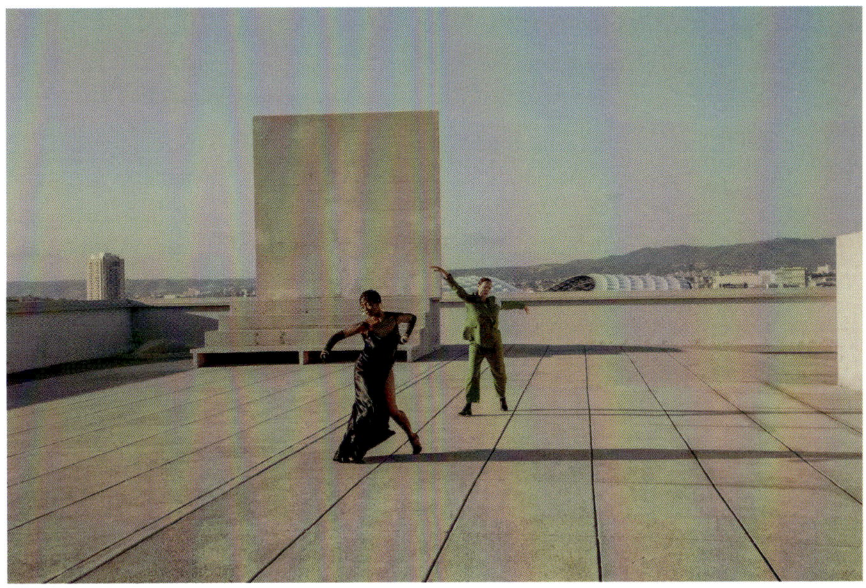

The trajectory of Gerard & Kelly's work over the past decade from the many machinations of the *Modern Living* series to the more recent films *Panorama* and *Bright Hours*, indicates the artists' ongoing investment in exploring the space in between dance, architecture and film, indeed in creating combinatory works that are "a hybrid between a dance film and a cinematographic essay" that rigorously attend to past forms, ideas, and lives in order to reimagine the present and future. As explored in this essay, however, notions of past, present, and future are not neat sequential categories for Gerard & Kelly. Neither is self and other. Recognizing opposites as dialectical, and nurturing their mutuality and interpenetration, the artists consistently disrespect existing categories in order to generate multiplicities of voices, times, identities, and meanings in and through their work. But multiplicity in and of itself is not enough. It cannot be an automatic positive value since it can also be simply a mess. With the use of the term "constellation" in the title of this essay and as it appeared here and there within this writing, I mean to differentiate Gerard & Kelly's method of mapping across affinities, associations, and dialectical pairings from mere juxtaposition or lazy accumulation as we see in so much contemporary art today. The specificity of what is constellated and the precision of how the constellation takes shape matter, and this precision and specificity is what really counts in the production of viable new meaning. To designate Gerard & Kelly's art as allegorical constellations is also to recognize how their work functions like a set of vectors, incorporating a sense of movement. And as such, as constellations, their work has no center. Theirs is an art without an interior, like the stars in the sky.

• • •

In the final segment of *Panorama*, sounds of thunder and rain announce what could be an ending or a new beginning. Perhaps this is the storm that Memory saw coming. Recalling the opening sequence of the film, the camera slowly pans down from the glass ceiling of the Bourse de Commerce to find, this time, Avenir in the middle of the rotunda, alone. Dwarfed by the grand architecture, he is dancing by himself circling the space under the dome. The delicately haunting and moody piano music of Julius Eastman competes with the sounds of the storm, rising then fading beneath loud claps of thunder. Miraculously, it is raining inside the building. The camera sees Avenir looking upwards, turning his head toward the glass ceiling and the source of the rain. Drops of water become streams, drenching her face as the dance continues while Eastman's rhythmic piano returns, insistent this time, as if to propel Avenir's movement onwards. The camera is now much closer, dancing with Avenir, catching quick passing glimpses of her face, torso, arms, hands, and shoulder, some of which are obscured by the fogging of the lens. Then cut to darkness, with Eastman's piano becoming louder and more ascendant, even urgent. Avenir's wet face reappears, very briefly. No more dancing. He confronts the viewer's gaze. Her expression is mysterious, not quite blank but also not expressive. Is there sorrow in those eyes, in his countenance? Is it worry? Anger? Resignation? Anticipation? Fear? Resolve? Uncertainty? Exhaustion? Before an answer could be had, Avenir disappears again as Eastman's music continues its surging, spinning, reaching search as final credits roll.

The ending of *Panorama* is a discomforting ambiguity. It does not offer a celebratory or energizing sense of the new beginning that awaits the Bourse de Commerce as a museum of contemporary art. Perhaps this is because we know all too well that art is not the antithesis of commerce. While many will continue to believe, or wish to believe, that art occupies a higher realm uncontaminated by money and commercialism, there is no real separation between the circulation and accumulation of finance capital and symbolic capital today. Art has become (or it always was) a highly sophisticated instrument of commercial exchange, even as it continues to offer other things like beauty, spiritual uplift, and enlightenment. A museum in the twenty-first century thus cannot be seen as a zone that is free of the marketplace since it is a market place, too, albeit of another kind that

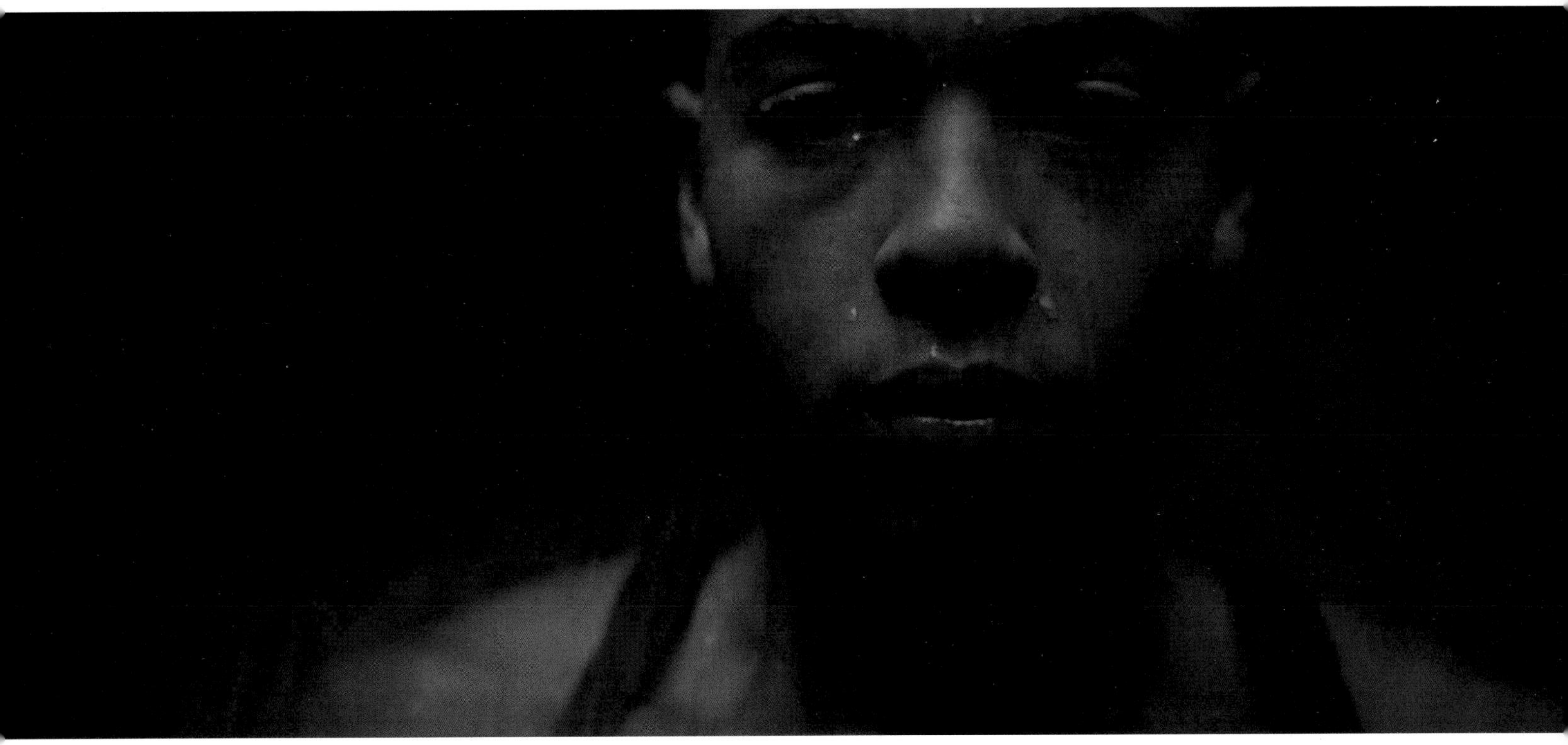

engages in highly abstracted and specialized commodity forms and modes of exchange. Although literal trading of art as commodities will not be happening at the Bourse de Commerce, it can be argued that the opening of the Pinault Collection at the historic site represents less the displacement of commerce by art and more the expansion of the currencies that pass through its halls—from wheat and corn, to now contemporary art. Like Avenir, and perhaps Gerard & Kelly, too, we await what is to come here with apprehension and optimism.

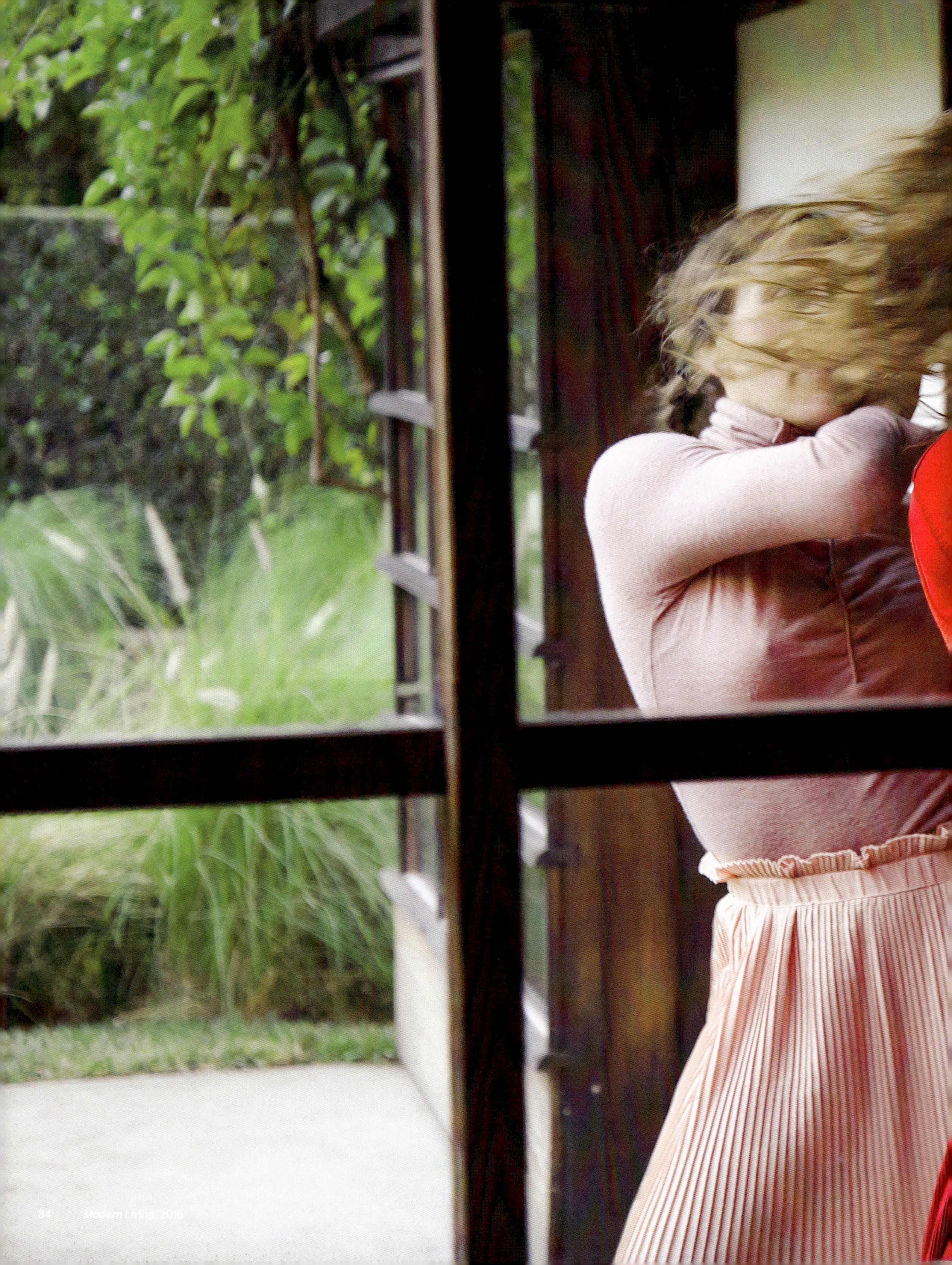

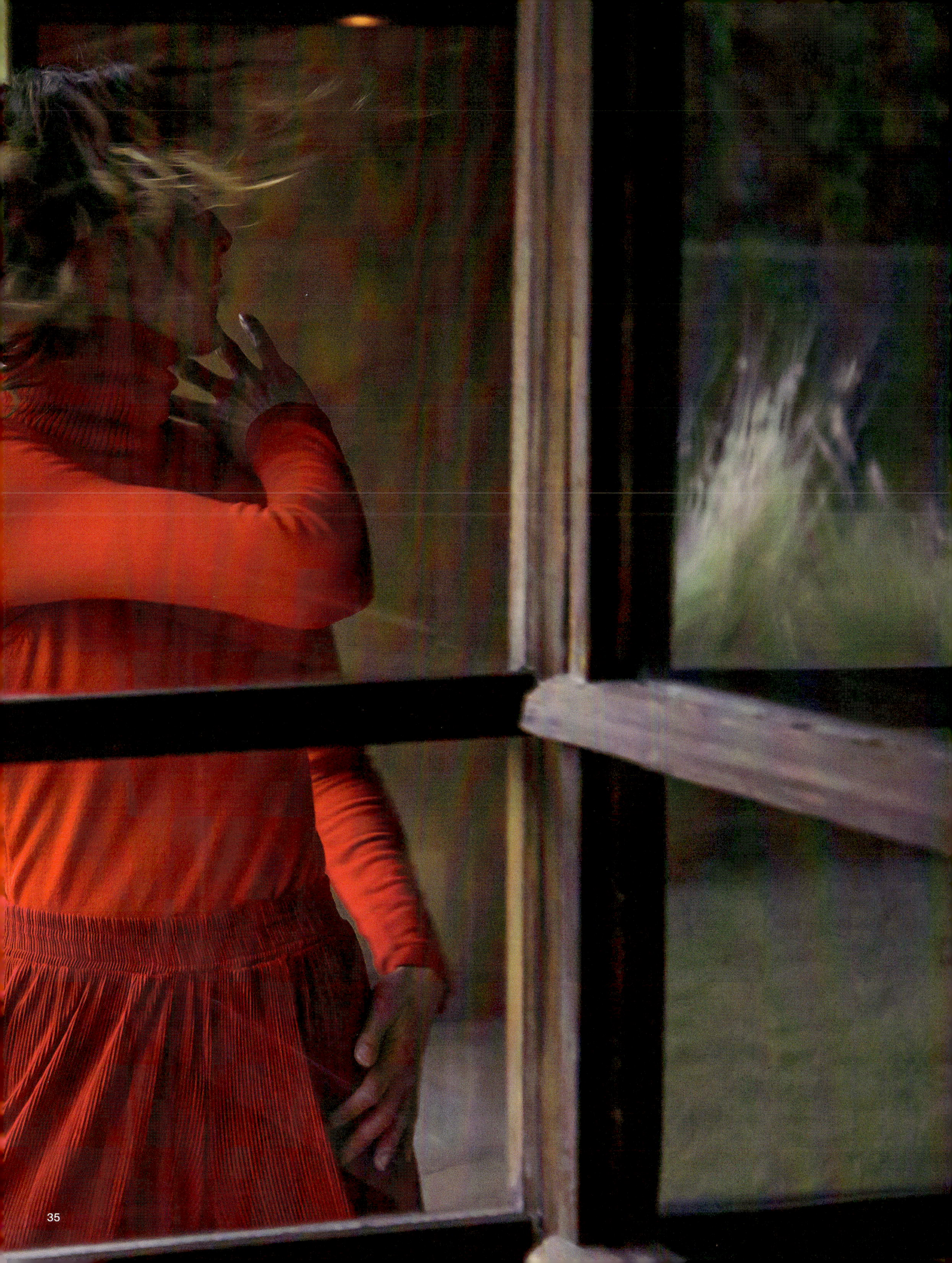

There, Where Subjectivity Flickers

Lou Forster in conversation with Gerard & Kelly

Conducted on January 20, 2021, and May 18, 2022, at the author's home in Paris and Gerard & Kelly's studio in Aubervilliers, France, this interview addresses the genesis of *Ruins* and the works that comprise the exhibition. The conversation develops against the backdrop of a shared experience: the author performed in the artists' *Timelining* alongside dancer and choreographer Lenio Kaklea from 2014 to 2017. An emphasis on the artists' collaborations with performers thus emerges in the interview, revealing the narratives of lived experience embedded in their works.

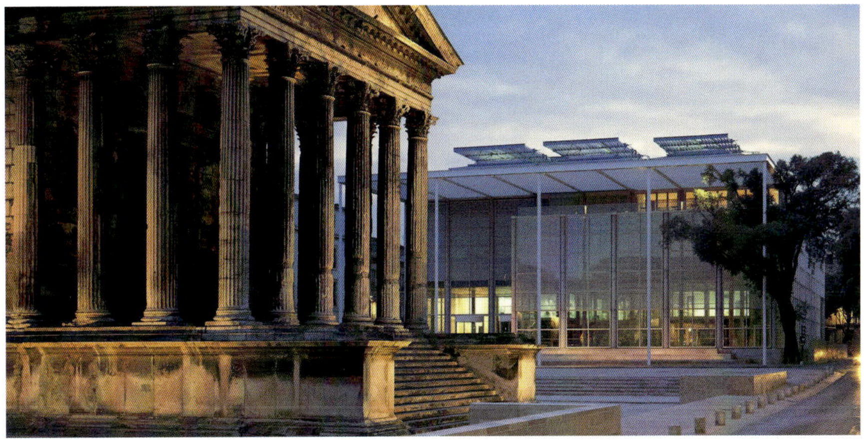

View of the Maison Carrée and Carré d'Art, Nîmes

Lou Forster

How did you approach the exhibition at Carré d'Art? Would you rightly call it a retrospective of your work, which started almost 20 years ago?

Ryan Kelly

When we arrived in Nîmes I was impressed by this postmodern site, which brings together in the same public square a 2,000-year-old Roman temple and a 30-year-old "glass box" by architect Norman Foster–the Maison Carrée and the Carré d'Art, respectively. It is a disconcerting sight, because the museum's architecture is at once a palimpsest and a ruin. In thinking about the exhibition, I sense that we keep coming back to this view, which makes me think of what Craig Owens and Douglas Crimp have written about the museum.[1] As a result, archives, history, abstract forms, temporality, narrative are all subjects that float through the exhibition.

Brennan Gerard

I wouldn't say it's a retrospective, but an overview of a little less than a decade of our work. The exhibition explores questions of relationships and intimacy through sculpture, film, and installation. Our performance practice is pushed to the very end of the exhibition. Although composed of autonomous works, it's indeed a site-specific exhibition. What is this site designed by Norman Foster? An architecture faithful to the modernist canon, dominated by the use of glass. Our project for this museum connects to the site not only in a discursive, but also in a phenomenological way. The first thing visitors will see as they walk up the stairs is the installation *Relay* (2018), a multi-colored vinyl work applied to the windows on the top floor of Carré d'Art, from which the old city of Nîmes can be seen. This work constantly changes because of the light passing through; there is a performative dimension to it. *Relay* is also the trace of performances we have made since 2016 as part of our *Modern Living* project. In this series, nine dancers transmit a gestural message throughout the architecture and site. The order of the colors in the installation is the

1.
See Craig Owens, "The Allegorical Impulse: Towards a Theory of Postmodernism (parts 1 and 2)", *Beyond Recognition: Representation, Power, and Culture* (Berkeley: University of California Press, 1994); and Douglas Crimp, *On The Museum's Ruins*, (Cambridge: MIT Press, 1993).

same as that of the monochrome costumes worn by the dancers in the performance. *Relay*, as the moving diagram of this choreographic action, is ultimately more faithful to the live event than any other form of documentation could be.

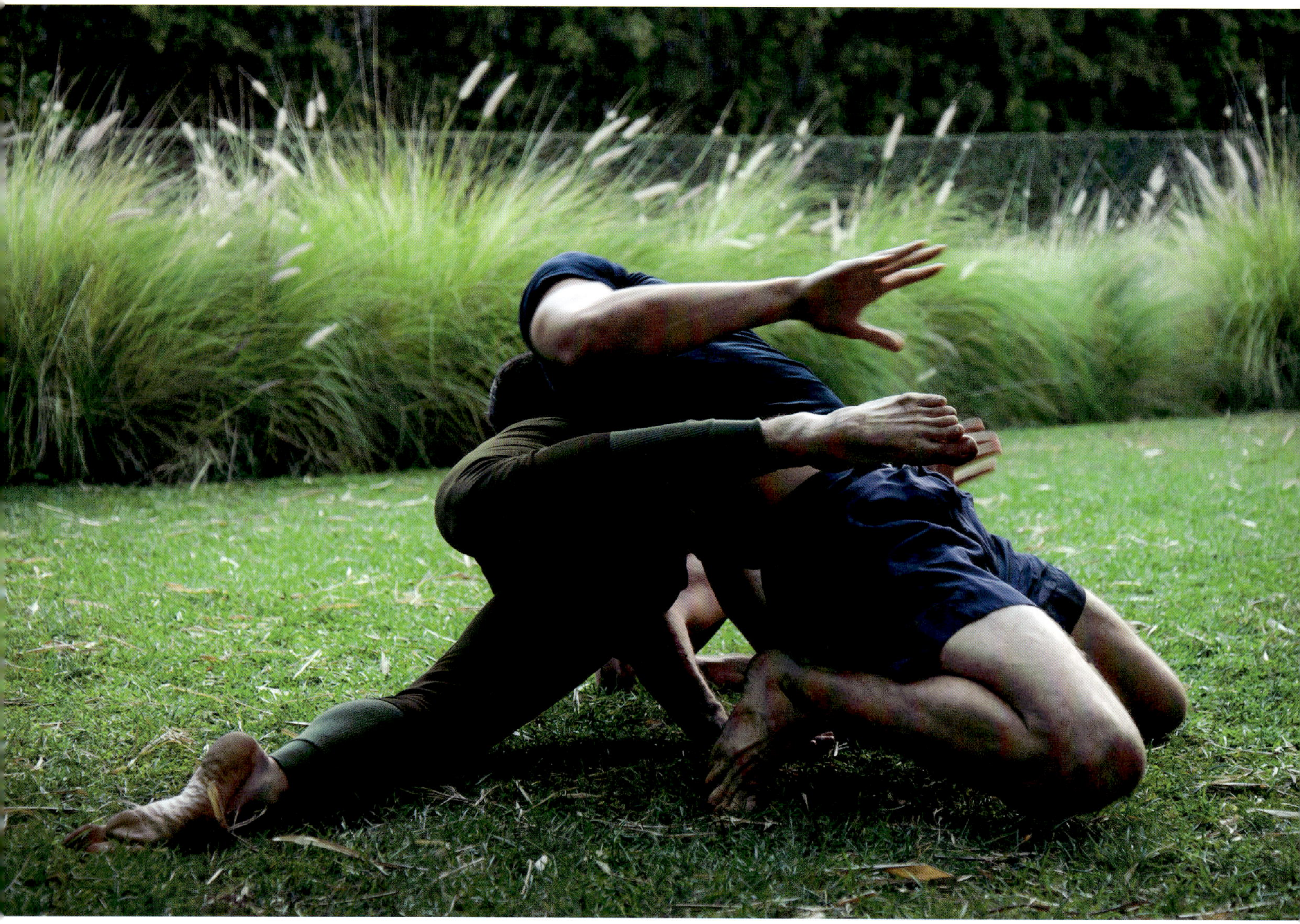

Modern Living

LF

Modern Living was developed in two phases. From 2016 to 2018, you worked in the United States in three iconic houses by modernist architects, Rudolf Schindler's house (1922) and the two Glass Houses by Philip Johnson and Ludwig Mies van der Rohe, built in 1949 and 1951 respectively. Since 2018 your activity has shifted to France, where you've been interested in several of Le Corbusier's dwellings—namely his Apartment-Studio in Paris (1934), the Villa Savoye in Poissy (1931), and the Cité Radieuse in Marseille (1952). Could you talk about the genesis of this project?

BG

It seems to me that *Modern Living* is an extension of our previous projects, *Timelining* (2014) and *Reusable Parts/Endless Love* (2011), in which we dealt with the question of the couple. Addressing the home was a logical next step. It corresponded to a moment when

Modern Living, 2016

2.
One should mention though some exceptions, such as *Sexuality and Space*, ed. Beatriz Colomina (New York: Princeton Architectural Press, 1992); Aaron Betsky, *Building Sex: Men, Women, Architecture, and the Construction of Sexuality* (New York: William Morrow,1995); Joel Sanders, *Stud: Architectures of Masculinity* (London: Taylor & Francis, 1996); Aaron Betsky, *Queer Space: Architecture and Same-Sex Desire* (New York: HarperCollins, 1997); Paul B. Preciado, *Pornotopia: An Essay on Playboy's Architecture and Biopolitics* (New York: Zone Books, 2014); and Mario Gooden, *Dark Space: Architecture, Representation, Black Identity* (New York: Columbia Books on Architecture and the City, 2016).

we ourselves were in search of a place to live. We realized how most domestic architecture is heteronormatively structured, and how these spaces could not accommodate the way we live and work together. It was around this time that we discovered the Schindler House in Los Angeles. It had been built in the 1920s for two young couples who decided to live in what amounted to a commune. Each member had his or her own space where he or she worked, while domestic tasks were divided equally. This way of living resonated so strongly with our own aspirations that we became interested in other houses and other modernist experiments where architects seek formal responses (glass walls, the free plan) to make our most intimate relationships possible.

RK

The design of space influences the way we live with others. In proto-queer spaces like the Schindler House, reproduction is no longer central to domestic space, and the relationship between inside and outside is redesigned. From the 1990s onwards, queer studies mainly focused on public space: nightclubs, gay bars, streets, docks, public toilets, and so on. And domestic space was most often described negatively, as a closet.[2] It seemed to us that less normative forms of sexuality had also transformed the domestic space, and that it was necessary to reclaim the home as a place that produces queer subjectivities, and to trace a genealogy of these other forms of inhabitation.

LF

Although you use a variety of mediums (film, sculpture, performance), the primary investigative tool for *Modern Living* is dance, in particular a score called "Clock" that allows you to produce choreographic materials that intersect with the conditions of space and time. What is this "Clock?" And how does it investigate the way these architects think about domestic space?

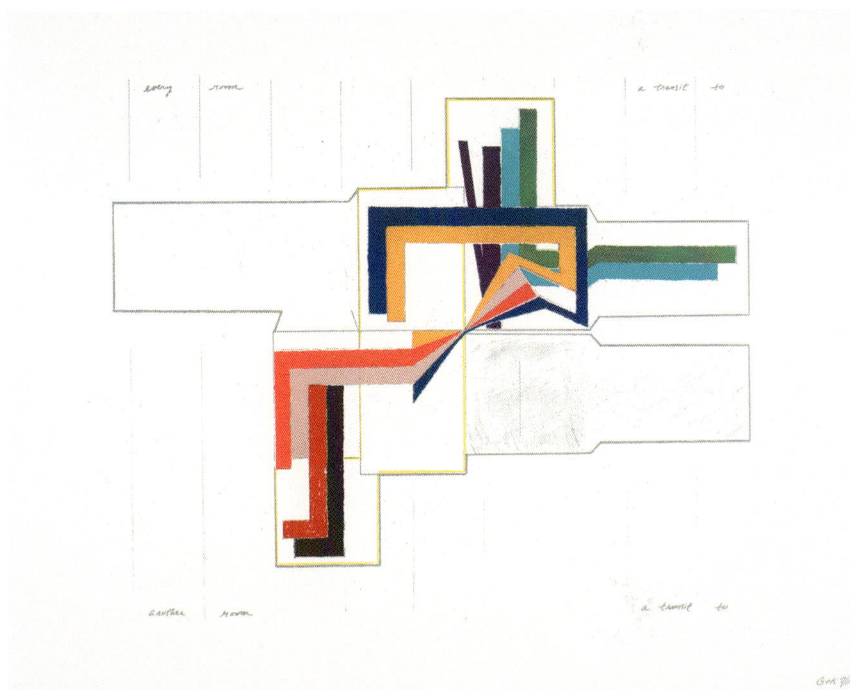

RK

When we started *Modern Living* we used "Clock" in the studio on a daily basis. In the practice, the dancer creates twelve gestures corresponding to the positions of numbers on the face of a clock (12 is in front of you, 6 is behind, and so on). The dancer then establishes a consistent oscillating movement somewhere in the body which acts as a time signature for their clock. If I had to define what a "Clock" is, I would say it's *une machine à habiter*, a vehicle for time travel, a way of organizing time and space. It's a way of manipulating the emptiness and banality of the studio, of dancing in the confined space of the domestic habitat, a way of inducing movement, a rhythmic interface between self and others. Working in the Schindler House we had to quickly create choreographic materials adapted to the scale of the rooms, to be performed by the dancers of L.A Dance Project. So this tool became an obvious choice for us.

BG

In "Clock," the performer associates personal memories with hours of the day. This process of recollection has an analytical dimension; it brings into play, or into representation, the formation of the subject who enunciates and who dances: where I come from, what are the events that have constructed my subjectivity. This task insists upon being present in the here and now, which challenges daily life mediated by all the telecommunication devices that clutter domestic space. Part of the film *Schindler/Glass* (2017) is based on the choreographic materials created through this process.

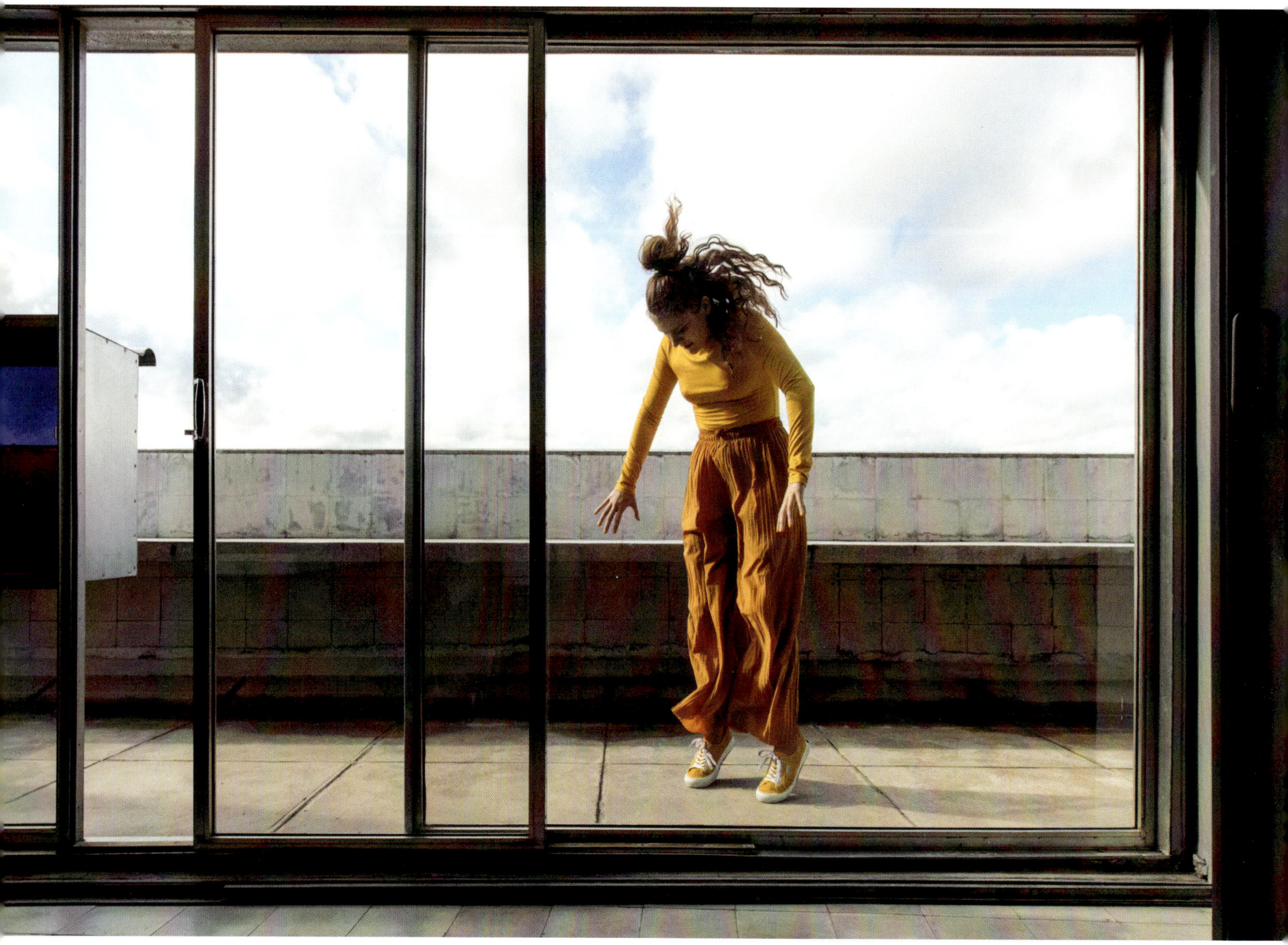

RK

In 2018, what had been a studio practice developed into a stand-alone performance entitled *Clockwork*. This piece is based on a score, it's repeatable, produced as a limited edition, and it can happen without us. It was formalized in the eponymous exhibition at Pioneer Works, New York, in 2018.

BG

One of the important influences for *Clockwork* is Félix González-Torres' *Untitled (Perfect Lovers)* (1991). Two identical clocks that over time fall out of sync. It models a type of relationship and functions as a protocol: you can buy these clocks anywhere. We were interested in importing this way of working into the field of performance.

RK

Clockwork and *Timelining*, another score-based performance, were developed at the same time, between 2010 and 2013, when we were in graduate school at the University of California, Los Angeles. A rather strange object, called *Recto Verso*, served as an early sketch for these pieces, where we were drawing circles on the floor. There are still some traces of this performance on the internet. It was a rudimentary form of "Clock" which later, in 2018, became *Clockwork*. It took us almost a decade to metabolize what had been a studio practice into an artwork.

BG

It's very complicated to create a choreographic tool that allows you to generate movements that are neither expressionistic, nor dependent on your state of mind at the time, nor tied to particular skills and techniques. This research corresponds to a period during which we worked with Simone Forti and a generation of artists who created tools to make works from their own bodies in space. But the legacy of Simone Forti, Yvonne Rainer, and Yoko Ono is not only formal, it also corresponds to a way of living. For example, Forti's *Dance Constructions* (1961) were performed in the loft where Ono lived. This interpenetration of the public and the private was constitutive of their way of living and making. With regard to the 1960s, I think our contribution is to show how these intersections of certain choreographic practices are a place where queer subjectivities are produced.

LF

Modern Living gave you the opportunity to make your first film *Schindler/Glass*. Could you go back and expand on its articulation with live performance?

RK

It became clear very quickly that the events we were making in these architects' houses were unique. They could probably not be redone or transposed elsewhere. The installation allows these performances to circulate, at least on some level. We were never interested in documentation, even for other performances. So, it seemed interesting to bring two places, the Schindler House and the Glass House, together in the virtual space of film.

BG

Initially we considered multi-channel video installations that would reproduce the live experience. But since we had already made the performances, it felt more interesting to explore filmic space.

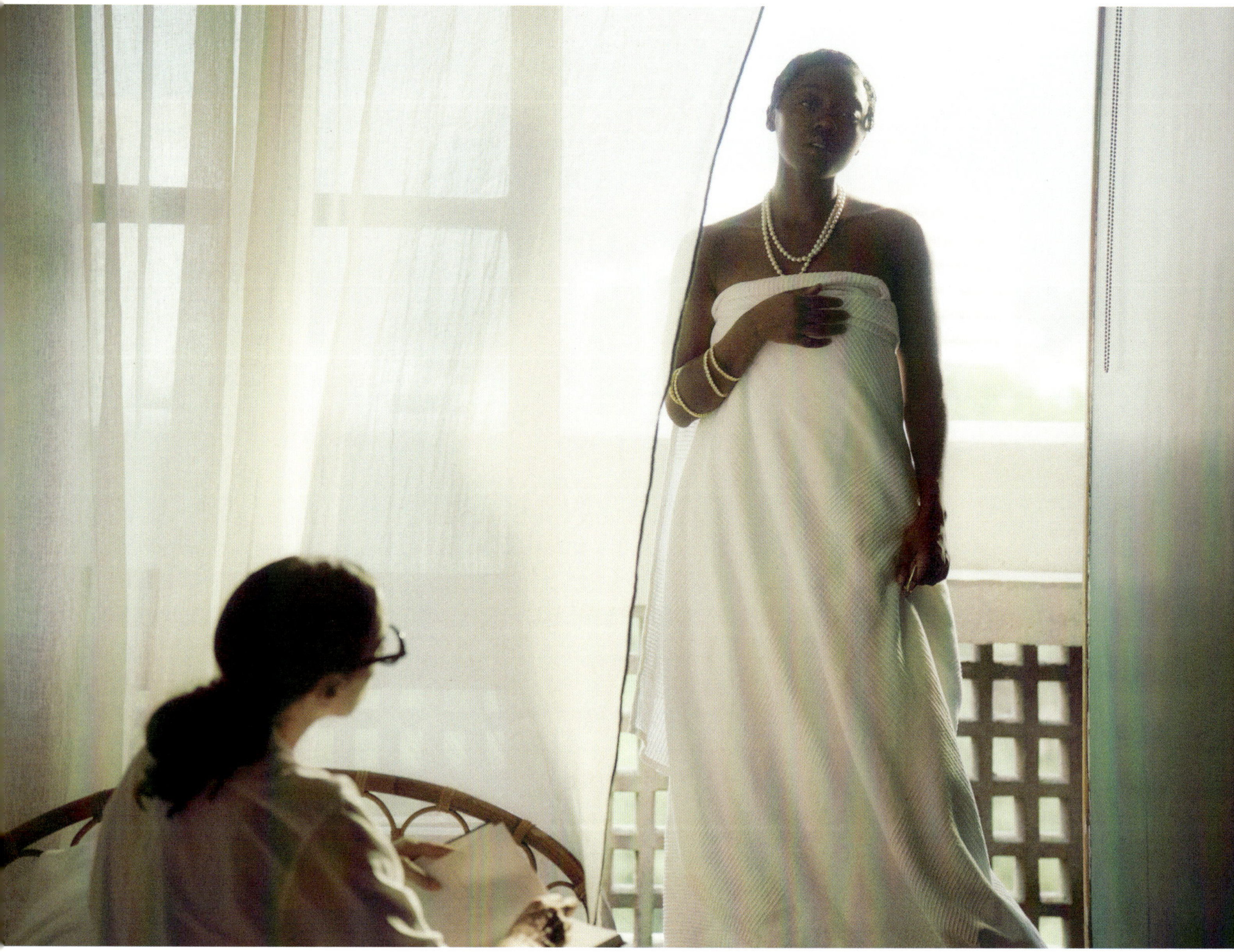

3.
Anne Anlin Cheng's account of this encounter was an important source of inspiration. See Anne Anlin Cheng, *Second Skin: Josephine Baker & the Modern Surface* (New York: Oxford University Press, 2010), 90–99.

Towards Fiction

LF

In terms of genre, *Schindler/Glass* sits at the intersection of a dance film and a film about architecture. With *Bright Hours* (2022) you create a fiction, the love affair between Le Corbusier and Josephine Baker—the details of which are not known, although the affair itself has been partially attested.

RK

To me this evolution seems linked to the materials we work with. Our decision to write fiction was not motivated by a loyalty to a genre, but by the discursive space in which we place ourselves. On issues of racial and colonial constructions, we find ourselves on the side of the privileged, which is not the case regarding sexuality. So, we needed a form of polyphony that only narrative could provide. The story we wanted to tell—the encounter between Josephine Baker and Le Corbusier—has been scarcely documented.[3] Consequently we were forced to fill in these gaps. What would have happened if Le Corbusier and Josephine Baker had had a romantic relationship while crossing

4.
For a summary of this studio co-led with architect Andrew James Holder, see Vrinda Kanvinde, "The Queer Home: Combining Architecture with Movement to Speculate on the Future of Housing," *Harvard University Graduate School of Design News*, May 20, 2022. https://www.gsd.harvard.edu/2022/05/the-queer-home-combining-architecture-with-movement-based-practice-to-speculate-on-the-future-of-housing/

the Atlantic? Might this affair have transformed Le Corbusier's vision of architecture? Or allowed us to understand Josephine Baker as one of the architects of modernity? This story would re-cast dancers, popular artists, women, and people of color as fully-fledged actors in the history of art. This speculative narrative proposes a plural vision of modernity. The underlying thesis of the film is that Josephine Baker is a modernist. If you take the paradigm of mechanization, Josephine Baker's particular dancing body can be described as a dancing machine. Baker cuts and juxtaposes choreographic materials in an artificial way, as in a film montage. She dances a bit of Martha Graham, alongside her interpretations of Afro-Caribbean dance, of jazz dance, and a snippet of Parisian cabaret. She works, like Picasso, with collage. It was viewing her through this way of dancing and choreographing that we began to see Baker as a modernist. That's also how we worked with Emara Neymour-Jackson, who plays the role.

BG
During the shooting with Emara and Jeanne Balibar, who plays Le Corbusier, we realized what a mechanical process it is to act or dance for the camera. You have marks, your movements are meticulous, every shift of the head is captured. The film set is a machine in motion, and the challenge is to find a subjective image that escapes the control of the actor and director. It's this *something* that has to happen at the time of shooting, on a conscious or unconscious level.

LF
In *Bright Hours*, you associate the meeting of Le Corbusier and Baker with a transformation in his approach to architecture. Whereas in the 1920s his works are marked by an adept use of whitewash, from 1931 onward he developed a polychromatic architecture. *Bright Hours* suggests that the discovery of color occurs through the encounter with Baker, and that it is not merely an architectural issue.

RK
We've been able to make this speculation because of a shift in the field of cultural criticism over the last ten years, during which the taboo against discussing intimacy between artists has been challenged. This allows for a renewed understanding of the relationships that structure cultural production.

A Framing Device

LF
In your work, you approach architecture as a framing device. This question appears in *Panorama* (2021), a film that revolves around the monumental painting in the Bourse de Commerce, now the Pinault Collection—the "Panorama du Commerce," created between 1886 and 1889.

BG
Through *Bright Hours* and *Panorama*, we're trying to infuse a dialectic into the experience of architecture. Today, architects work primarily with computers and digital images. When we taught at the Harvard Graduate School of Design, we introduced movement practices to the students, so that they might ultimately embody a certain perception of space.[4] Conversely, our experience with Le Corbusier's work has led us to relativize some of the critical discourse that regards his

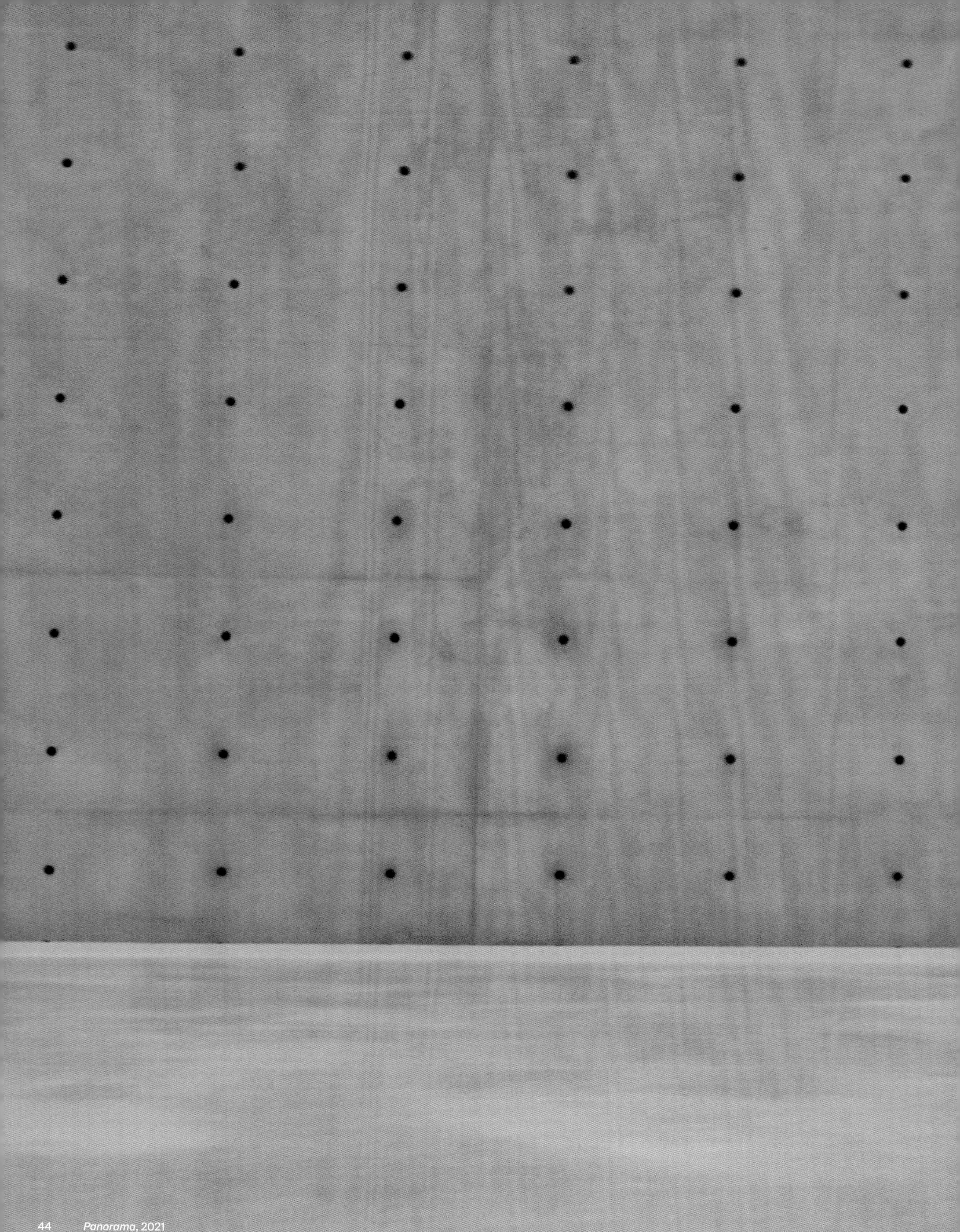

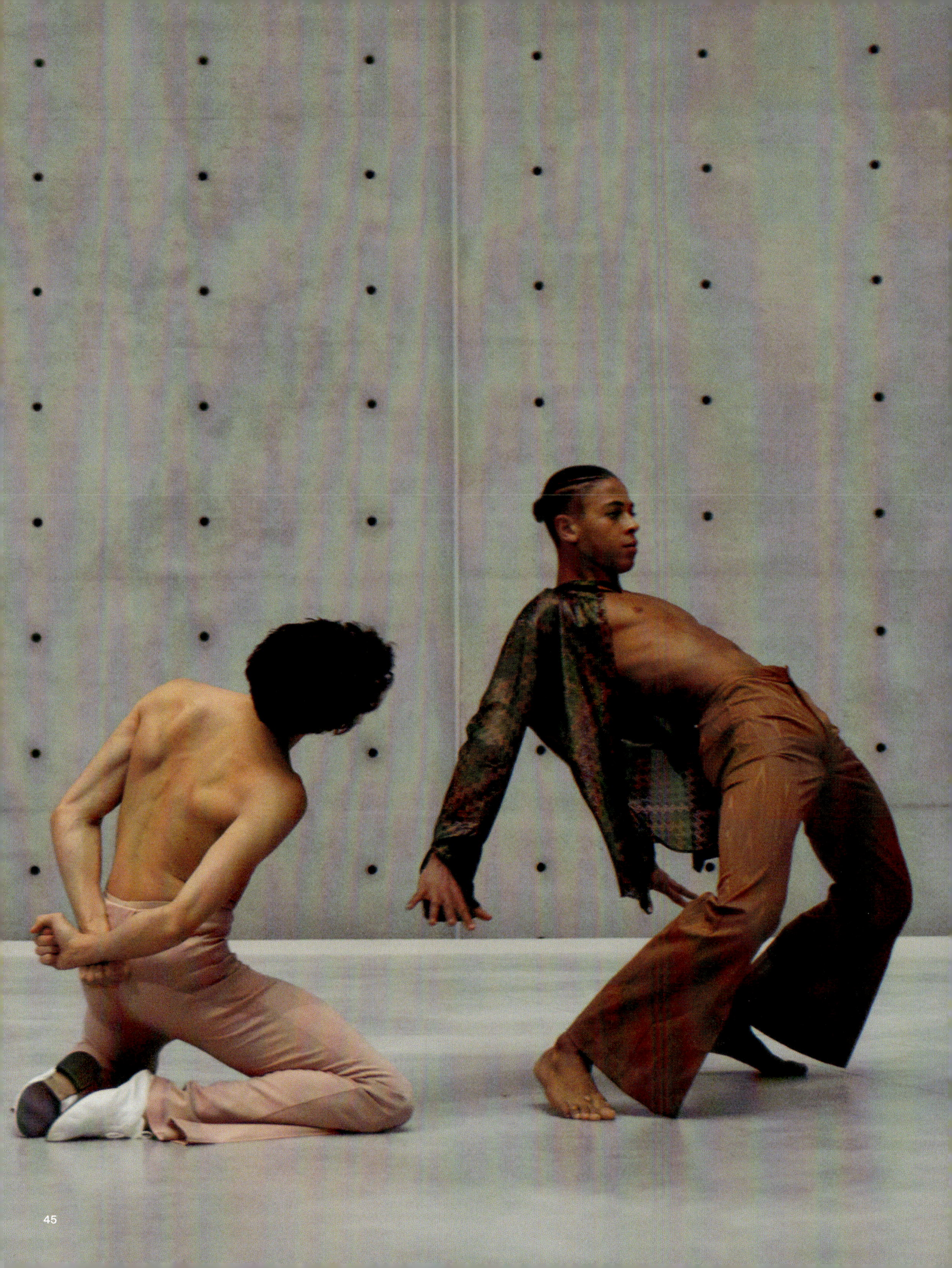

architecture as an optical device. I'm sensitive now to the way his approach is linked to the body, how he designed on a human scale.

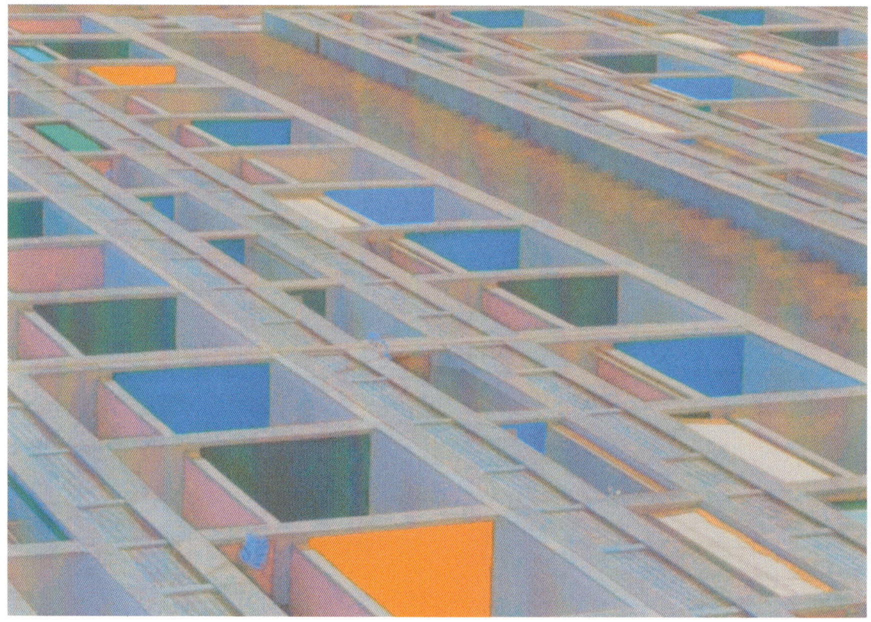

RK

One thing that impressed us when we first visited the Bourse de Commerce, while Tadao Ando's intervention was under construction, was that the "Panorama du Commerce" is the only permanent artwork. And that this monumental painting had been restored. It was a surprising choice. The painting depicts a stereotypical representation of colonial subjects, and it is this history of violence committed in the name of a racist state that occupies a central place in the museum. The panorama is also a framing device for the building, which Ando understood perfectly with his concrete cylinder. In the film, we follow this framing while occupying the central space under the weight of the cupola. But we also use the peripheral space in the shadow of the dome. It's in this marginal space where, in an ironic way, something on the order of truth is expressed: the intersecting history of violence and commerce.

BG

The "Panorama du Commerce" is designed to place the viewer at the center of the Bourse. He is the unmarked term, the heteronormative white European man who possesses a certain capital. The characters represented in the painting frame this empty center. In our film, the painting is viewed from the margins. Our approach is indebted to the work of Douglas Crimp, Craig Owens, and Mary Kelly, and how they have conceived of the frame as a device—even if in the film we do this with a dose of camp.[5] *Panorama* also has a reparative dimension. We see this in the embodiment of three characters—Memory, Allegory, and Avenir—as performed by Soa de Muse, Germain Louvet, and Guillaume Diop. Their relations are structured not by violence, but by a kind of conviviality, pleasure, intimacy, and anger directed against the positions assigned to them by the painting. The film is less a work of institutional critique than a discursive critique of the interlocking institutions of heteronormativity, capitalism, and colonialism.

LF

I'm glad you mention the performers, because in a way the film performs a shift from the panoramic form of representation to that of the portrait. It could be seen as a portrait of three dancers.

5.
Craig Owens authored the English translation of Jacques Derrida's text "Parergon" in *La vérité en peinture* (Paris: Éditions Flammarion, 1978). This text played an important role in the development of his own reflections on the frame. See Craig Owens, *Beyond Recognition. Representation, Power and Culture* (Berkeley: University of California Press, 1994). Owens' writing influenced Douglas Crimp in his exhibition *Pictures*, presented in 1977 at Artists Space, New York. Crimp admits as much in *Before Pictures* (Chicago: University of Chicago Press, 2016). Finally, this question of the frame is equally interrogated by the artist Mary Kelly, with whom Gerard & Kelly studied at the Interdisciplinary Studio of the University of California, Los Angeles. See her collection of essays in *Imaging Desire* (Cambridge: MIT Press, 1996).

BG

I think portraiture is an interesting genre. Yvonne Rainer's *Lives of Performers* (1972) is certainly not an immediate reference, but it makes sense to us in the way that Rainer's subject is always first and foremost the artist, the performer. *Panorama* is about creating a space in which the subjectivity of the artist flickers before the eye of the viewer.

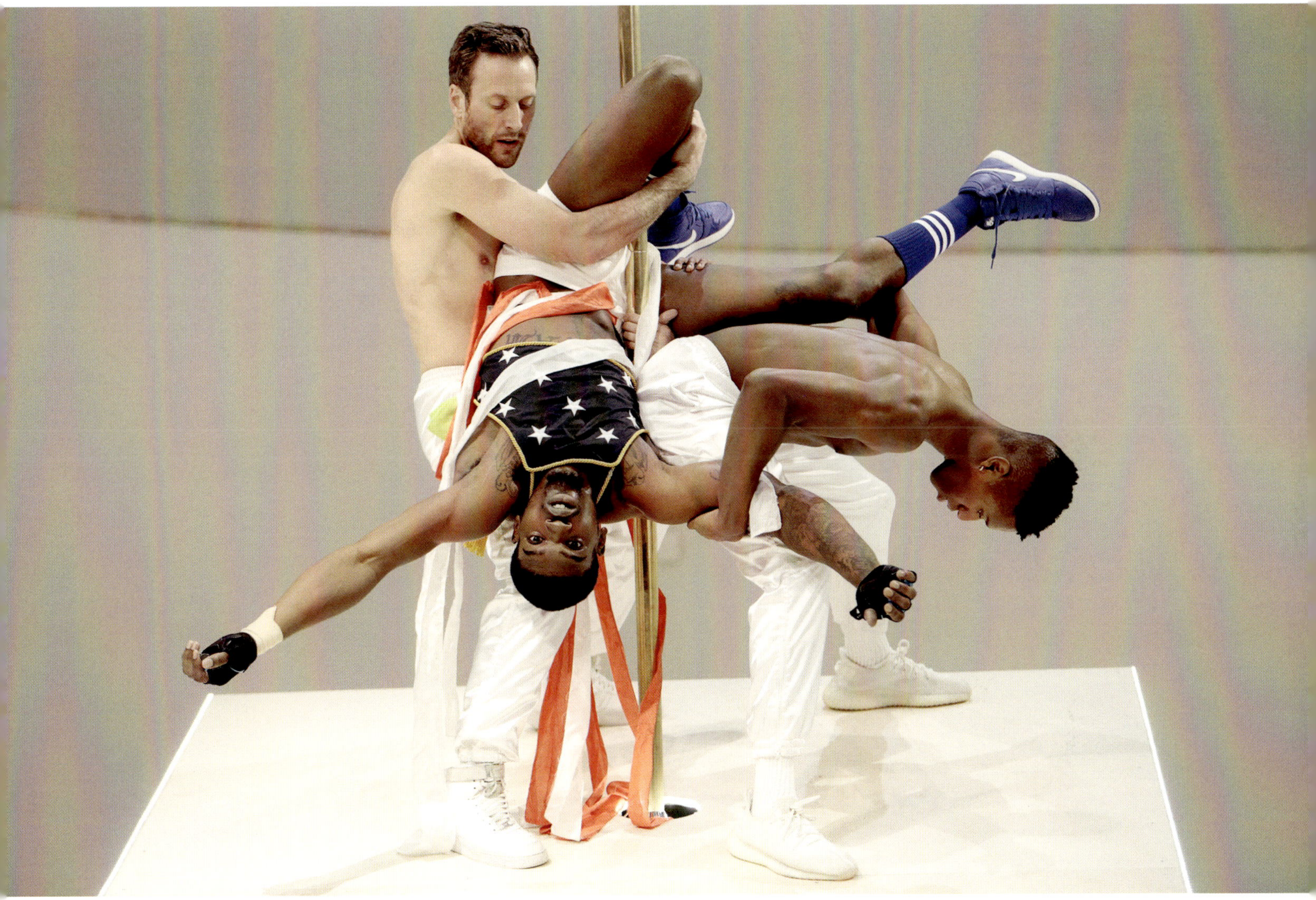

Dance Constructions

LF

You mentioned Simone Forti's *Dance Constructions*. Of the performative works you've created, *State of* (2019) relates most directly to this definition of a dance piece arranged or structured by an inclined plane, a pole, a dancer, and a "flag costume."

BG

These references to art history are very personal to us, as we've worked with both Simone and Yvonne. When we created *State of* we probably didn't think consciously of these references because these artists have transmitted to us ways of working that have become atavistic. *State of* could be seen as a cross between Rainer's *Trio A With Flags* (1970) and Forti's *Slant Board* (1961). While working with Forty Smooth, one of the pioneers of pole dancing in the New York City subway system, we learned there was a movement called the flag, which involves levitating the body to a horizontal position. How does the body get perpendicular to the vertical pole? This physical, sculptural, and choreographic question guided our work. And then, of course, there was the decision to incorporate the American flag: who can represent the United States, and who is represented by the national anthem?

RK

In a surprising way, *State of* also relates to the specific architecture of Carré d'Art and the Maison Carrée. When we researched the history of this Roman temple, we learned that it had fascinated Thomas Jefferson. He commissioned an architect to make a model of it and sent this model to America. He then used that model to design the Virginia State Capitol in Richmond. Only two of the fifty state capitols in the United States are based on a Classical model. Seventy years after its construction, the Virginia State Capitol became the seat of the Confederacy during the Civil War. The American South deployed this symbol of civilization and Enlightenment reason to defend the barbarism of slavery.

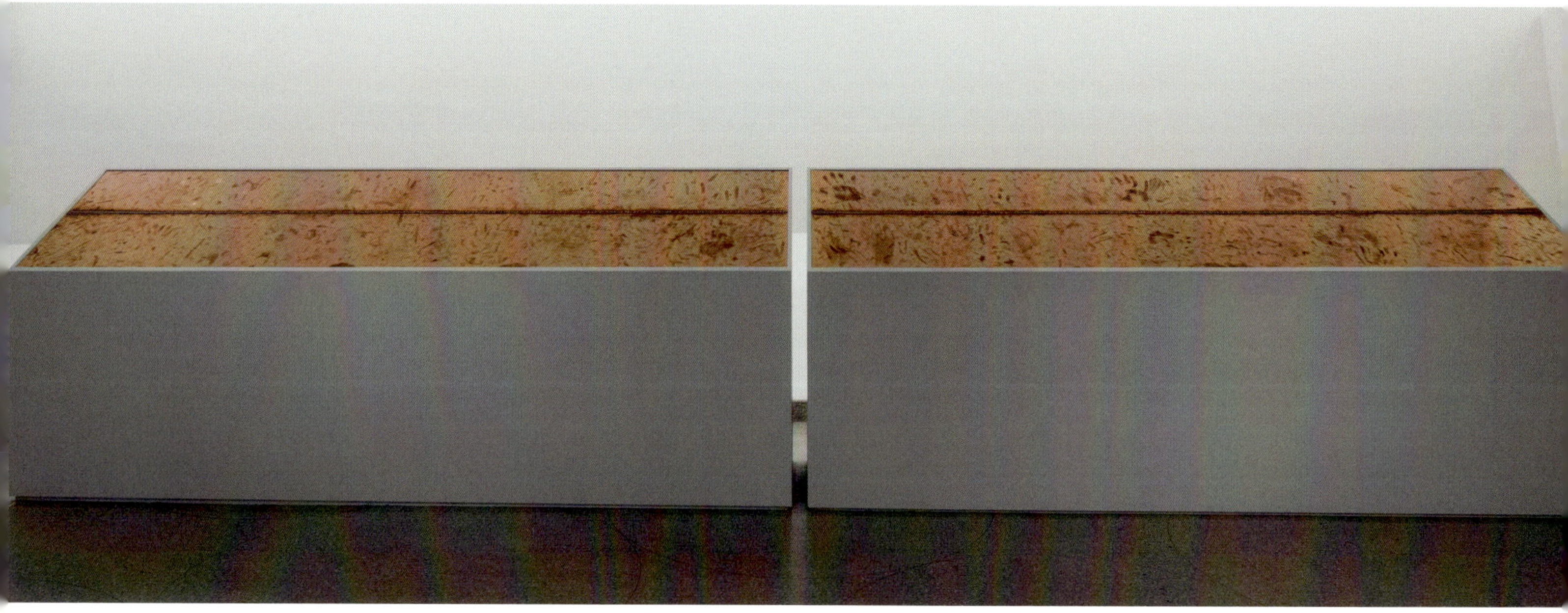

Reading and Writing

LF

Writing and reading play an important role in your artistic practice. You write scores that in *Timelining* or *Clockwork* lead the performers to produce texts themselves. You write the scripts for the films you make. You also create sculptures like the *Transcripts* series (2014) that implicate the visitor in a certain relationship to reading.

BG

Both writing and drawing are parallel practices to film and performance. Whenever we work with these mediums, we face constraints of time and money. We also have to deal with the perishable materiality of the body and the voice, whereas in writing there is a form of freedom. The exhibition allows these multiple practices to co-exist in their different states. *Transcripts* are sculptures composed of two pieces of copper. They transcribe in Braille fragments of our chronologies as they were spoken in the performance *Timelining*. To read the work,

Transcript 2 (Shock and Awe in front of I met you / I met you in front of moved to NYC / moved to NYC in front of graduated college / graduated college in front of stolen election / stolen election in front of my uncle died / my uncle died in front of boyfriend's lisp / boyfriend's lisp in front of Newports // Weapons of Mass Destruction in front of I met you / I met you in front of first cigarette / first cigarette in front of Chevy Cavalier / Chevy Cavalier in front of aware of AIDS / aware of AIDS in front of Haley's Comet / Haley's Comet in front of), 2014 it's necessary to approach and touch them. Copper is a material that indexes fingerprints. Thus, each physical reading of the work leaves the trace of the act of reading.

RK

Transcripts refer back to our relationship as the source of this exhibition. They allow us to measure the time that has passed since 2014. They inscribe our interpersonal history alongside the histories of the Schindler House, French colonialism, the Maison Carré, the American Civil War. Found inside these fragments are citations, public and private events that may also structure the visitors' relationships to the exhibition, to me, to us. Some elements of the *Transcripts* will correspond to the particular history of a given spectator, and others will not. The work functions as a key, allowing you to position yourself in this ruin, in this postmodern archive that is the exhibition. Lou, you, yourself, performed *Timelining* with Lenio Kaklea. What was your experience with the piece?

LF

I remember being impressed with the set of writing techniques you shared with us as we produced our timelines. It likely has to do with your experience as choreographers, in which you place the performers in a process of creation drawn from their own lives. In my training as an art historian, one learns first of all to write from the outside, which does not impede forms of reflexivity. In working with you, I've experienced the opposite movement.

BG

I think we both try to emphasize writing as a physical and subjective practice. This brings us back to your first question about the exhibition, in which we address reading and looking as embodied experiences.

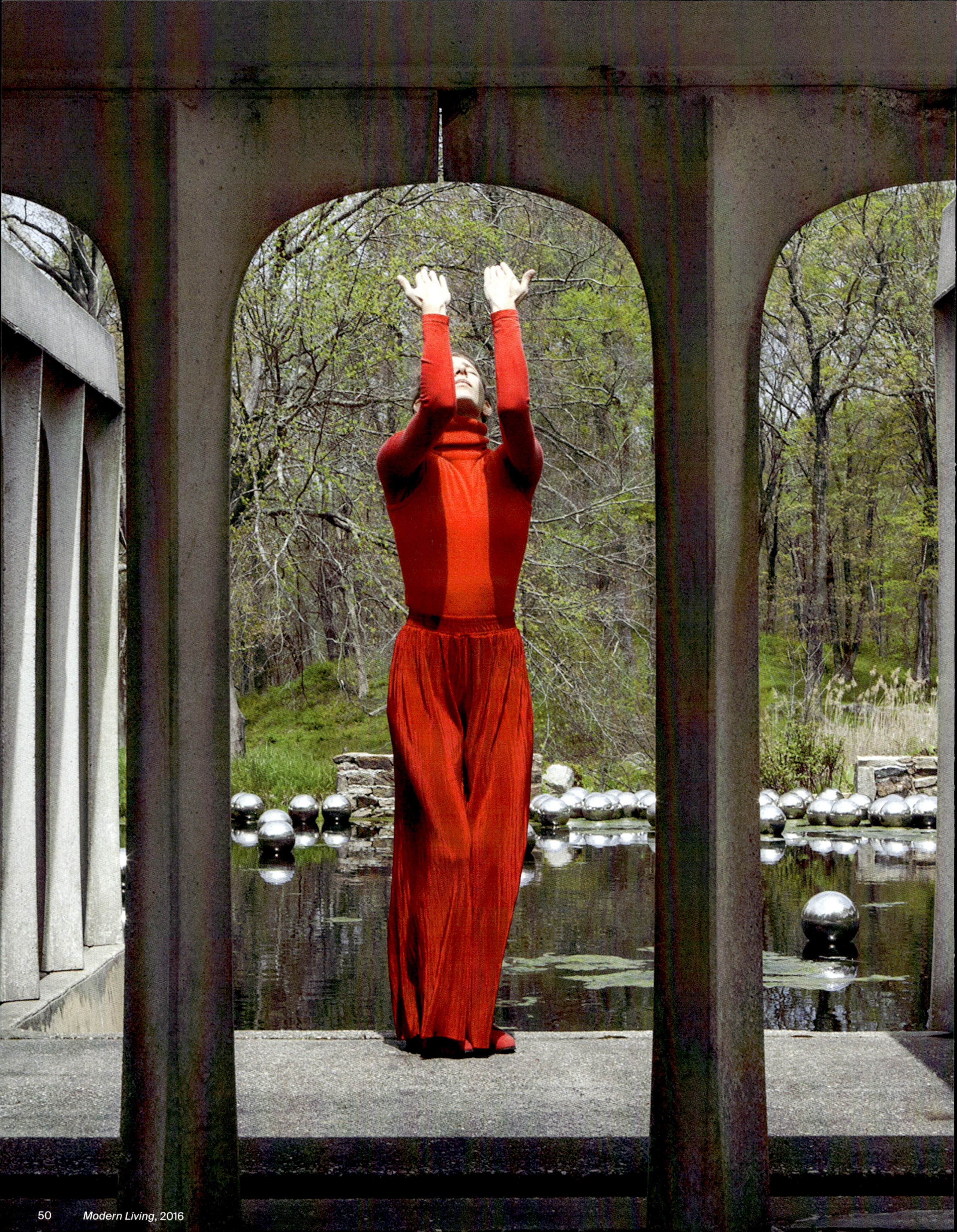

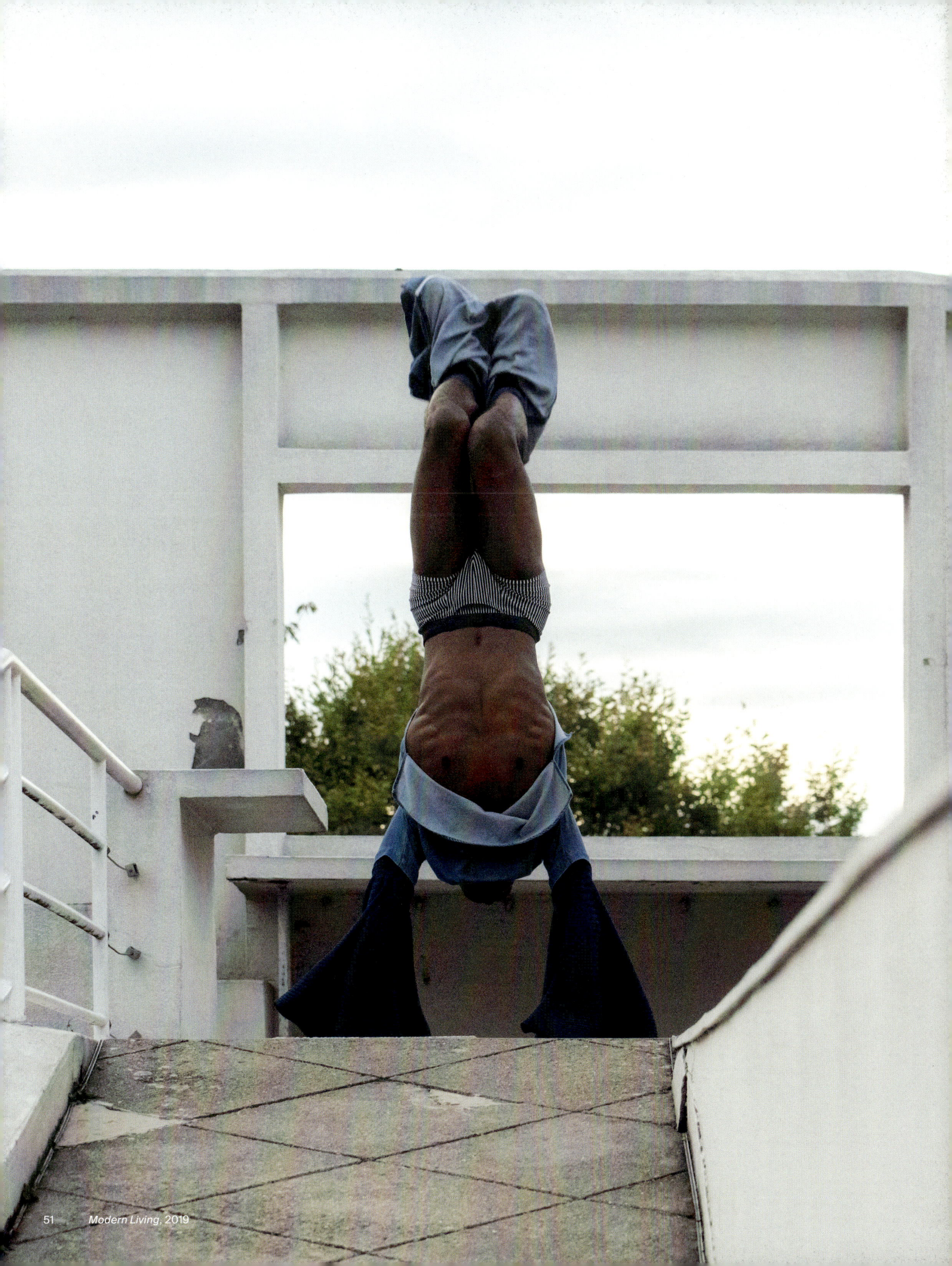

Ruins

Installation views / Vues d'exposition

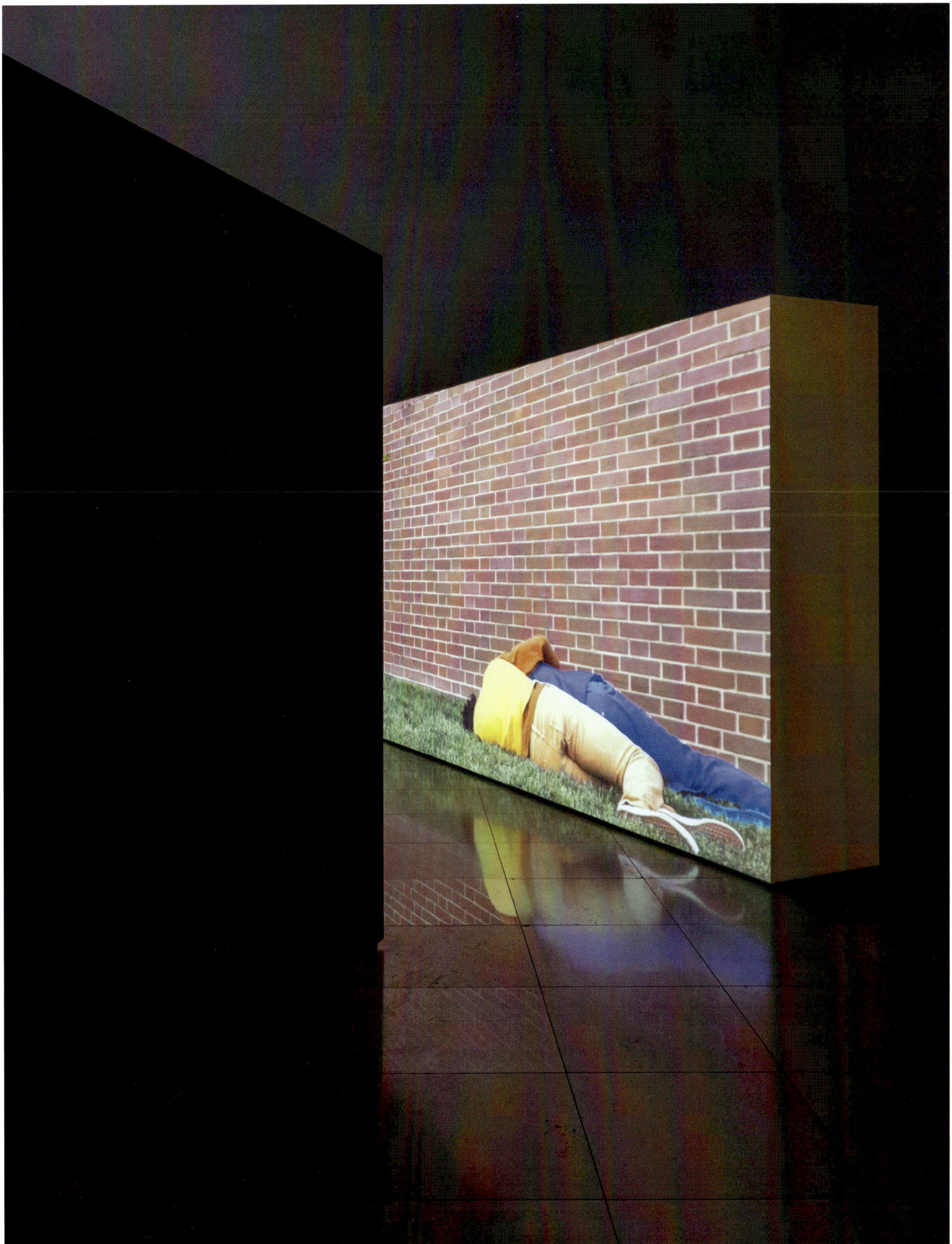

 Schindler/Glass, 2017

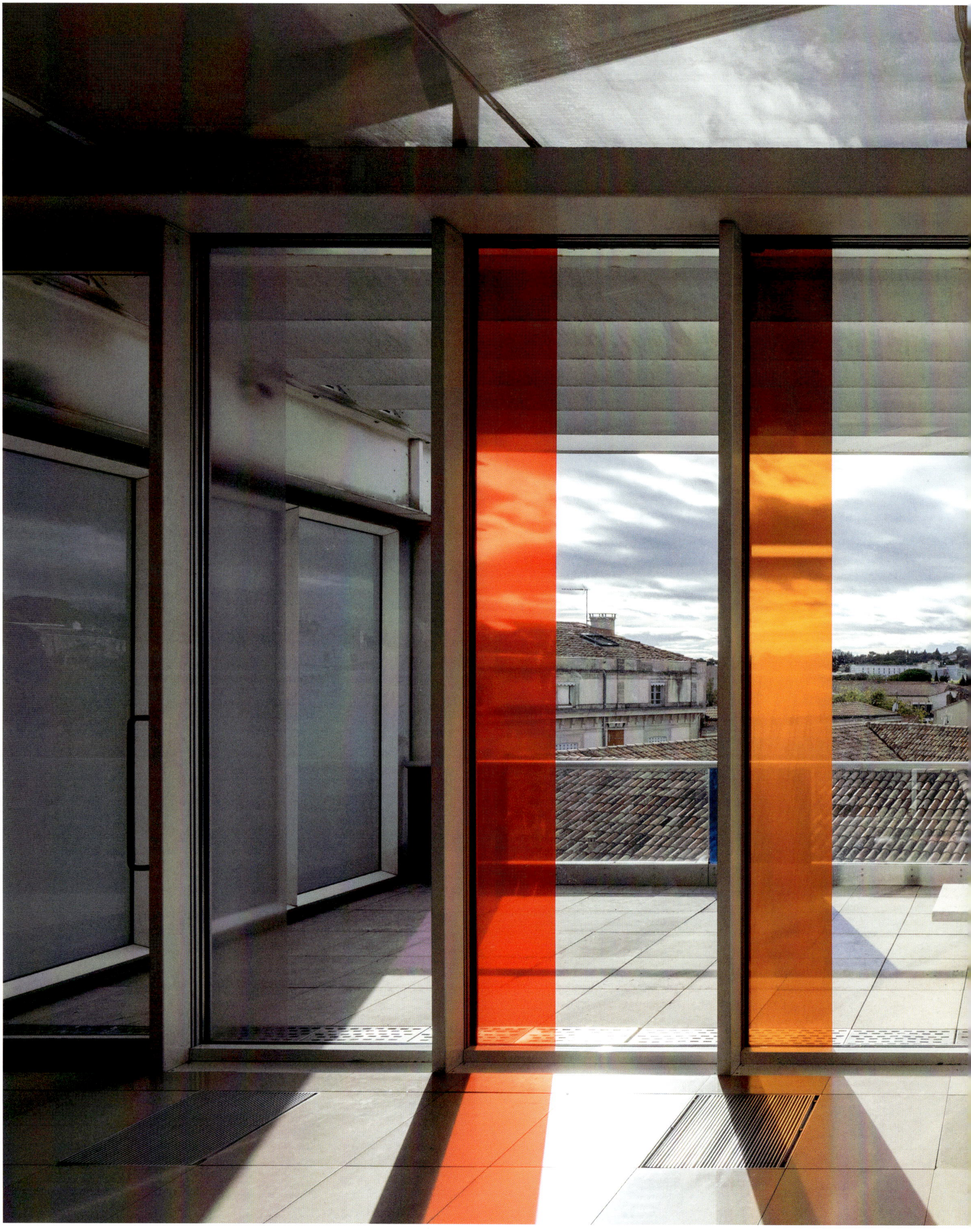

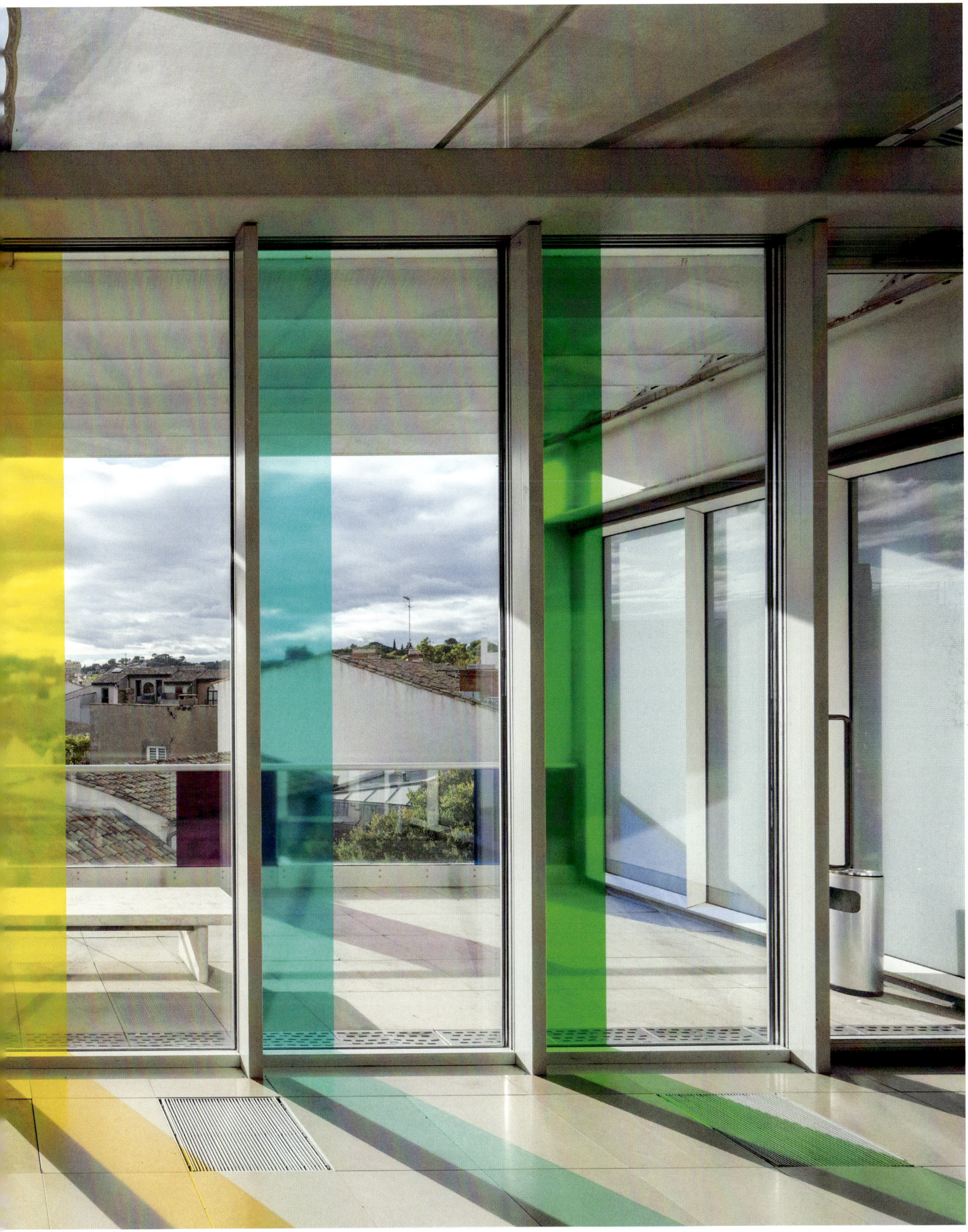

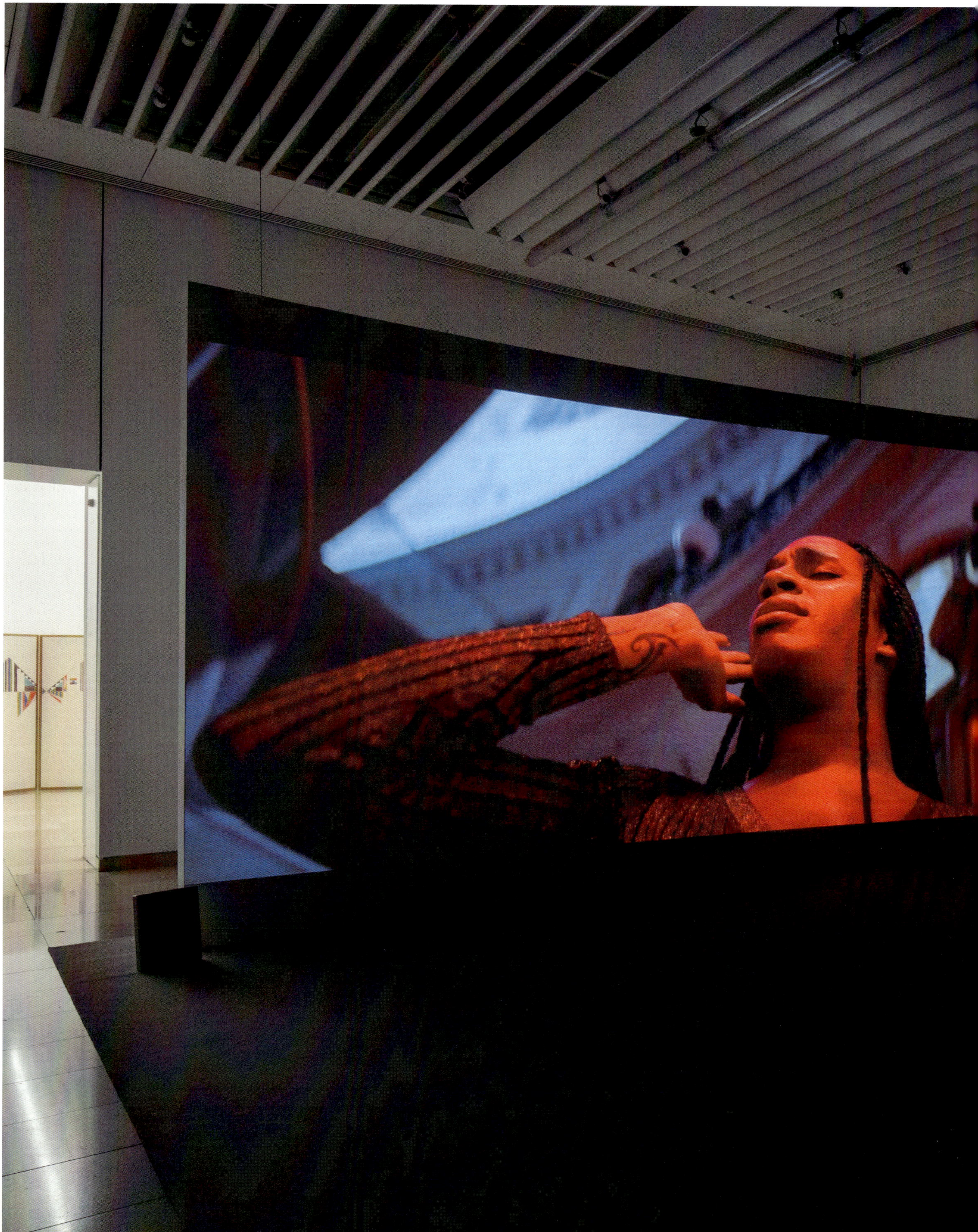

 Panorama, 2021; Eileen Gray, *Monte Carlo Sofa*, 1929

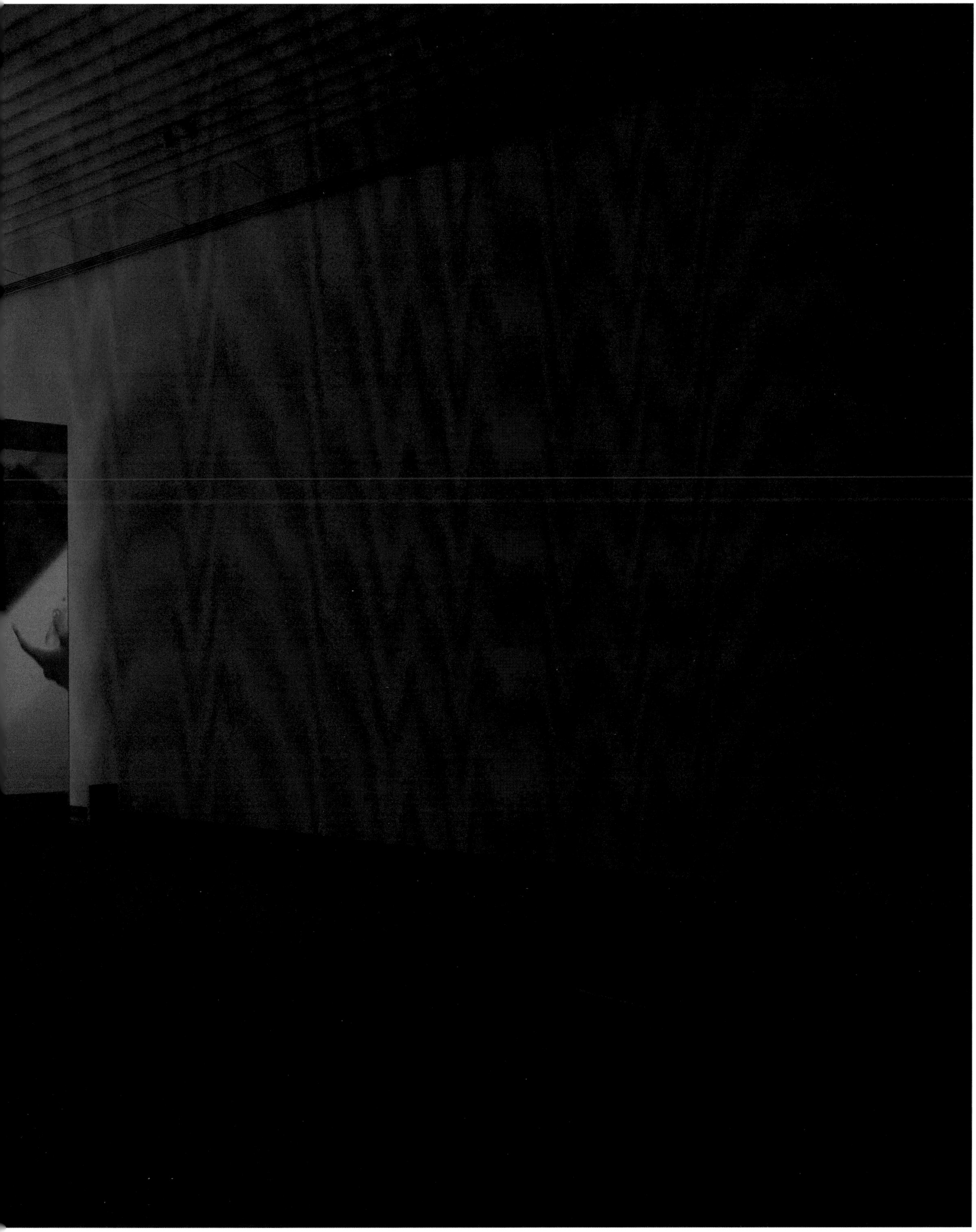

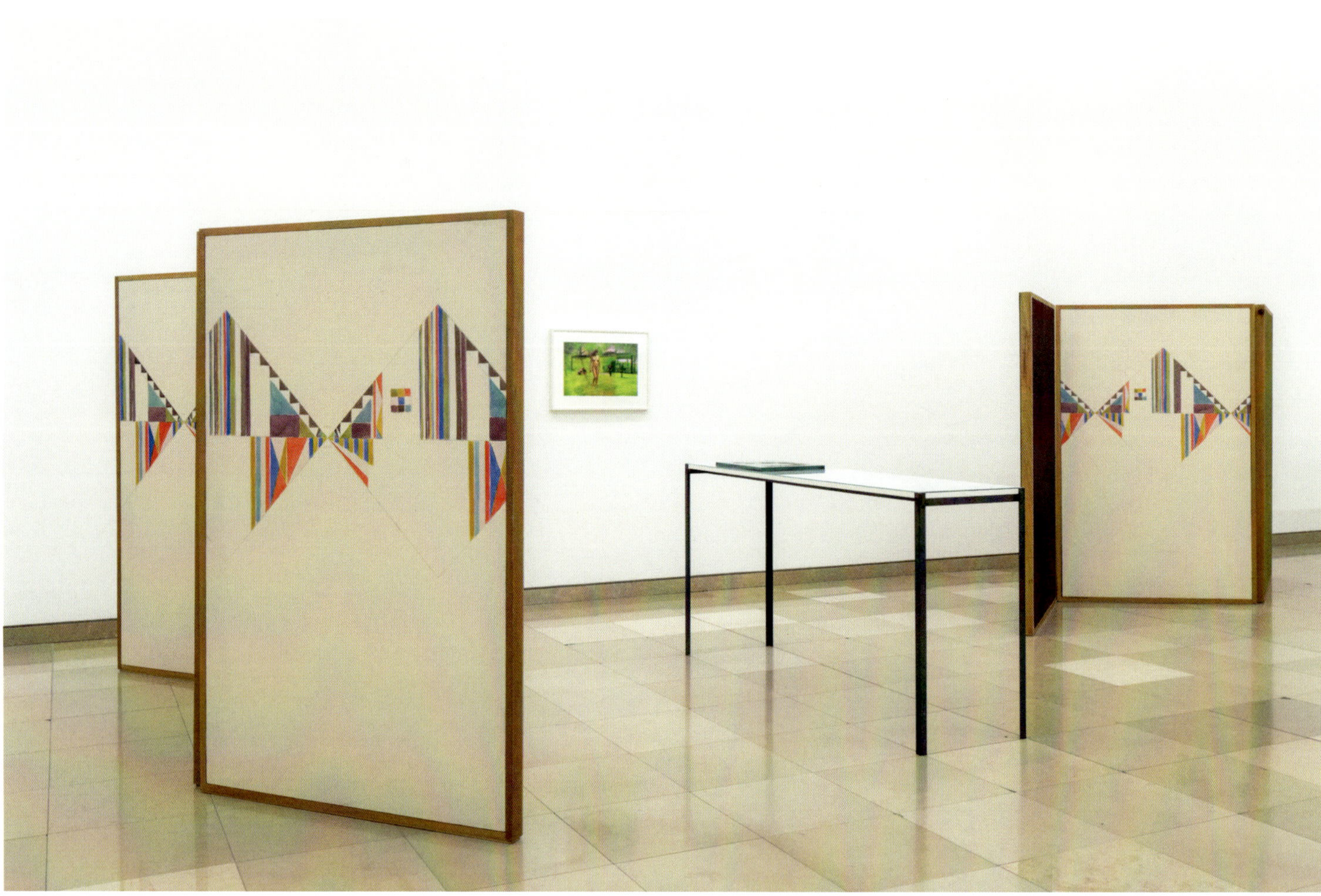

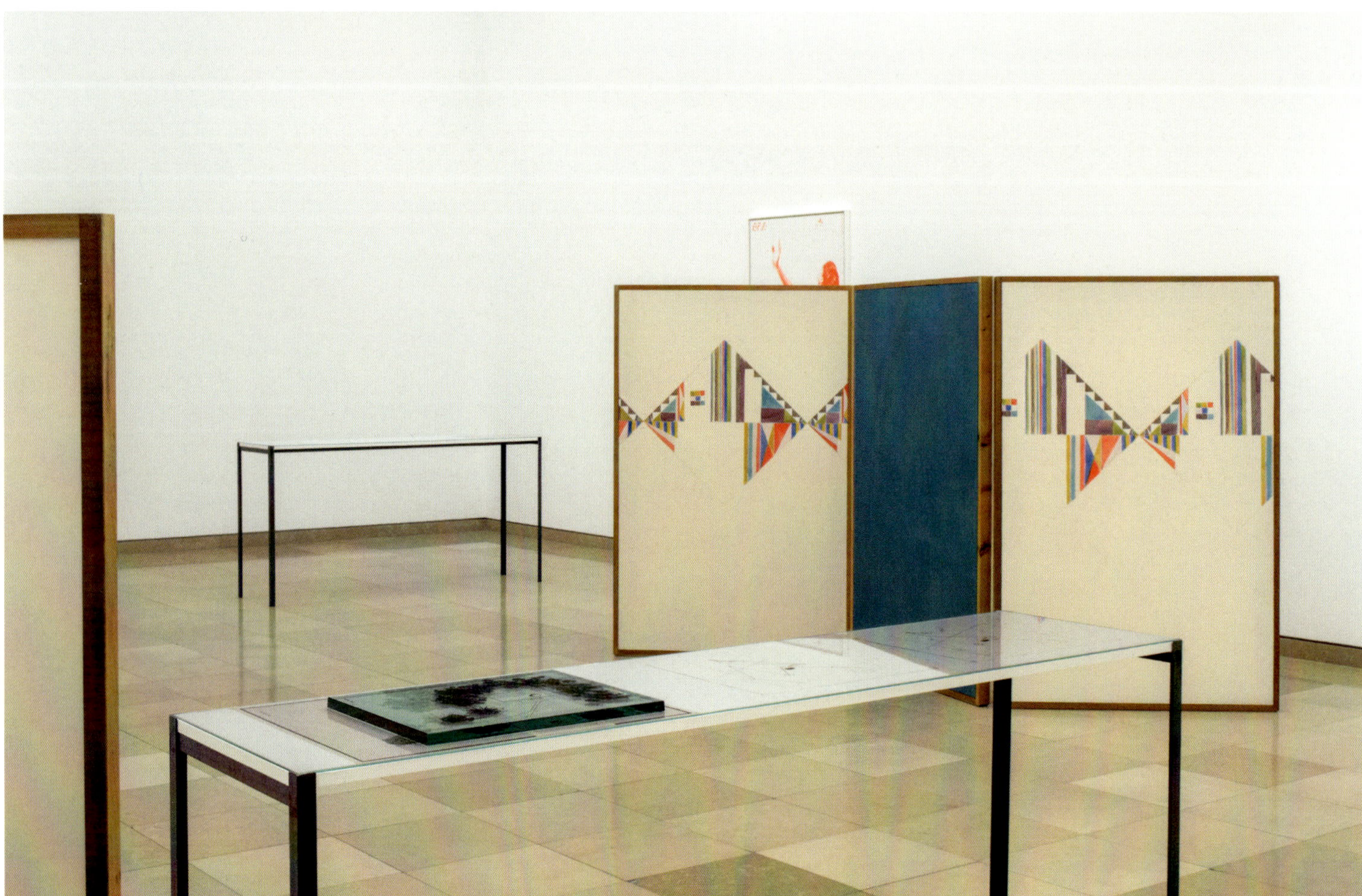

 Above: *The family is a system of regeneration I & III*, 2018; James Welling, *5097*, 2016 / Below: *The family is a system of regeneration II*, 2018

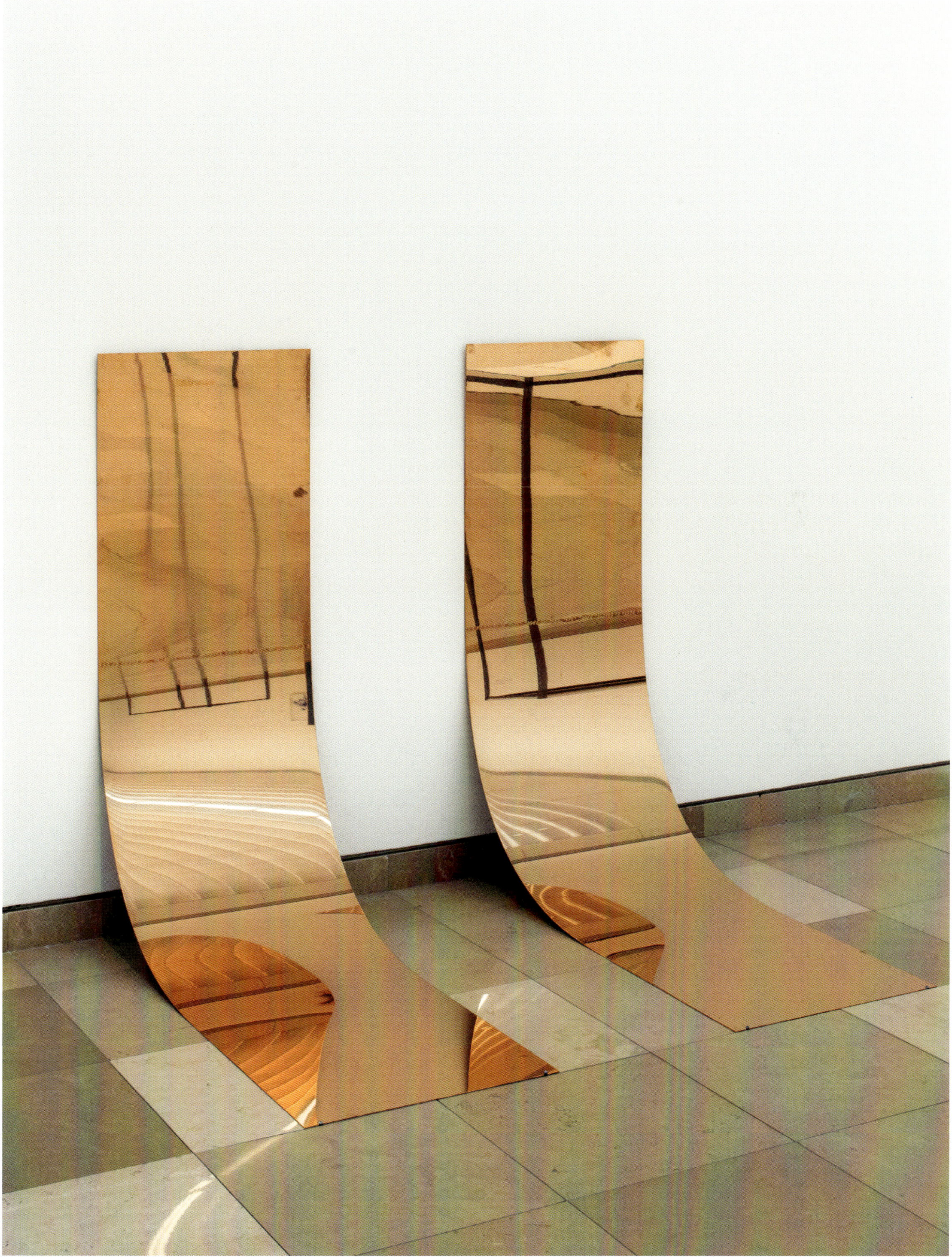

 Transcript 1 (Now in front of Whitney died / Whitney died in front of LA bike rides // Now in front of drove cross country / drove cross country in front of), 2014

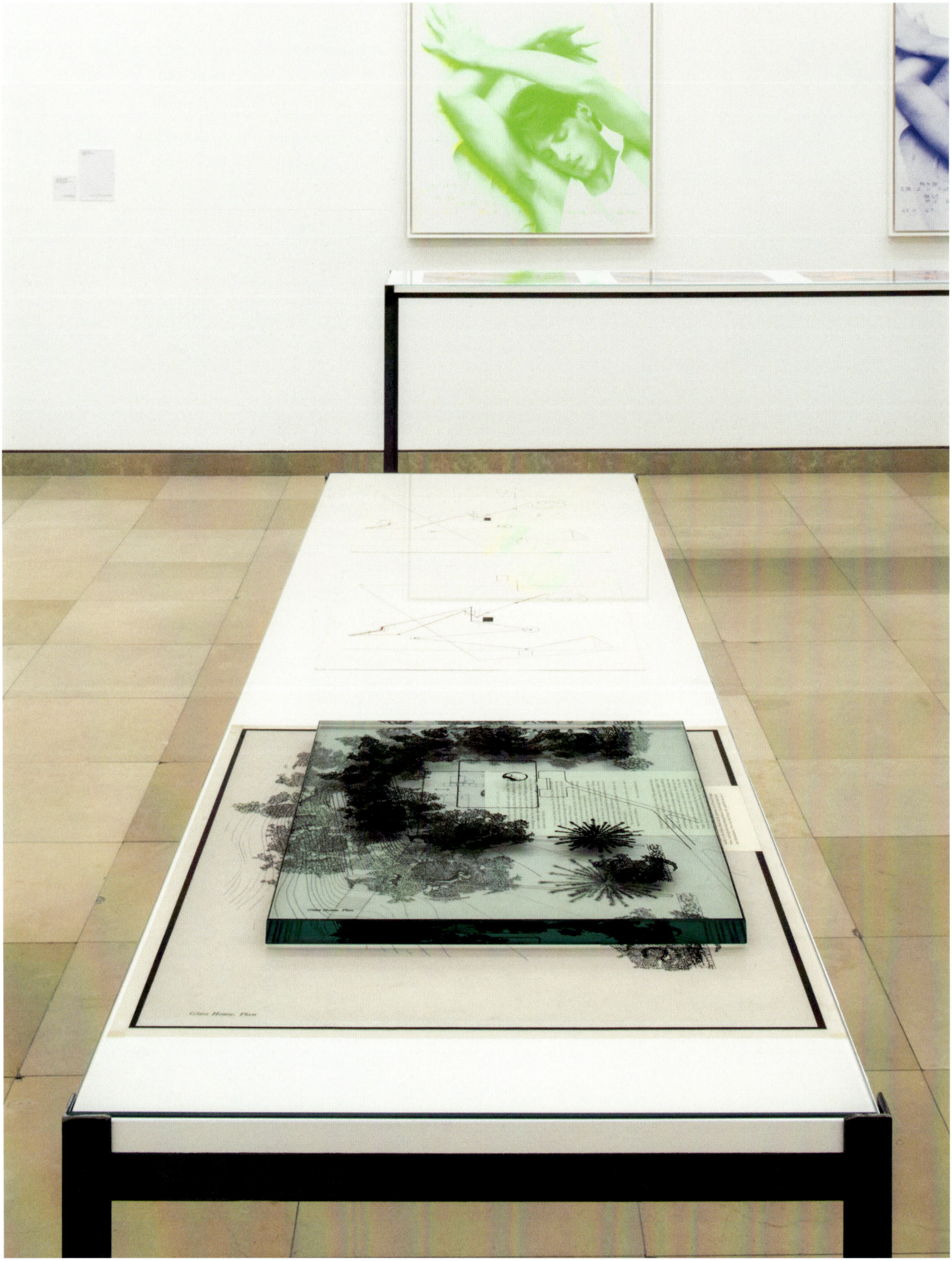

 Private, 2018

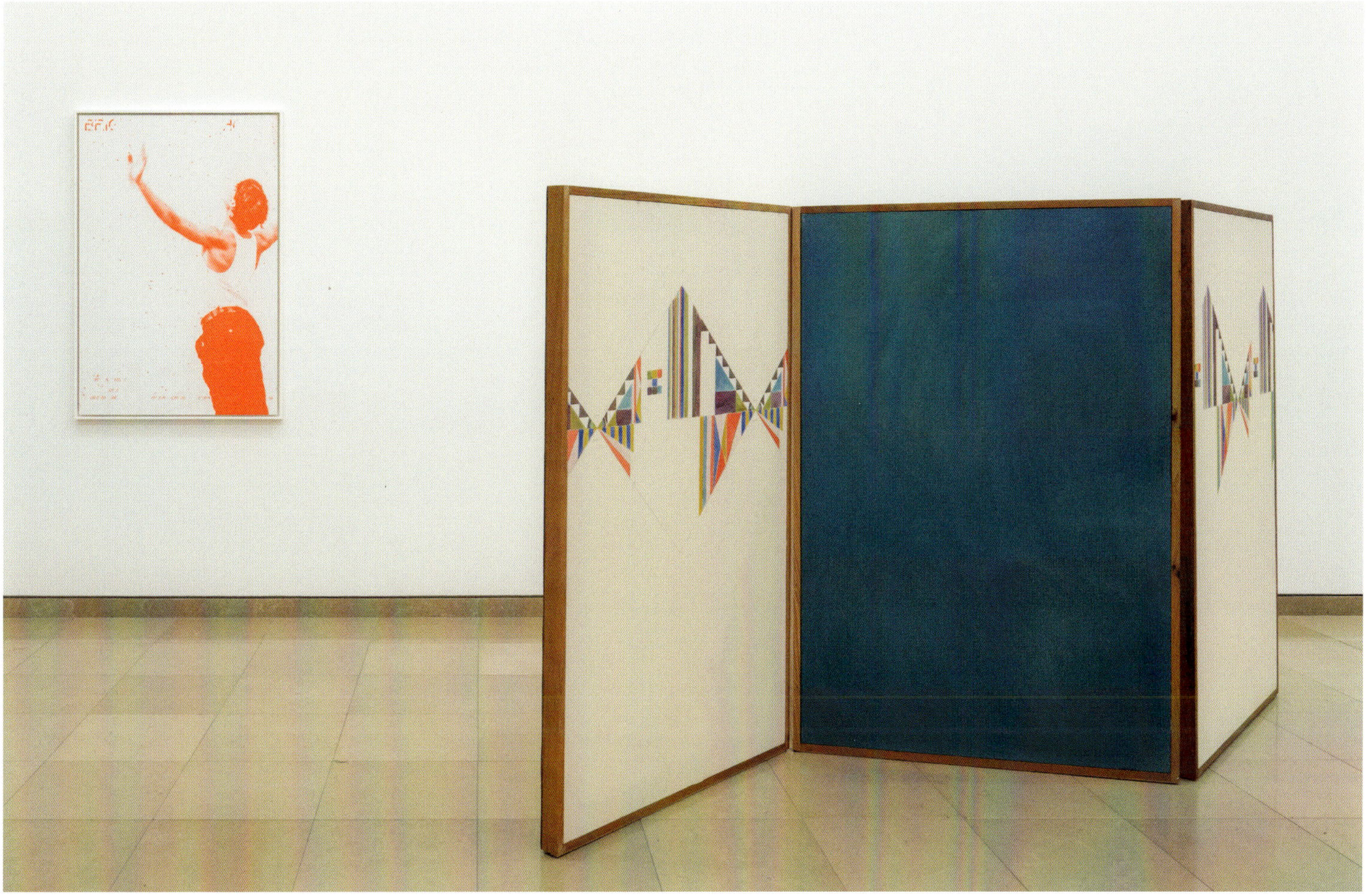

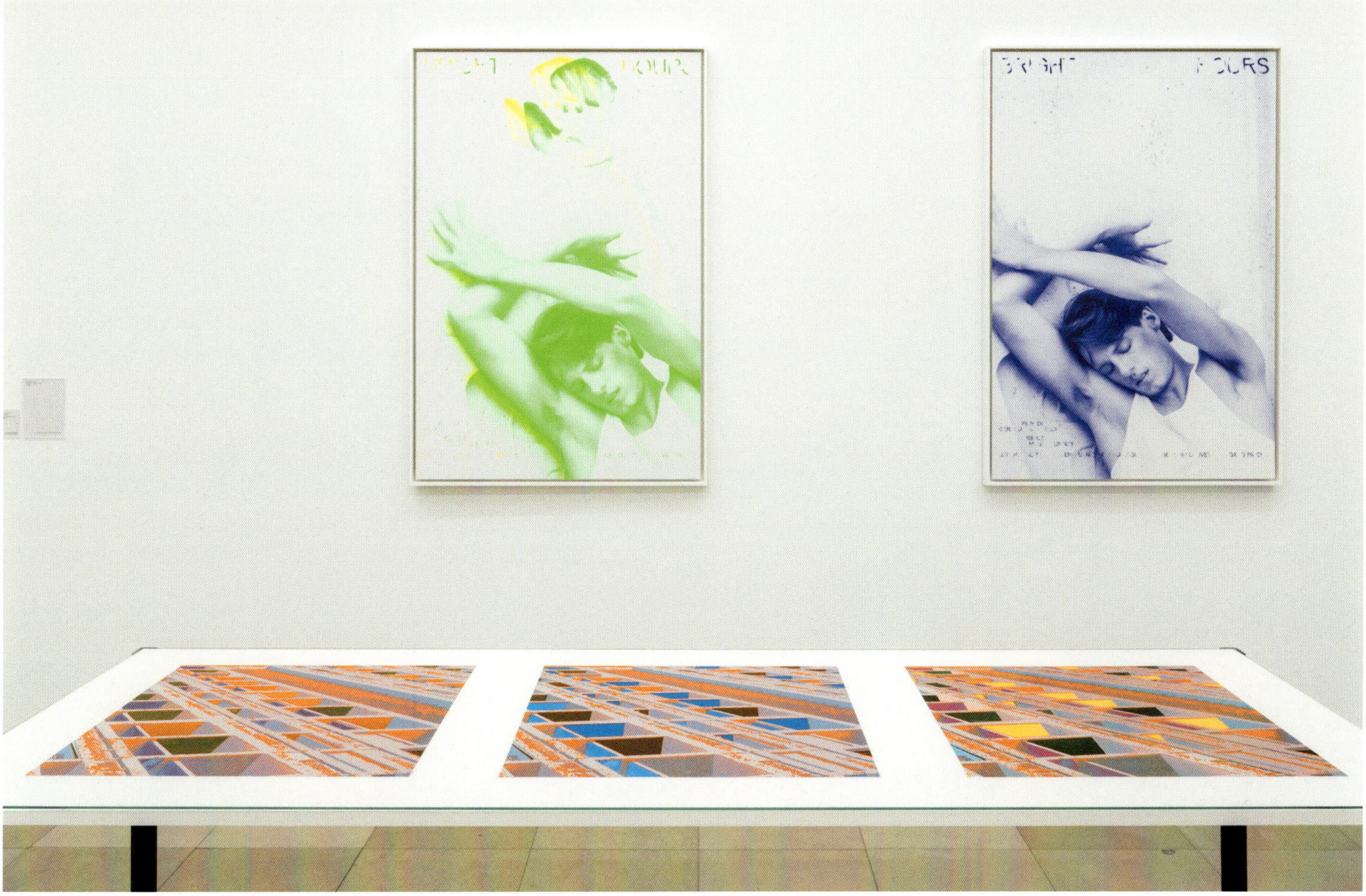

Above: *Affiche*, 2022; *The family is a system of regeneration II*, 2018 / Below: *Affiche*, 2022; *Facades II*, 2022

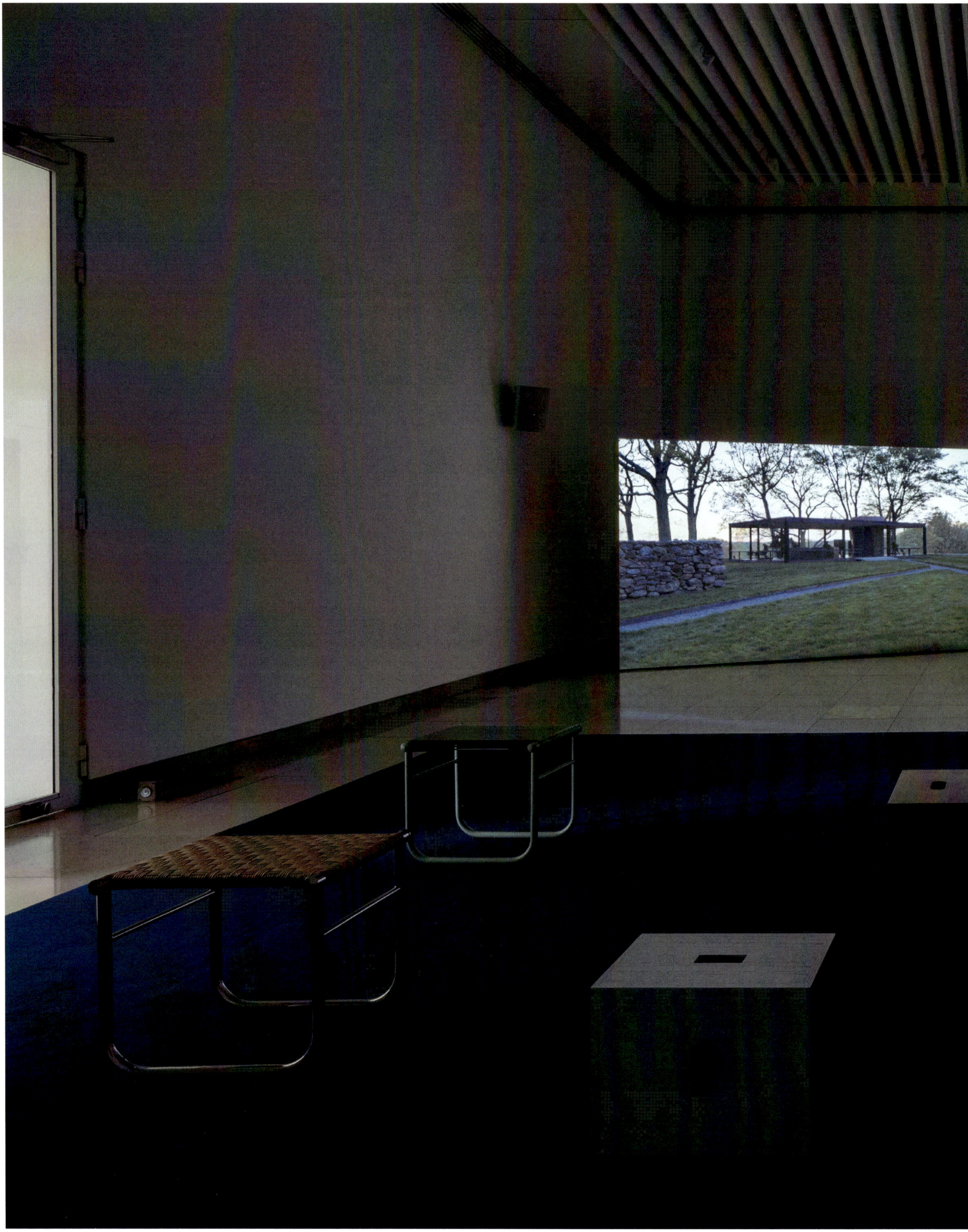

 Schindler/Glass, 2017; Charlotte Perriand, *LC 9 Tabouret*, 1929; Le Corbusier, *LC 14 Tabouret Cabanon* and *LC 14 Tabouret Nantes Rezé*, 1952

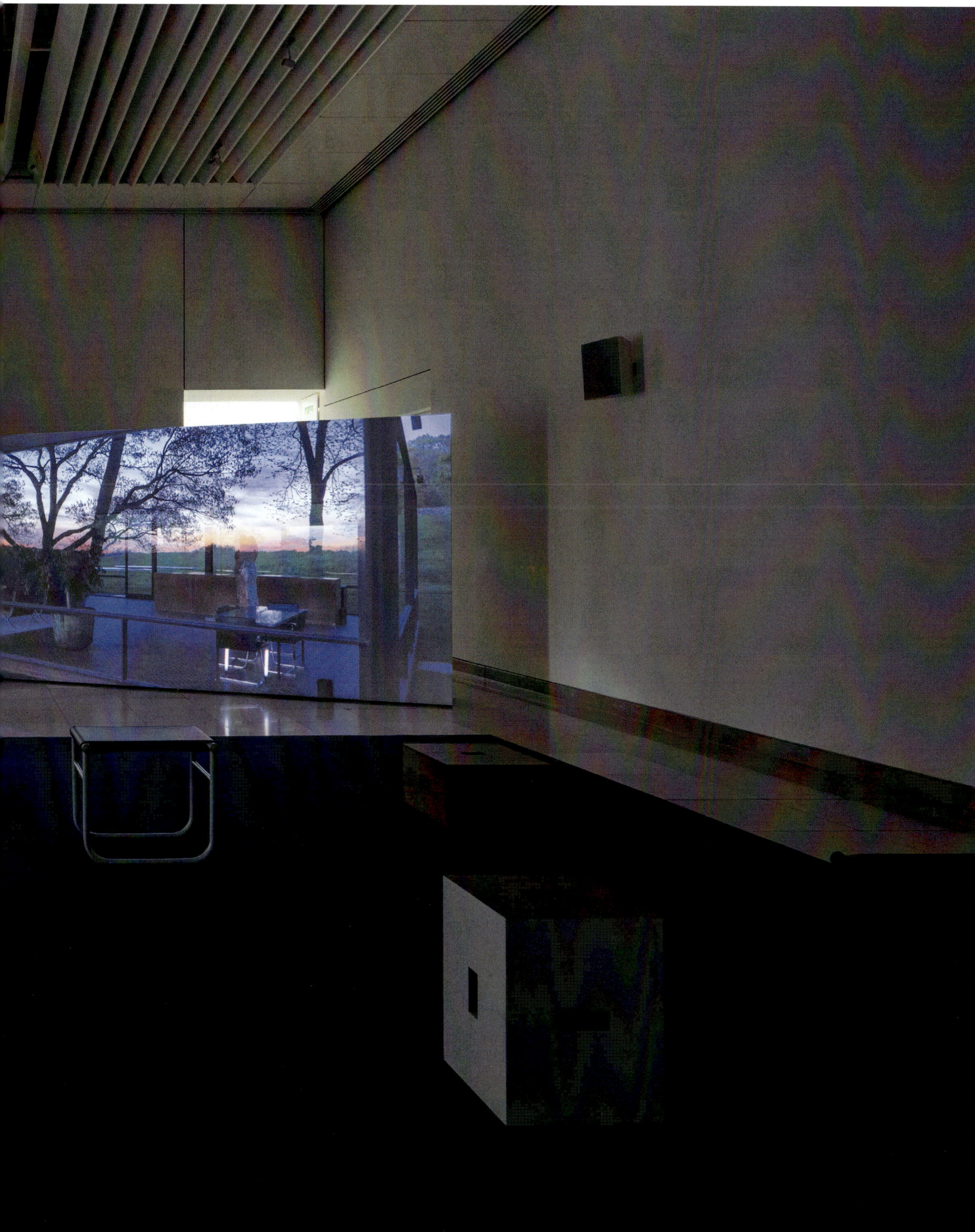

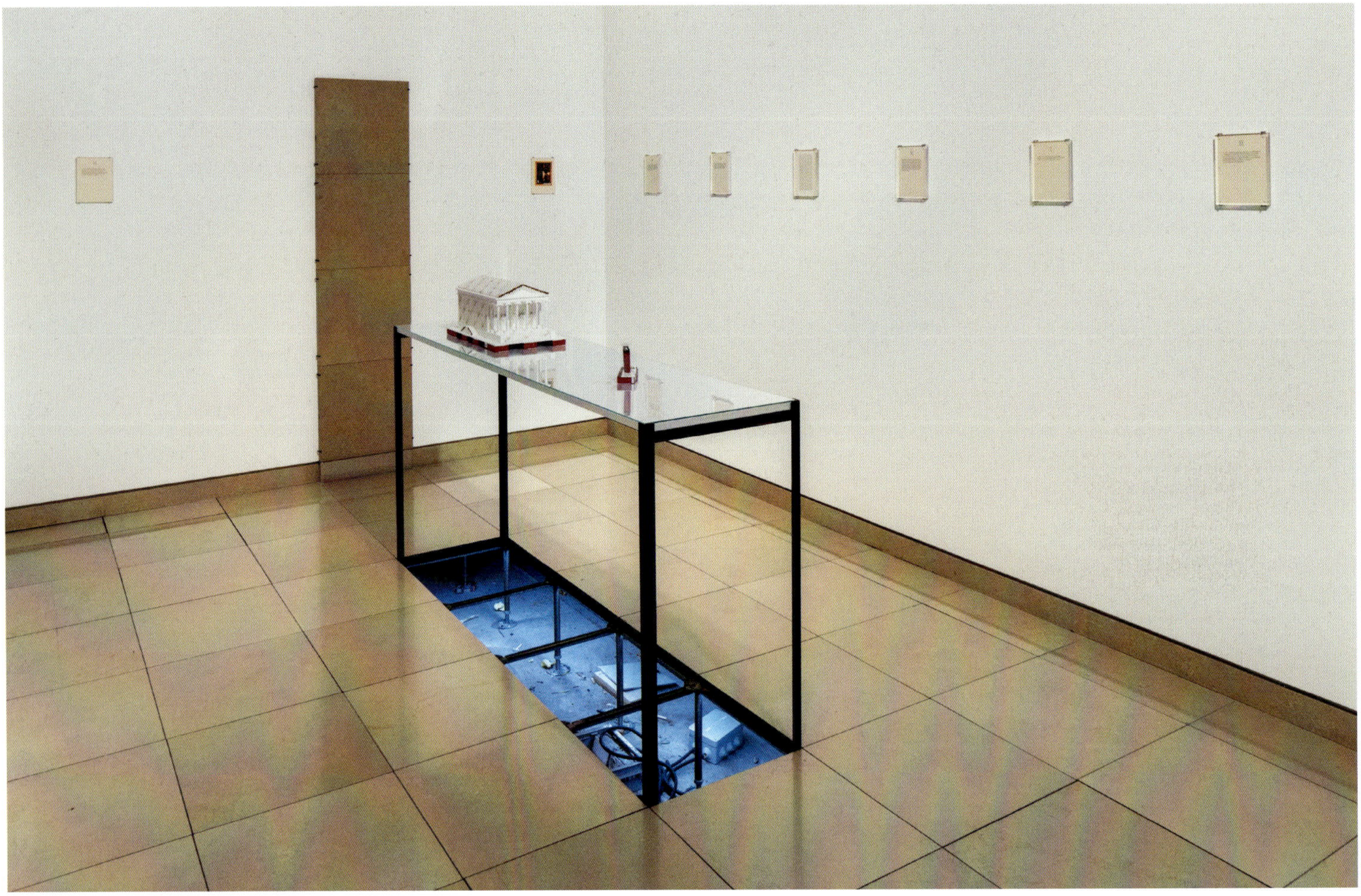

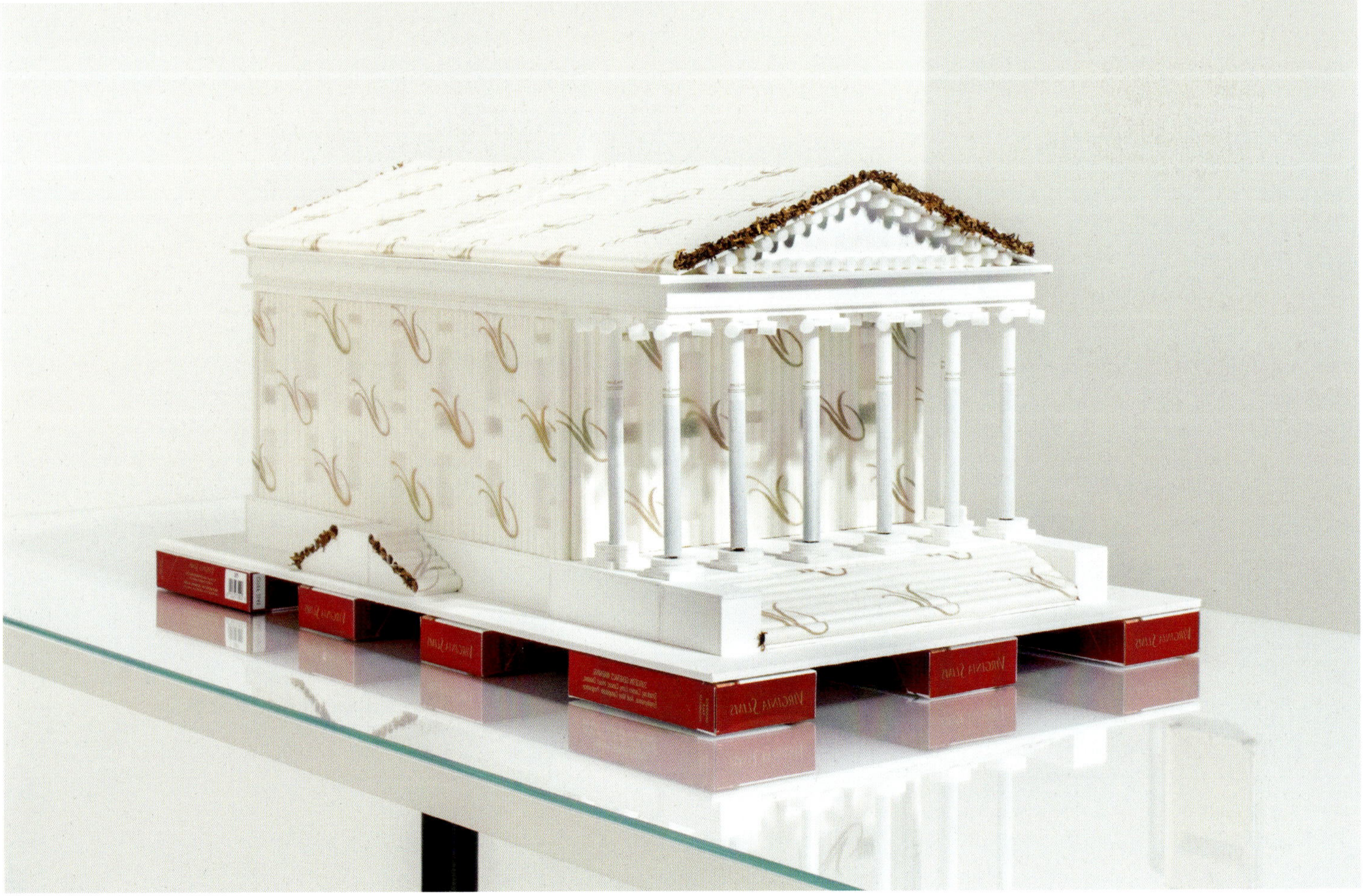

 Ten Thousand Recollections, 2022

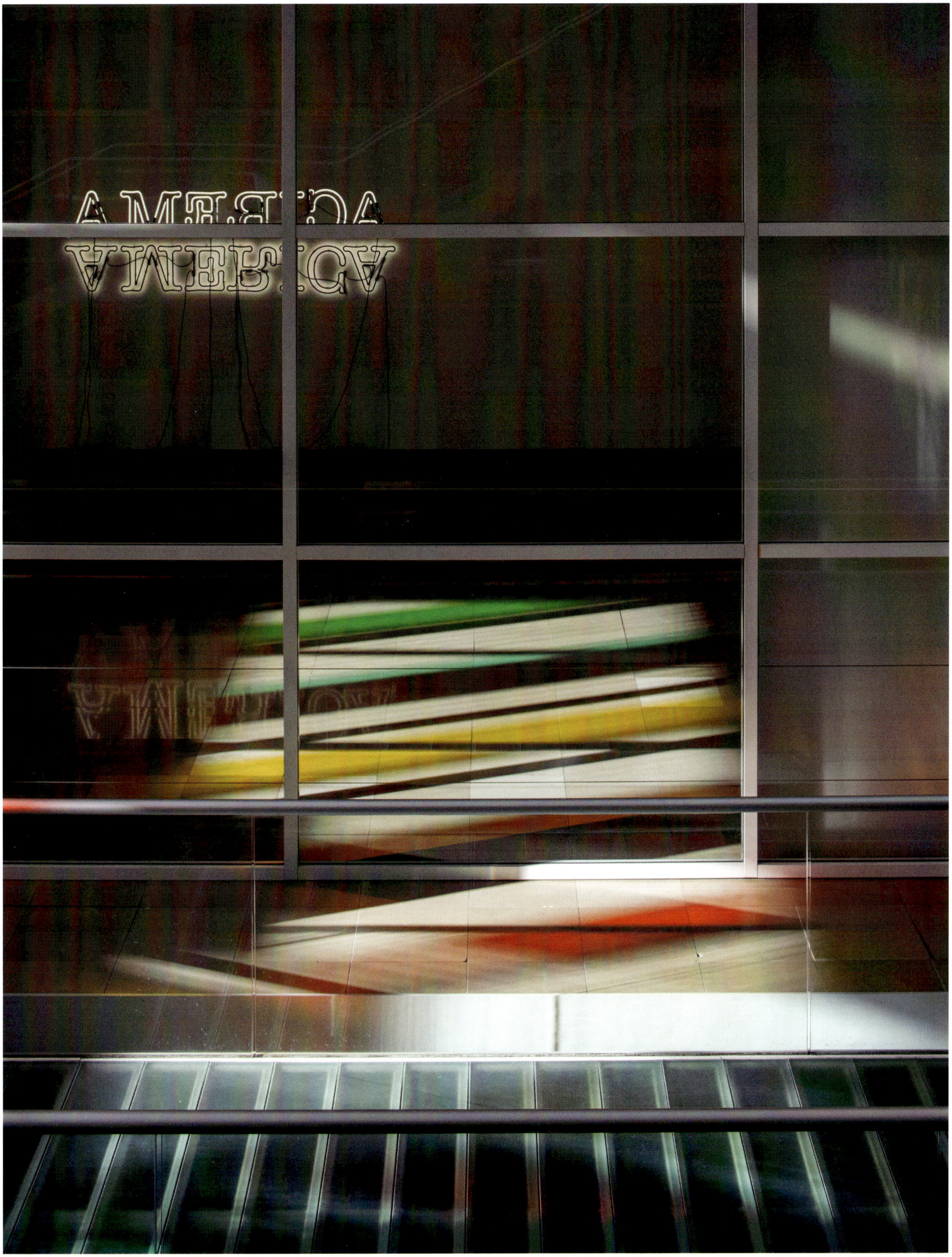

 Relay, 2018; Glenn Ligon, *Double America*, 2012

Transcript 1 (Now in front of Whitney died / Whitney died in front of LA bike rides // Now in front of drove cross country / drove cross country in front of), 2014

Polished copper embossed with Braille
Two parts: 241 × 56 × .15 cm each

Transcript 3 (in front of leaving Ohio / leaving Ohio in front in front of my baby brother's curls / my baby brother's curls in front of the smell of fresh cut grass / the smell of fresh cut grass in front of "she sells seashells by the seashore" / "she sells seashells by the seashore" in front of Patient Zero / Patient Zero in front of I was born // my sister was born in front of I saw an ocean / I saw an ocean in front of I was born), 2014

Polished copper embossed with Braille
Two parts: 241 × 56 × .15 cm each

Score Drawing SH. 2, 2016

Graphite on paper
35.5 × 43 cm

Schindler/Glass, 2017

HD video on two channels, color, sound, 35 min.
Collection Carré d'Art–Musée d'art contemporain de Nîmes
With L.A. Dance Project | Stephanie Amurao, Anthony Bryant, Aaron Carr, Julia Eichten, Morgan Lugo, Nathan Makolandra, Robbie Moore, Rachelle Rafailedes, Lilja Ruriksdottir
Music: SOPHIE, Lucky Dragons
Directors of photography: Javier Bosques, Alex Salinas-Albrecht
Editors: Kate Abernathy, Abigail Collins
Costume design: Stacey Berman
Post-production: Harbor Picture Company

Score Drawing SH.3, 2018

Silkscreen and letterpress on rag paper
35.5 × 46 cm

The family is a system of regeneration I, 2018

Acrylic paint and graphite on canvas, Western redcedar
192.5 × 372 × 6.5 cm

The family is a system of regeneration II, 2018

Acrylic paint and graphite on canvas, Western redcedar
192.5 × 372 × 6.5 cm

The family is a system of regeneration III, 2018

Acrylic paint and graphite on canvas, Western redcedar
192.5 × 372 × 6.5 cm

Private, 2018

Sandblasted glass, torn book page, vellum
49.5 × 64 × 2 cm

Untitled (for Edith), 2018

Blue nightgowns and inkjet print on photo paper
5.5 × 3.5 m

Relay, 2018

Transparent vinyl on windows, nine colors
Dimensions variable

State of, 2019

Plywood, brass, LED light strips, flag costume, performance, 60 min.
With Ryan Kelly, Forty Smooth, Quenton Stuckey
Costume design: Rio Uribe/Gypsy Sport, Stacey Berman
Production: & Compagnie
Presented with the support of FUSED: French-US Exchange in Dance

Score Drawing (Glass House 1), 2020

Graphite on paper
36 × 43.5 cm

Score Drawing (Glass House 2), 2020

Graphite on paper
36 × 43.5 cm

Score Drawing (Schindler House), 2020

Graphite on paper
28 × 57 cm

Score Drawing (This house is not white), 2020

Letterpress, silkscreen, and graphite on rag paper
33 × 45.5 cm

Score Drawing (Villa Savoye), 2020

Graphite on paper
28 × 57 cm

Clockwork (Score Drawing), 2021

Silkscreen and letterpress on rag paper
41 × 51 cm

Panorama, 2021

4K video, color, sound, 22 min.
With Guillaume Diop, Germain Louvet, Soa de Muse
Music: Julius Eastman
Director of photography: Clément de Hollogne
Editor: Félix Rehm
Costume design: Camille Assaf
Production: & Compagnie with the support of Pinault Collection
Post-production: Harbor Picture Company

Bright Hours, 2022

4K video, color, sound, 25 min.
With Jeanne Balibar, Germain Louvet, Emara Neymour-Jackson, David Paycha
Script collaboration: Loïc Barrère
Music: Moses Sumney
Director of photography: Clément de Hollogne
Editor: Grégoire Brice
Costumes: Glen Mban
Coproduction: & Compagnie, Caviar
With the participation of HVH Films
Powered by Dropbox
With the support of the Ministère de la Culture – Direction générale de la création artistique, Carré d'Art–Musée d'art contemporain de Nîmes, Fondation d'entreprise Hermès as part of its New Settings program, CCN – Ballet National de Marseille, Harbor Picture Company
Presented by Cinéma Sémaphore, Nîmes

Affiche, 2022

Silkscreen on paper
Three parts: 100 × 150 cm each

Facades I, 2022

Silkscreen on rag paper
35.5 × 51 cm

Facades II, 2022

Silkscreen on rag paper
Three parts: 35.5 × 51 cm each

Gerard & Kelly in collaboration with Elsa MH Mäki
Ten Thousand Recollections, 2022

Mixed media installation: ink-jet prints on recycled paper, 15 parts: 15 × 21 cm each; architectural model in paper straws, loose tobacco, tracing paper, rolling paper, paper filters, museum board, Virginia Slims cigarettes and packaging; vintage lighter, glass bell jar, graphite on aluminum foil; displaced marble floor tiles
Overall dimensions variable

Unless otherwise noted, all artworks are courtesy of the artists and Marian Goodman Gallery. / Sauf indication contraire, toutes les œuvres sont courtesy des artistes et Marian Goodman Gallery.

Other works in the exhibition / Autres œuvres en exposition

Eileen Gray
Monte Carlo Sofa, 1929

Chrome-plated tubular steel, cotton
60 × 280 × 95 cm
Courtesy of ClassiCon

Charlotte Perriand
LC 9 Tabouret, 1929

Painted tubular steel, leather / polished chrome, wicker
46 × 51 × 37 cm
Courtesy of Domus

Le Corbusier
LC 14 Tabouret Cabanon, 1952

Solid chestnut
43 × 43 × 27 cm
Courtesy of Cassina

Le Corbusier
LC 14 Tabouret Nantes Rezé, 1952

Birch with oak veneer, paint
43 × 43 × 27 cm
Courtesy of Cassina

James Welling
5097, 2016

Archival pigment print on rag paper
52.5 × 70 cm
Courtesy of the artist

Avant-propos

Jean-Marc Prevost

Depuis plusieurs années, Carré d'Art a ouvert sa programmation et la collection à la performance et à la danse contemporaine avec les expositions d'Anne Imhof, Emmanuelle Huynh et Jocelyn Cottencin, Tarik Kiswanson ou l'exposition *A Different way to move: Minimalismes, New York, 1960-1980.* Dans cette exposition était évoquée la complexité des relations de la Post-Modern Dance avec les formes de l'Art Minimal. Le caractère éphémère de la danse signifiait la possibilité d'échapper aux régimes de marchandisation et réification de l'art. Avec le temps, les choses ont radicalement changé, la performance entrant de façon légitime dans l'espace du musée et même parfois ses collections. Il est toutefois certain que ce corps sujet a encore aujourd'hui pour fonction une critique de la représentation par sa seule présence si ce n'est que le geste est toujours différent, continuellement rejoué et lié au contexte et au temps où il advient. Faire entrer les corps dans l'espace du musée, c'est aussi un questionnement de la mémoire des gestes, de la transmission en interrogeant les limites du musée. « Elle révèle d'un désir – de la part des interprètes comme du public – d'expériences en contrepoint de nos vies en ligne : immédiateté incarnée, présence collective partagée, proximité physique, sens du lieu, méditation intérieure en compagnie d'autres personnes[1]. » C'est comme si, paradoxalement, le « white cube » du musée, pensé comme un dispositif neutre et froid, permettait de renouer avec une certaine forme d'intimité.

Gerard & Kelly, artistes venant du champ chorégraphique, entrent avec cette exposition de façon manifeste dans celui des arts visuels avec la présentation d'installations vidéo, sculptures, et œuvres sur papier. C'est d'une certaine façon, le passage du champ de l'expérimentation des corps à leur représentation que l'on pouvait déjà trouver dans le passage de leurs performances à la réalisation de films. La spatialisation des installations dans les salles du musée peut être vue comme une mise en abyme où le corps du spectateur surgit dans l'espace d'exposition.

Leur travail s'est entre autres développé depuis plusieurs années autour du projet *Modern Living* qui se présente comme une série de performances et films dans laquelle ils interrogent des projets architecturaux qui déjouent l'usage bourgeois et patriarcal traditionnel. Ils sont intervenus dans la Schindler House à West Hollywood en Californie et la Glass House de Philip Johnson dans le Connecticut, des architectures que les architectes ont conçues pour eux-mêmes et leurs proches abritant des relations aussi expérimentales que leurs conceptions. La maison devient le cadre de performances où les interprètes apprennent à vivre ensemble. C'est en quelque sorte une façon de repenser les notions de genre, de couple et d'espace intime à partager. Schindler a conçu sa maison en 1922 pour deux couples dans une ébauche de vie communautaire. Johnson a pensé la sienne, construite en 1949 dans la forêt, pour abriter la vie avec son partenaire David Whitney.

Une production récente, *Panorama* (2021), a été filmée à la Bourse de Commerce qui abrite aujourd'hui la collection Pinault. Ce bâtiment, à l'origine halle au blé, a été transformé au XIXe siècle en un bâtiment à la gloire du commerce et de la finance. Les peintures dans la rotonde datant de 1889 sont les témoignages idéalisés des échanges avec les nations européennes et américaines mais aussi les colonies en Afrique et en Indochine. Trois danseurs de différentes origines, cultures et formations, habitent l'espace épuré de Tadao Ando chargé de l'histoire des puissances impérialistes européennes. Au discours qui se déploie dans la rotonde, répond une fragilité des corps dans l'espace monumental mais aussi l'affirmation de gestes qui sont la manifestation d'identités multiples.

Dans *Bright Hours* (2022), Gerard & Kelly se sont intéressés à la Cité Radieuse de Le Corbusier et en particulier à sa relation avec Joséphine Baker après leur rencontre en 1929 entre São Paulo et Paris sur un paquebot transatlantique. C'est la rencontre de la radicalité d'un architecte moderniste blanc européen et d'une danseuse afro-americaine à laquelle est associée la libération du corps.

À travers ces performances, films et installations, Gerard & Kelly rendent visible des histoires et situations inconnues et nous entrainent vers une relecture par le geste chorégraphique des icônes architecturales qui nous entourent. Une autre histoire peu connue s'inscrit fortuitement dans le projet d'exposition. Thomas Jefferson, ambassadeur en France de 1785 à 1789 avant de devenir le troisième président des États-Unis, a visité Nîmes. Il tombe amoureux de la Maison Carrée qui deviendra source d'inspiration pour le capitole de Richmond en Virginie. Les États-Unis sont une nouvelle nation et il prend la Maison Carrée, temple romain du Ier siècle comme modèle. Richmond qui par ironie de l'histoire deviendra de 1861 à 1865 la capitale de la Confédération des états esclavagistes. La Maison Carrée deviendra l'arrière-plan de *State of* (2019), performance avec trois danseurs interrogeant les symboles du nationalisme à partir du drapeau et de l'hymne américain.

1.
Claire Bishop, « Black Box, White Cube, Gray Zone : Dance exhibitions and audience attention », dans *Performance Works*, Mousse Publishing, p. 66.

À travers les vestiges du rêve du futur :

l'art des constellations allégoriques de Gerard & Kelly

Miwon Kwon

... l'*inter*prétation est un dés*inter*nement .[1]
—Craig Owens, 1980

Dans *Panorama*, le temp vécu et le temp à venir sont réunis par un art à la signification ambivalente et trouble. Dans ce film de 22 minutes les artistes américains Brennan Gerard et Ryan Kelly basés à Paris depuis 2018 ont créé « un hybride entre film de danse et essai cinématographique[2] ». *Panorama* voit trois muses – Mémoire, Avenir et Allégorie[3] – s'inviter sur le site historique de la Bourse de Commerce dans le centre de Paris[4]. Tourné fin 2020 après l'achèvement de la refonte et de la rénovation du bâtiment par Tadao Ando et avant son ouverture au public, *Panorama* marque un moment très précis dans la transformation de la séculaire bourse de commerce en un musée d'art contemporain dédié à l'accueil et à la présentation de la vaste collection personnelle de l'homme d'affaires François Pinault[5]. En tant que tel, *Panorama* peut être considéré comme l'inauguration informelle et non officielle d'une nouvelle institution artistique française qui s'appellera désormais « Bourse de Commerce – Pinault Collection ». Occupant conceptuellement l'espace du trait d'union dans la dénomination qui relie l'identité très ancienne du bâtiment en tant que site d'échanges commerciaux et sa nouvelle identité d'espace d'exposition consacré à « l'art de notre temps[6] », *Panorama* montre autant qu'il illustre le déplacement du commerce de l'art dans ce monument néoclassique dont l'architecture originale, en particulier son dôme de fer et de verre, était autrefois saluée comme la quintessence de l'art le plus avancé de son temps.[7]

Si le moment précis de la mise en scène et du tournage de *Panorama* ne dépendait pas entièrement de Gerard & Kelly (certes, le moment de la réalisation du projet était quelque peu inopiné[8]), la réunion de Mémoire, Avenir et Allégorie pour ce qui pourrait être interprété comme un nettoyage rituel du bâtiment avant son ouverture au public a été conçue avec la plus grande précision. Rappelant le trope des trios de déesses de la mythologie classique et d'autres trios de sœurs du destin des temps anciens et de la littérature qui pouvaient voir ou déterminer le destin des humains, les trois muses de *Panorama* dansent, chantent et parlent tout en confrontant les histoires et les possibles futurs inscrits dans l'ancienne et la nouvelle architecture de la Bourse de Commerce.

Tout d'abord, *Panorama* adresse et répond à la vision de grandeur de la France telle que capturée dans le projet décoratif central du bâtiment, la grande peinture murale allégorique « Panorama du Commerce », également connue sous l'intitulé « France triomphante », achevée à l'origine en 1889 pour l'Exposition universelle et minutieusement restaurée pour la réouverture du bâtiment en tant que musée d'art contemporain[9]. S'enroulant à 360 degrés tout autour de la rotonde comme une frise sous l'énorme dôme, le panorama mesure 10 mètres de haut et 140 mètres de long et dépeint l'horizon du progrès français devant être réalisé à travers les échanges et le commerce mondiaux tel qu'il était projeté à la fin du XIXe siècle[10]. Peint par cinq artistes différents, chacun s'étant vu assigné différentes régions du monde, ce panorama est essentiellement un collage, une construction faite de différentes sections rassemblées afin de créer un ensemble apparemment continu et fantastique. Si certains spécialistes ont noté le manque de cohérence picturale dans l'œuvre, en partie dû à l'implication d'un trop grand nombre d'artistes, ce « Panorama du Commerce » présente néanmoins une vision idéologiquement unifiée du monde reflétant l'ambition, pour ne pas dire la portée triomphaliste de la France à l'époque moderne.[11]

Après un bref prélude composé d'extraits d'archives légèrement dégradées de vues extérieures et intérieures de la Bourse de Commerce qui installent le décor du film et établissent l'âge avancé du bâtiment, *Panorama* entraine bientôt le spectateur dans la clairière centrale sous la rotonde telle qu'Ando l'a conçue. On y trouve Mémoire, figure solitaire sur la toile de fond minimaliste du cylindre de béton – 9 mètres de haut et 30 mètres de diamètre – que l'architecte japonais a intégré dans le vide central du bâtiment. Vêtue d'un élégant costume couleur magenta, parfaitement coiffée de longues tresses et les ongles impeccablement manucurés, Mémoire est assise sur le sol, pieds nus, les genoux ramassés sous elle comme en imploration. Elle chante doucement, et tout en augmentant le volume de sa voix, elle essuie (ou plutôt caresse) délicatement le sol avec une éponge imbibée d'eau. Avenir regarde, à travers des reflets réfractés de son propre visage. Puis apparait Allégorie qui de même « nettoie » l'architecture d'Ando. Debout à l'étage supérieur et surplombant la présence de Mémoire dans la rotonde en contrebas, il trace une ligne sur le rebord supérieur du cylindre de béton avec une éponge humide coincée dans sa bouche[12]. Puis la présence fugitive d'Avenir parle, apparemment de loin, ou peut-être d'un autre temps, avec une question pour Mémoire : « De quoi te souvenais-tu ? »

La réponse de Mémoire est une énumération de choses remarquées dans le panorama – des objets, des personnes, des bâtiments, des paysages, des activités ou des interactions. Elle crie, son regard scrutant et balayant les différentes scènes de la peinture murale :

Un léopard[13]
Une carrière
Un chef indien protège son visage
Deux enfants autochtones se tiennent la main
Maman?
Mother
Mama we
Dé esclave poté yon pyebwa
The train

The spear
Tonnage de coton
Hectares de blé
Un arc et une flèche
A ship in the clouds
Columbus dans le cumulus castellanus
Columbus up my anus!
A la vache !
Cows, cowboys… a bull?
Un blanc barbu à son bureau [puis comme si elle se corrigeait]
Hmm… un comptable caucasien
I guess

Mousse couvre pierre
Un bateau à vapeur
Une usine au loin qui crache du jaune
Un pont
A lighthouse
Horses, horses, horses
A monkey
Two monkeys
Chapeau napoléonien
Tricolore
Wicker basket
A Chinese man sells yellow silk
Geisha geisha geisha

Two tattooed Michaelangelos tug a canoe
American flag
The American flag–
[commence à chanter « God Bless America »]
–a cherub's ass

Et le nom du peintre gravé dans la roche,
E. Luminais[14]

Les souvenirs de Mémoire couvrent ici un très vaste ensemble, des emblèmes de la production industrielle moderne (carrières, usines et leurs « crachats » jaunes) aux nouveaux moyens de transport (bateaux à vapeur, ponts, navires, trains), de diverses denrées (hectares de blé, tonnes de coton, paniers en osier, soie jaune) aux animaux exotiques et domestiques (léopard, singes, taureau, chevaux, vaches) en passant par les marchands et les ouvriers d'origines étrangères (chef indien, enfants indigènes, esclaves, geishas, un Chinois, cow-boys). Mêlé à cet inventaire éclectique, Mémoire rappelle en outre avec une irrévérence mordante une série de symboles de la puissance occidentale présents dans le panorama (Colomb et sa caravelle, un homme blanc barbu comptant son argent, le chapeau de Napoléon, le cul d'un chérubin), sans oublier les couleurs tricolores françaises et les étoiles et rayures américaines, d'autant plus soulignées par de courtes phrases mélodiques de « La Marseillaise » et de « God Bless America » chantées par Mémoire. Elle termine sa promenade dans le passé par l'évocation d'Évariste-Vital Luminais, le peintre à qui l'on doit la section Amérique du Nord du panorama, dont le nom, note-t-elle, est gravé dans la pierre, confirmant son statut d'artiste plongé dans l'Histoire. Puis, après une brève pause pour se recomposer, Mémoire conclut tranquillement et de manière prémonitoire : « Une tempête arrive. »

Ce dont Mémoire se souvient de manière fugaces et fragmentaires comme dans un rêve troublé ou dans un collage encombré, c'est un empilement historique de résidus. Il s'agit d'autant de rappels et de plans d'un avenir projeté par le modernisme européen et le capitalisme industriel sur le monde au cours du XXe siècle. Il se déploie sur des terres et des peuples lointains pour en extraire les richesses. Il n'est peut-être pas surprenant que Mémoire prédise l'arrivée d'une tempête[15]. Debout dans cet avenir que le « Panorama du Commerce » projetait, les spectateurs et les spectatrices d'aujourd'hui connaissent les nombreuses impasses dans lesquelles cette vision a entrainé l'humanité. Car si la peinture murale « décrit le triomphe du commerce à travers les continents, de la Russie enneigée à un Nouveau Monde émergent et aux marchés d'Orient[16] », le XXe siècle a également connu partout dans le monde des entreprises colonialistes qui au nom même du progrès, du développement et de la modernisation ont invariablement traités les êtres humains et les territoires comme des marchandises à prendre, à vendre et à échanger. Le siècle dernier a également connu des progrès technologiques et des nationalismes tribaux qui ont nourri la concurrence et la volonté de domination plus que le partage ou la collaboration, menant à l'horreur des guerres mondiales, des destructions sans précédent, des atrocités humaines insondables et des catastrophes naturelles[17]. Mais en dépit de l'annonce de cette tempête – ou peut-être à cause d'elle – Mémoire, Avenir et Allégorie convergent dans la rotonde. Et dansent.

Bien sûr, l'art sert très souvent de palliatif, sinon de mécanisme rédempteur. Comme par magie, l'art peut transformer le bestial en beau et les déchets en or. L'art peut non seulement élever, mais aussi travestir, dissiper ou excuser ce qui serait le cas échéant inacceptable, horrible et méprisable. Vu sous cet angle, la séquence d'ouverture de *Panorama* qui semble proposer le « nettoyage » comme leitmotiv – Mémoire frottant le sol de la Bourse de Commerce et ses exhortations servant de métaphores de l'exorcisme de tous les péchés historiques qui auraient pu se produire littéralement et symboliquement dans son périmètre et au-delà – pourrait faussement être interprétée comme un acte rédempteur de la part de Gerard & Kelly. Mais comme le révèlent les séquences de danse et de performance qui suivent, les péchés du passé ne peuvent être ni lavés ni recouverts. Après le « nettoyage », s'amorce une prise de conscience du passé et une contemplation inquiète de l'avenir. La danse de Mémoire, d'Avenir et d'Allégorie face à une tempête à venir n'est ni l'expression d'un deuil ni celle d'une célébration. Elle n'est pas une tentative de transcendance ou d'absolution. Le trio exprime plutôt des exigences – vis-à-vis de l'Histoire, de la société, des dieux. Ils exécutent une relecture provocatrice et ludique des récits et des valeurs hérités d'époques révolues qui ne dorment ni ne meurent, mais persistent encore dans le présent. Ainsi, en dansant, ils affirment collectivement et de manière répétitive :

Je suis une maison vide
Une maison sans intérieur
Je suis une surface
Qui demande le droit d'être multiple[18]

Ici, les muses affirment un modèle d'identité et de subjectivité qui n'est ni ancré dans, ni motivé par une essence intérieure fixe et stable. Le cœur du « je » est une vacance. Le soi/l'identité comme réceptacle vide signifie qu'il ne peut être connu ou « rempli » que par l'effet des inscriptions qui sont soit imposées de force à sa surface – par le langage, les codes culturels et sociétaux, les systèmes juridiques, les héritages historiques, etc. –, soit adoptées de manière performative et continuellement recodées (souvent en résistance aux inscriptions imposées). Et en tant que tel, le « je » est impermanent, non fixé. Le mouvement perpétuel est le corolaire du fait d'être vivant, dépendant de moments, de lieux et de désirs particuliers. Ainsi, lorsque Mémoire, Avenir et Allégorie affirment être une maison vide et revendiquent le droit à être multiples, en réaction au mythe d'une identité nationale unifiée dépeinte comme triomphante de l'altérité et de la différence dans le panorama, il faut comprendre ce que cette requête a de politique et d'existentiel. Leur demande remet en cause la croyance dominante en des identités cohérentes et singulières (des individus comme des cultures et des nations) qui craint, refuse ou réprime la différence, à l'intérieur et dans le monde. Plus précisément, Mémoire, Avenir et Allégorie appellent la maison Pinault à embrasser la multiplicité.

On pourrait aussi dire qu'une maison vide, sans intérieur, fait référence à l'ouverture au cœur même du bâtiment de la Bourse de Commerce. Selon Gerard & Kelly, la prise en compte de l'histoire du *Panorama* dans un engagement critique face à la peinture murale décorative du XIXe siècle est en grande partie inspirée par la « poétique brutale » de Tadao Ando. Les artistes décrivent l'imbrication architecturale d'Ando d'un cylindre de béton démesuré à l'intérieur de la rotonde existante comme, d'une part, un encadrement physique du panorama qui entoure l'intérieur du bâtiment et, d'autre part, et peut-être plus important encore, comme une « proposition radicale pour confronter et réfléchir au passé tout en réinventant le monde au présent[19] ». Ando a lui-même présenté l'assemblage de la rotonde et du cylindre de béton en forme de silo comme reliant le passé au présent et à l'avenir. L'architecte a déclaré : « J'espère que la superposition de la rotonde et du cylindre, de l'ancien et du nouveau, donnera lieu à une série d'espaces encore plus puissants et variés et créera un lieu animé approprié au soutien de la culture de la ville pour la prochaine génération[20]. » Si cette déclaration semble d'une grande platitude, comme le sont généralement les communiqués de presse, il est néanmoins important de réaliser que la refonte et la rénovation conçues par Ando ne correspondent pas à la réhabilitation standard d'un bâtiment qui « respecte » l'ancien en introduisant le nouveau de manière convenue.

Le travail d'Ando à la Bourse de Commerce, comme dans tant d'autres de ses projets, ne consiste pas simplement à opposer des contraires dans le même espace, comme le passé et le présent, par exemple. Son architecture procède plutôt à une rigoureuse *interpénétration* des qualités généralement considérées comme opposées – passé et présent, ancien et nouveau, clair et sombre, nature et culture, abstraction et figuration, dur et doux, présence et absence, masculin et féminin, Est et Ouest, etc. Plus précisément, l'architecture d'Ando révèle la dynamique et le mouvement mutuellement constitutifs, la *dialectique* entre des opposés qui *maintiennent leurs identités de manière relationnelle*. En ce sens, affirmer que cette architecture parvient à une harmonie miraculeuse, une synthétise ou une réconciliation des contraires, comme on a coutume de le dire, ne serait pas exact à cent pour cent, et, ce bien que l'architecte l'ait lui-même déclaré [21]. Le mouvement dialectique ne débouche pas sur une stase opérant une synthèse, une réconciliation ou une résolution. L'utilisation par Ando du terme « superposition » pour décrire son geste architectural d'insertion d'un cylindre de béton à l'intérieur de la rotonde existante nous rapproche un peu plus de cette dialectique, mais elle reste encore en deçà de ce que Gerard & Kelly décrivent comme une « poétique brutale », une proposition radicale. Car l'architecture d'Ando à la Bourse de Commerce ne se résume pas uniquement à la juxtaposition du passé et du présent ou à leur accumulation, comme l'addition de strates temporelles. Elle réalise plutôt une superposition, ou une interpénétration, ainsi que noté précédemment, des contraires, du passé et du présent. Dans cette architecture, le passé n'est pas tant un point de référence historique distant, distinct du présent (une couche de temps différente pourrait-on dire), mais fait immédiatement *un avec le maintenant*, inséparable du présent et, par extension, du futur. La « superposition » architecturale d'Ando permet ainsi l'expérience non seulement de la temporalité non linéaire, mais aussi de la *multiplicité* des temps *à l'intérieur* du présent. Hier est aujourd'hui est hier est demain est aujourd'hui... Un peu comme un palimpseste, son travail matérialise le temps comme toujours déjà multiple[22]. L'intérêt de Gerard &

Kelly pour la co-articulation du passé, du présent et du futur dans *Panorama*, leur évocation d'identités multiples et de multiples temps dans le film, résonne profondément avec cette dialectique de l'architecture d'Ando.

La notion d'identité et de temps comme multiples, et performatifs aussi, est explicitement démontrée dans une séquence ultérieure de *Panorama* dans laquelle Mémoire, Avenir et Allégorie imitent trois figures représentées dans une petite scène de la section Amérique du Nord du panorama. La hiérarchie des relations de pouvoir est sans ambiguïté dans cette scène peinte : une femme blanche distinguée, assise sur un coussin de soie verte sur un socle de pierre, est accompagnée d'une jeune femme noire, sa servante sinon son esclave[23], qui la sert en tenant un grand parasol. Protégée du soleil brûlant, la maîtresse sur son trône de fortune lève les yeux vers le parasol et au-delà vers le ciel. Elle ne remarque pas le jeune garçon amérindien par terre, agenouillé à ses pieds, portant vers elle à deux mains et avec déférence l'offrande d'un oiseau exotique. Cette organisation figée des rapports de pouvoir selon la race et le genre, entre blanc et non blanc, entre maître et esclave, prend vie et se désagrège simultanément tandis que Soa de Muse, Guillaume Diop et Germain Louvet prennent des poses pour reproduire la scène peinte. En imitant ou en se référant à l'interaction triangulée dans la vignette panoramique, ils changent de rôle de manière ludique, brouillant ainsi la hiérarchie de leurs positions. Ce faisant, leurs identités de Mémoire, Avenir et Allégorie, les rôles que chacun personnifiait respectivement dans le film jusque-là (et qu'ils reprendront à nouveau) se superposent lorsqu'ils adoptent et abandonnent les rôles de la fille noire, de la femme blanche, du garçon indigène, du colonisateur, du donneur de cadeaux, du serviteur, etc. En même temps, les trois interprètes sont en fait de beaux Parisiens cosmopolites du XXIe siècle, des danseurs et des artistes professionnels. Les identités métisses de race, de genre et de sexualité de Soa, Guillaume et Germain sont peut-être plus fluides et plus libres que ce qui est représenté ou autorisé avec les personnages de la peinture murale du XIXe siècle, mais tous trois jouent néanmoins des rôles attribués et construisent eux aussi leur identité.

Alors que la caméra s'éloigne lentement des trois interprètes principaux qui, comme évoqué précédemment, incarnent de multiples identités et occupent différents temps, la théâtralité artificielle de la situation se révèle avec le va-et-vient de femmes et d'hommes assistants techniques pour les costumes, les éclairages, les accessoires, les habillages, le maquillage, etc. qui traversent le cadre de l'image. Le recul de la caméra brise le « quatrième mur » pour montrer une organisation différente du pouvoir et de l'autorité qui structure *cette* scène (laquelle déconstruit l'organisation du pouvoir et de l'autorité dépeinte dans une scène historique datant de plus d'un siècle). La caméra montre finalement Brennan Gerard et Ryan Kelly debout dans l'ombre derrière leur caméra, côte à côte, dirigeant tranquillement l'équipe et les interprètes et supervisant toute la mise en scène en tant que Gerard & Kelly, une position d'auteur qui est intrinsèquement divisée et multiple. Cette image est aussi une reconnaissance introspective du rôle des deux artistes en tant que créateurs de la construction figurative de *Panorama* et de leur position d'œil derrière l'œil même qui *les* regarde. Fait important, cependant, si cette révélation introspective renvoie aux discours postmodernistes sur la politique du regard, Gerard & Kelly contournent la binarité oppositionnelle qui structure ces approches[24]. Cette séquence ne s'arrête pas à la révélation critique de l'autorialité. La caméra poursuit son voyage. Passant devant les artistes, elle trace son chemin jusqu'à rejoindre les trois interprètes encore en répétition ou en préparation, pour donner vie à cette scène issue du panorama. La caméra désormais plus proche de la reconstitution voit que la correspondance entre la scène du XIXe siècle et son double du XXIe siècle est presque parfaite, prête à être capturée en film ou en photographie pour l'éternité. Un instant, cependant. Soa, Guillaume et Germain, avant de prendre leurs positions finales de garçon amérindien (Mémoire), de femme blanche (Avenir) et d'esclave (Allégorie), insistent pour prendre un selfie de groupe pour commémorer ce moment pour eux-mêmes, affirmant leurs propres identités « réelles » et posant pour l'objectif de l'un de leurs téléphones (même si cet intermède est aussi pour la caméra de Gerard & Kelly). À la suite de cette interruption impertinente de la « vraie vie », qui introduit un tout nouveau sens du temps et ne perturbe que momentanément la réalité artificielle de la reconstitution, une voix masculine invisible lance un « COUPEZ » pour mettre fin à la séquence.

La (re)présentation d'identités multiples et leur transposition dans cette partie du film entraînent une interpénétration du passé et du présent, comparable à l'architecture d'Ando, ainsi que le brouillage du temps et de l'espace de représentation et du temps et de l'espace « réels » (tout cela étant d'autant plus complexe du fait de l'imbrication de la politique du regard). Elle devient un espace de multitemporalité et de polyvocalité qui ne laisse pas le passé reposer en paix ou se perdre dans l'oubli. En tant que tel, le palimpseste s'impose comme une métaphore appropriée pour le travail de Gerard & Kelly. Il désigne une page dans laquelle les inscriptions passées ont été remplacées par de nouvelles inscriptions, mais demeurent enchâssées dans le texte original. La signification de la nouvelle inscription n'est donc pas indépendante des inscriptions antérieures ; elles partagent le même corps. Ou plus clairement, tel que l'exprime Google, un palimpseste est quelque chose « de réutilisé ou de modifié mais qui préserve des traces visibles de sa forme antérieure », comme par exemple Soa, Guillaume et Germain qui reproduisent et modifient simultanément les positions du trio dans la scène panoramique, ou Mémoire, Avenir et Allégorie réécrivant d'une manière radicale l'histoire des Trois Destins (ou Moirai) de la mythologie grecque et les différentes adaptations ultérieures par d'innombrables écrivains, artistes et cinéastes au fil du temps.

Dire de *Panorama* que c'est un palimpseste revient à dire que sa structure en tant qu'œuvre d'art est comme un texte, une nouvelle inscription qui agit sur des textes antérieurs (le « Panorama du Commerce », la Bourse de Commerce), se souciant de leurs traces et les transformant pour le présent. L'œuvre d'art tout à la fois parasite et émerge des inscriptions données/passées, réinterprétant à nouveau leur signification comme un supplément. Ce qui rappelle les réflexions du théoricien et critique d'art américain Craig Owens, qui, dans son essai fondateur de 1980, « The Allegorical Impulse: Toward a Theory of Postmodernism », remarquait la résurgence de l'allégorie pourtant proscrite par le modernisme et identifiait le palimpseste comme le premier paradigme de l'allégorie. Il déclarait : « Dans la structure allégorique, [...] un texte est *lu à travers* un autre, aussi fragmentaire, intermittente ou chaotique que puisse être leur relation ; le paradigme de l'œuvre allégorique est donc le palimpseste.[25] » Pour Owens, l'allégorie est « une attitude autant qu'une technique, une perception autant qu'une procédure », et elle se produit à « chaque fois qu'un texte est doublé par un autre[26] ». Il poursuit : « l'allégoriste n'invente pas une image mais la confisque » et « revendique son importance culturelle, se posant comme son interprète. Entre ses mains l'image devient autre chose [...] Il ne restaure pas un sens originel qui aurait été perdu ou effacé ; l'allégorie n'est pas de l'herméneutique. Il ajoute plutôt un autre sens à l'image. Mais s'il ajoute, il ne le fait cependant que pour remplacer : le sens allégorique supplante un sens antérieur ; c'est un supplément.[27] »

Réfléchir à la théorisation d'Owens pourrait conduire à penser que toutes formes d'interprétation, de commentaire ou de production artistiques qui impliquent une sorte de réécriture appropriative d'un texte premier ou antérieur serait allégorique. Mais le critique a précisé que les relations allégoriques doivent être considérées comme quelque chose qui se passe *à l'intérieur* de l'œuvre d'art, structurant sa logique même. Et il en a fait une caractéristique distinctive, une tendance générationnelle, que l'on retrouve dans les pratiques artistiques postmodernistes de son temps. Il a souligné d'autres attributs de la pulsion allégorique dans son essai tout en déconstruisant simultanément les racines profondes de son interdiction, de sa suppression et de sa marginalisation dans l'esthétique moderniste et l'histoire de l'art, remontant à la peinture française du XIXe siècle (incidemment le moment même de la réalisation du « Panorama du Commerce ») et aux débats qui l'entouraient[28]. S'il n'est pas approprié ici de procéder à une analyse exhaustive de la pensée complexe d'Owens, il convient d'en rappeler certains des points essentiels afin de mieux comprendre dans quelle mesure la pratique artistique de Gerard & Kelly, au-delà de ce qui a déjà été dit sur *Panorama*, prolonge encore l'attitude, la technique, la perception, et le procédé allégoriques théorisés par le critique.

Tout d'abord, Owens considère que « le travail allégorique est synthétique ; il franchit les frontières esthétiques. » Plutôt que de tendre vers la pureté d'un médium ou d'un genre comme l'auraient voulu certains modernistes, une œuvre allégorique les mélange et les confond. « Cette confusion de genre », ajoutait le critique, « réapparaît aujourd'hui dans l'hybridation, dans des œuvres éclectiques qui combinent de manière ostentatoire des médiums artistiques auparavant distincts[29]. » L'art de Gerard & Kelly qui amalgame et combine sans relâche la danse, la sculpture, la chorégraphie, le dessin, l'installation, le film, le *design*, l'écriture et même l'architecture – dans les espaces « vrais » d'une maison particulière et d'un musée ainsi que dans des espaces de représentation comme une scène, une salle de projection et une galerie d'exposition – fait en effet intervenir de nombreux médiums et genres, floutant ainsi les catégories artistiques établies. Le lecteur se souviendra qu'au début de cet essai, le duo d'artistes décrivait *Panorama* comme « un hybride entre un film de danse et un essai cinématographique[30] », une description précise de son statut indéterminé et de sa multiplicité identifiable. Ce type d'hybridation, présente dans *toute* la production artistique de Gerard & Kelly au-delà de *Panorama*, se rapproche également de l'affirmation d'Owens selon laquelle l'allégorie manque généralement de respect pour la distinction entre le visuel et le verbal. L'allégorie propose une réciprocité entre les mots et les images – « les mots sont souvent traités comme des phénomènes purement visuels, tandis que les images visuelles sont proposées comme des écrits à déchiffrer ». À cet égard, l'allégorie est « pictogrammaticale » selon Owens, comme un hiéroglyphe ou un rébus[31]. Comme déjà démontré, le travail de Gerard & Kelly fait également intervenir le langage des hiéroglyphes et des rébus. Mais avec l'intégration de la chorégraphie et de la danse comme éléments centraux ou moteur de leur travail, les mots et les images et leur réciprocité sont conjugués dans le registre du geste et du mouvement dans leur art, fusionnant et se dissolvant dans le temps.

Cette qualité transitoire et éphémère de l'art de Gerard & Kelly confirme un autre aspect de l'allégorie mis en évidence par Owens : un penchant pour la pratique *in situ* par laquelle les œuvres sont calibrées en réponse aux conditions existantes de réalisation ou de présentation, et sont donc « impermanentes, installées dans des lieux particuliers pour une durée limitée, leur impermanence fournissant la mesure de leur qualité circonstancielle[32] ». Certes, à l'époque à laquelle Owens écrivait, en 1980, la notion d'*in situ* n'était pas encore complètement développée[33]. Il n'est donc pas surprenant qu'il ait mis en avant l'ancrage *physique* d'une œuvre dans son site comme une qualité déterminante et qu'il ait jugé l'œuvre de Robert Smithson, *Spiral Jetty* (1970) en particulier, comme exemplaire. Le critique a déclaré : « L'œuvre spécifique au site aspire souvent à une monumentalité préhistorique ; Stonehenge et les lignes de Nazca sont considérées comme des prototypes. Son " contenu " est souvent mythique. » Et l'œuvre « semble s'être fondue physiquement dans son cadre, intégrée à l'endroit où nous la rencontrons[34]. » Il faut noter que même dans ce qui se lit comme une conceptualisation dépassée et limitée de la spécificité du site, Owens a toujours reconnu que la relation entre l'œuvre et son site devait être comprise comme *dialectique*. Selon Owens, l'œuvre de Smithson au Grand Lac Salé invite à une « *lecture* du site, non seulement en termes des spécificités topographiques, mais aussi de ses résonances psychologiques. L'œuvre et le site s'inscrivent donc dans une relation dialectique[35]. » C'est-à-dire que la *Spiral Jetty* est aussi un palimpseste. Selon Owens, ce terrassement canonique, en tant que lecture allégorique du site, une inscription dans ses nombreuses couches d'inscriptions sédimentées, est dans le même temps le doublement dialectique du site[36].

L'intérêt pour *l'in situ* en tant que modèle exemplaire d'une œuvre allégorique contemporaine a conduit Owens à affirmer de manière révélatrice que ces œuvres, en devenant un emblème de la fugacité et de la qualité éphémère de *tous* les phénomènes, est le « memento mori du XXe siècle[37] ». Cette affirmation fait suite à une déclaration antérieure : « L'allégorie est constamment attirée par le fragmentaire, l'imparfait, l'incomplet – une affinité qui trouve son expression la plus complète dans la ruine, que [Walter] Benjamin identifiait comme l'emblème allégorique par excellence. Ici, les œuvres de l'homme sont réabsorbées par le paysage ; les ruines représentent donc l'histoire comme un processus irréversible de dissolution et de décomposition, une distanciation progressive des origines[38]. » En effet, Owens postulait que les ruines, en tant que rappels non seulement du passé mais aussi du passage de toutes choses identifiées comme de l'entropie dans le cas de Smithson, avait nourri l'*in situ*, et non l'inverse. Pour un allégoriste, la ruine est attrayante non seulement en raison de ses qualités de fragment imparfait et incomplet, mais aussi parce que ces qualités témoignent d'un sens particulier du temps et de l'histoire, tous deux conçus comme allant inévitablement vers la décomposition, la désintégration et la perte. « L'allégorie émane de la volonté de préserver les traces de quelque chose qui est mort ou sur le point de mourir[39]. » Pour approfondir ce sens du temps qui s'impose à l'allégoriste (comme en témoigne sa fascination pour les ruines), Owens insistait sur l'analyse des écrits de Charles Baudelaire sur la modernité par Benjamin, récupérant le célèbre écrivain de la vie moderne comme défenseur de l'allégorie. Tout en reconnaissant « le transitoire, le fugace, le contingent » comme caractéristiques saillantes de son présent moderne, Baudelaire voyait aussi dans l'agitation de son Paris son déclin et sa disparition futurs. Il comprenait l'avenir comme un passé perdu, une ruine du présent, tout comme les cités antiques de Grèce et de Rome disparues n'étaient plus disponibles au poète[40]. Owens soutenait que pour Baudelaire et d'autres, cet intérêt pour les ruines était associé à une sensibilité exacerbée à la disparition et à l'inaccessibilité du présent dans/pour l'avenir, reflétant cette tendance temporelle particulière de l'allégorie à se tourner vers l'avenir tout en faisant face au passé[41].

Compte tenu de tout ce qui a été évoqué jusqu'ici, il n'est peut-être pas surprenant de découvrir que la ruine est également un concept générateur essentiel pour Gerard & Kelly, même si le sens qu'ils accordent à ce terme peut être nuancé par rapport à celui trouvé dans les œuvres de Baudelaire, Benjamin, Smithson et Owens[42]. Le duo d'artistes a plus d'une fois déclaré l'importance de la ruine pour sa qualité heuristique dans leur approche de bon nombre de leurs projets. Ils ont notamment déclaré concernant *Panorama* :

> Le [« Panorama du Commerce »] se détache du reste du bâtiment comme une relique, hostile à la simplicité d'Ando. Il est en décalage avec les aspirations de notre société contemporaine, multiculturelle et cosmopolite. C'est une ruine qui murmure depuis un autre monde, à travers le gouffre du temps, pour partager une vision de l'histoire dont les effets violents sont encore présents dans les perceptions contemporaines que nous avons de nous-mêmes et des autres.[43]

En caractérisant le « Panorama du Commerce » de relique et de ruine, les artistes soulignent la désuétude des conventions picturales académique de cette composition. Cette peinture murale conventionnelle et archaïque représente, aussi, une éthique politico-économico-nationaliste qui a porté le capitalisme industriel euro-occidental et ses entreprises colonialistes et impérialistes partout dans le monde. Tous deux semblent être dépassés aujourd'hui, rendus caducs, anachroniques, ou pour reprendre les mots des artistes, « en décalage avec les aspirations de notre société contemporaine, multiculturelle et cosmopolite ». Mais dire que le « Panorama du Commerce » et ce qu'il représente est une ruine ne revient pas à dire qu'il n'est pas pertinent ou révélateur de notre époque. Comme le reconnaissent les artistes, certains des rêves futurs figés dans le « Panorama du Commerce » ne sont pas complètement morts. Ils poursuivent leur existence en tant que ruines. Et dans la mesure où elles fournissent littéralement la preuve d'un lien avec le passé, bien que de manière incomplète et fragmentaire, les ruines offrent également l'opportunité de réinventer les futurs passés et les passés futurs, c'est-à-dire notre temps. Ce qu'Owens considérait comme le socle théorique de l'œuvre de Baudelaire – « l'amalgame du passé et du présent[44] » – et, ainsi que je l'ai décrit plus tôt, cette interpénétration du passé et du présent, est également figé dans les ruines ; ce qui offre ce que Gerard & Kelly ont décrit comme une chance de « réfléchir au passé tout en réinventant le monde au temps présent ».

• • •

Étonnamment, le duo a également qualifié des bâtiments modernes, beaucoup plus récents que la Bourse de Commerce, de ruines. Contrairement au site de *Panorama*, ils sont de petites structures, des maisons privées, conçues à l'origine pour être habitées par un nombre limité de personnes. Quoique d'échelle et de taille beaucoup plus réduites que celles de la Bourse de Commerce, chaque bâtiment n'en reste cependant pas moins monumental dans sa stature d'édifice canonique du modernisme architectural du XXe siècle. Mais ces bâtiments modernes, destinés à abriter des vies nouvellement émancipées et libérées qui allaient redéfinir la domesticité, la famille, l'intimité et la vie privée, sont toutes maintenant des maisons vides, ouvertes au public telles des reliques historiques, ce que les artistes appellent des « ruines du modernisme[45] ». La Schindler House conçue par Rudolf M. Schindler à West Hollywood en Californie, États-Unis (1922), la Villa Savoye de Le Corbusier à Poissy en France (1931), la Glass House dessinée par Philip Johnson à New Caanan dans le Connecticut aux États-Unis (1949), et la Farnsworth House réalisée par Mies van der Rohe à Plano dans l'Illinois aux États-Unis (1951) ont chacune servi d'espace pour des mises en scène de spectacles de danse *in situ* écrites et chorégraphiées par Gerard & Kelly. Ces performances ont continué à évoluer (et évolue toujours) au-delà des événements à proprement dit en films/vidéos, en sculptures, en performances, en installations et en expositions. Elles composent leur série *Modern Living*, débutée en 2016.[46]

Tels des archéologues confrontés aux vestiges insaisissables d'une civilisation révolue, Gerard & Kelly ont abordé ces célèbres demeures à la fois pour récupérer des aspects de leurs histoires perdues et pour rechercher des indices pouvant ouvrir des voies possibles à la « réinvention du monde au temps présent ». Comprenant l'architecture comme une autre forme de chorégraphie, les artistes ont activé les structures-carcasses de ces bâtiments avec des corps vivants pour exhumer les souvenirs et les rêves ainsi que les identités et les relations auxquels les concepteurs de ces maisons aspiraient ou sont parvenus à réaliser. À la Schindler House, avec son plan en forme de roue conçu à l'origine pour loger deux couples de jeunes mariés, les artistes ont montré l'ambition cachée de parvenir à un modèle de vie communautaire qui contourne l'idéologie du couple et de la famille hétéronormatifs[47]. La maison non seulement brise la division entre intérieur et extérieur avec des murs coulissants ; elle rejette également la convention d'espaces destinés à des fonctions déterminées, des pièces exclusivement dédiées à manger, à cuisiner, à dormir, se rassembler, avoir des relations sexuelles, lire, jouer, travailler, etc. Offrant la possibilité d'espaces ouverts, partagés et combinatoires, Schindler et son épouse, la compositrice Pauline Gibling, ont imaginé des relations ouvertes, partagées et combinatoires entre les habitants[48]. Dans la Glass House, Gerard & Kelly se sont inspirés du jeu architectural intelligent de Johnson autour de la notion de « secret de polichinelle », explorant comment l'incroyable exposition visuelle offerte par la transparence complète du prisme rectangulaire fonctionne paradoxalement pour dévier et occulter les vues. L'architecture ici révèle *et* « enferme » simultanément la vie à l'intérieur, manifestant à la fois le désir de voir et d'être vu et celui, tout aussi fort, de rester indétectable et invisible. Le traitement architectural de ce désir apparemment contradictoire en tant qu'attribut fondamental de la Glass House est particulièrement significatif étant donné qu'il protégeait l'identité homosexuelle de Johnson et sa relation à long terme avec son compagnon de vie, le conservateur David Whitney. La confusion délibérée entre transparence et opacité de la maison a permis de cacher à la vue de tous la vie quotidienne et l'intimité d'un couple homosexuel à une époque où cela était considéré comme déviant et criminel.[49]

L'installation vidéo à deux canaux de Gerard & Kelly intitulée *Schindler/Glass* de 2017 constelle ces deux bâtiments en une paire avec des segments des films des spectacles de danse dans les deux maisons présentées sur deux murs autoportants qui paraissent parfois ne faire qu'un en fonction du déplacement du spectateur à travers l'espace d'exposition. Disposés côte-à-côte mais séparés ces deux murs font de la projection du film un faux diptyque. Il s'agit d'une traduction sculpturale de la ligne conceptuelle de cette œuvre et de la série *Modern Living* en général, portant dans l'espace physique de la salle l'interrogation sur la notion de « couple », le duo banal, la plus petite unité identitaire au-delà du soi individuel. C'est-à-dire que *Schindler/Glass* va au-delà des histoires originales des deux maisons en tant que maisons d'architectes spécifiques conçues pour des couples spécifiques d'architectes-artistes. L'œuvre présente, d'une part les caractéristiques uniques des deux bâtiments qui déterminent une vision et un mouvement, soulignant comment leur architecture (ré)ordonne les interactions et les relations ainsi que les fantasmes et les désirs, finalement une cartographie de modèles alternatifs de vie privée, de vie domestique et d'intimité. Et d'autre part, *Schindler/Glass* extrapole et met en évidence des modèles divergents de collectivité et de socialité – au-delà du couple, la famille, une communauté, voire éventuellement une société et une nation – qui sont également inscrits dans la forme et l'histoire de ces structures datées.

La Schindler House et la Glass House sont toutes deux des adaptations des idéaux modernistes européens du début du XXe siècle pour une nouvelle façon de construire et de vivre (et par extension, de façonner la société), transplantée et réalisée sur le sol nord-américain, l'une sur la côte ouest sous le soleil de Los Angeles, qui au début des années 1920 était loin de la métropole urbaine qu'elle est devenue aujourd'hui, et l'autre sur la côte est dans une agréable petite ville de banlieue blanche qui n'a pas vraiment changé aujourd'hui. Dans ces contextes contrastés, les deux maisons, construites à près de vingt ans d'intervalle, offrent des visions (utopiques) contrastées de la cohabitation et des rencontres humaines. Dans la partie Glass House du couplage *Schindler/Glass*, qui vient en premier et compte pour près de la moitié du film, la chorégraphie de Gerard & Kelly introduit séquentiellement trois couples distincts – ils pourraient être frères ou sœurs ou amants – chacun se déplaçant par duos chorégraphiques tout en égrenant un ensemble de chiffres. ... *trois, quatre, trois, quatre, cinq, cinq, cinq, cinq... dix, dix, onze, onze, onze, onze, onze, douze,...*[50] Ce comptage à l'ouverture du film pourrait être un jeu, comme les enfants qui suivent leurs propres règles de jeu mystérieuses et singulières. Mais compter, c'est aussi marquer le temps et marquer les pas, une méthode d'apprentissage, de répétition et de mémorisation des mouvements par rapport au temps, une activité particulièrement familière aux danseurs[51]. Cette comptabilité vocalisée du temps accompagne les interactions internes des trois couples, soulignant ainsi leur synchronicité (unicité) à certains moments et leur déconnexion (séparation) à d'autres. Ce comptage se termine finalement avec la déclaration d'« Infinité » prononcée par l'un des danseurs. Puis le son et l'image se tournent radicalement vers la présence d'un nouveau groupe de personnes à l'intérieur de la Glass House, des hommes et des femmes tous vêtus des mêmes costumes noirs, alignés en grille et exécutant des mouvements identiques. Leur chant d'un air semblable à un hymne est bientôt rattrapé par ce qui pourrait être le son de lourdes bottes sur le sol, le rythme métronomique de pas faisant écho à la mathématique rythmique de l'architecture modulaire de Johnson. Et alors que la caméra s'éloigne de cette scène de rassemblement quasi militaire apparait une vue de la Glass House disparaissant dans l'obscurité, s'effaçant dans ses propres reflets dans un décor chaud de soleil couchant.[52]

Superposée à l'image fondue de la Glass House, la Schindler House apparaît progressivement, en particulier sa cheminée extérieure dont le feu étincelle dans la nuit. La maison s'éveille aux sons de carillons et de gongs qui vibrent dans l'air, annonçant un appel matinal organique et quelque peu primal (contrairement aux rythmes électroniques et aux paysages sonores qui enveloppaient précédemment la Glass House)[53]. La plupart des danseurs vus à la Glass House réapparaissent ici, cette fois répartis individuellement en des points déterminés partout dans et autour de la maison. La caméra est active, cadrant deux ou trois danseurs à la fois pour accentuer le cadre architectural de Schindler dans lequel ils se retrouvent, tout en rivalisant avec cette même architecture, traversant les murs et les fenêtres pour créer des coordonnées visuelles et spatiales cinématographiques alternatives entre les interprètes. Ce segment d'ouverture est un hommage rendu par Gerard & Kelly à *Roof Piece* (1971) de Trisha Brown[54] et à ses neuf danseurs imitant chacun à tour de rôle de courtes séquences de mouvements interprétées par un autre danseur à distance. La réactivation de la chorégraphie simple de Brown à la Schindler House, un doublage allégorique d'un texte antérieur au sens d'Owens, démontre sous une forme très condensée et abstraite le processus fondamental de transmission de la connaissance. L'imitation est une méthode d'apprentissage fondamentale pour les enfants comme pour les danseurs, et c'est aussi une forme de connexion et de communication, autant dire un relais d'une personne à une autre[55]. Observer et répéter est aussi, bien sûr, un mode de reproduction qui résonne profondément à la fois en termes biologiques et idéologiques dans le contexte du questionnement permanent de Gerard & Kelly sur le couple.

Les couples et le comptage vus à la Glass House se retrouvent à la Schindler House, avec cependant une plus grande diversité de couplages et de regroupements des artistes ici, et une plus grande fluidité de mouvement entre les espaces intérieurs et extérieurs. Il y a en fait une décomposition générale des frontières dans les scènes suivantes, avec une multiplicité de relations établies entre les danseurs – ils s'embrassent, résistent, rejettent, giflent, imitent, tiennent, tirent, s'allongent, suivent, sautent et se soutiennent mutuellement par paires ou en groupes qui changent continuellement. Leurs mouvements canalisent la multiplicité sans fin des possibilités d'habitation offertes par les différents espaces de la maison. Manifestant un sens ludique exubérant et même une forme d'infantilisme par moments, les danseurs finissent par se transformer en un troupeau sauvage sur la pelouse. De là, ils déclarent de manière hostile : « La famille est un système de régénération ». La déclaration est ambiguë dans ce qu'elle peut être comprise comme une critique de la structure familiale conventionnelle (qui est un appareil de reproduction idéologique des valeurs sociales normatives) et en même temps un appel à la régénération des familles d'un type différent, telle que celle que nous voyons à l'écran. Puis le troupeau s'effondre, les danseurs s'écroulent comme si la vie avait soudain été aspirée hors de leur corps. La scène évoque une mort collective d'innocents, résonnant avec le sombre sous-entendu de la comptine *Ring Around the Rosie* (« et nous tombons tous »)[56] et les dramatiques carnages fréquemment rapportés dans la presse de fusillades de masse ou de guerres. Ces références ne sont pas si éloignées des corps apathiques de ces danseurs sur le sol de la Schindler House.

Mais ce n'est pas la fin, et le mouvement reprend à nouveau. Lentement, la caméra suit le réveil des danseurs, capturant la régénération de la vie. Dans la séquence finale du film, Gerard & Kelly rendent hommage à une autre pionnière de la danse, Simone Forti, et à son extraordinaire construction de danse de 1961, *Huddle*[57]. Floutant la séparation entre soi et les autres, les danseurs glissent langoureusement au-dessus, autour et au-dessous les uns des autres, l'indépendance de leurs membres et de leurs corps se perdant dans l'unité de l'ensemble. Ce mouvement de blottissement est comme un flux fondu, et le gros plan intime de son informité évolutive donne même l'impression que la caméra fait partie du processus. Il faut noter que cette régénération ne s'élève pas. Son énergie ne cherche pas à atteindre le ciel. Elle se déplace latéralement, restant proche de la terre, immergée dans son propre processus de constant renouvellement à mesure que l'image se fond en noir.

En ce sens, *Schindler/Glass* propose deux visions modernes très différentes d'un corps collectif, deux modèles différents d'être ensemble et séparé à une échelle qui dépasse celle du couple. Si la séquence de la Glass House se termine par le spectre d'une armée fasciste, avec des individus préservant leur singularité dans un champ de similitude régularisée, on trouve à la Schindler House un empilement enchevêtré de corps qui tend vers l'effacement de la frontière entre soi et l'autre. Dans ce dernier, il y a un débordement extatique du soi, presque une convergence orgiaque et anarchique des corps et des désirs qui fait écho à la contre-culture hippie émergée dans les années 1960 que le cliché associe généralement à la Californie. Dans la précédente partie, en revanche, règnent la maitrise et la discipline des corps qui offrent une esthétique décomplexée de l'hyper-rationalité et de l'ordre qui produit sa propre forme de plaisir érotique. Qu'elle soit ou non réductible à l'opposition classique entre les impulsions apolloniennes et dionysiaques, la constellation dyadique de Gerard & Kelly de la Glass House et de la Schindler House dans *Schindler/Glass* semble concevoir les deux sites comme un couple dialectiquement lié, ensemble et séparé, faisant écho aux ruines de l'héritage esthétique et politique complexe du modernisme.

Ces explorations du couple et de l'allégorie comme modes d'investigation se sont poursuivies dans les performances de Gerard & Kelly à la Farnsworth House (2017) et à la Villa Savoye (2019), toutes deux intégrées à leur série *Modern Living*. À la Farnsworth House, l'architecture est interrogée à travers l'analyse de la relation du couple architecte-cliente – Mies van der Rohe et Edith Farnsworth – révélant comment la perfection immaculée de l'architecture du bâtiment et sa rhétorique libératrice ont échoué à répondre aux besoins domestiques et aux réalités d'une cliente pourtant très progressiste. Invoquant la présence du Dr Farnsworth à travers la voix et le mouvement, Gerard & Kelly mettent en lumière la politique de genre enracinée et répressive qui anime cette maison et son inscription ultérieure dans l'Histoire en tant que monument de l'architecture de style International. Contrairement à *Schindler/Glass*, dont les performances de danse se sont traduites en une installation cinématographique, le programme pour deux danseurs à la Farnsworth House a lui donné lieu à des sculptures de grande taille. *Untitled (for Edith)* et *Skin and Bones* (2018) reprennent dans la matière des aspects de la Farnsworth House et de son histoire en tant que constructions palimpsestes[58]. De même, la soirée de performance à la Villa Savoye ne s'est pas directement développée en film. Ici, sur le site d'un autre monument de l'architecture de style International, Gerard & Kelly orchestrent la réunion de l'architecte franco-suisse Le Corbusier et de la chanteuse et danseuse afro-américaine Joséphine Baker, permettant à leurs interprètes de traduire les écrits et les concepts de l'architecte en mouvements et les chansons et les danses de la chanteuse en relations spatiales[59]. Le fait historique de la liaison entre Le Corbusier et Baker est porté au-delà de la performance in situ à la Villa Savoye et sert de fil rouge au dernier film de Gerard & Kelly, *Bright Hours* (2022). Installés à la Cité Radieuse à Marseille, la plus connue et la plus célèbre des Unités d'habitation de Le Corbusier, le duo évoque cette rencontre amoureuse entre un homme européen blanc et une femme américaine noire sur un bateau de croisière en 1929 et réfléchit à son impact non seulement sur le couple, chacun portant en soi le fardeau de sa propre histoire et de ses désirs, mais aussi sur les formes innovantes du bâtiment et ses aspirations utopiques.

La trajectoire de l'œuvre de Gerard & Kelly au cours de la dernière décennie depuis les nombreuses machinations de la série *Modern Living* jusqu'aux films plus récents *Panorama* et *Bright Hours* affirme l'engagement constant des artistes dans l'exploration des interstices entre danse, architecture et cinéma par la création d'œuvres combinatoires, « hybrides entre film de danse et essai cinématographique », qui s'attardent résolument sur les formes, les idées et les existences passées pour réinventer le présent et l'avenir. Comme le montre cet essai, cependant, les notions de passé, de présent et de futur ne sont pas des catégories séquentielles strictes pour Gerard & Kelly. Tout comme ne le sont pas le soi ou l'autre. Reconnaissant les contraires comme dialectiques et nourrissant leur réciprocité et leur interpénétration, les artistes méprisent les catégories existantes pour générer une multiplicité de voix, de temps, d'identités et de significations dans et par leurs œuvres. Mais la multiplicité en soi ne suffit pas. Il ne peut s'agir d'une valeur positive automatique, puisqu'elle peut tout aussi bien générer une grande confusion. Avec l'utilisation du terme « constellation » dans le titre et en différents points de cet essai, je veux différencier la méthode de Gerard & Kelly visant à cartographier des affinités, des associations et des paires dialectiques d'une simple juxtaposition ou d'une accumulation paresseuse comme nous le voyons trop souvent dans l'art contemporain aujourd'hui. La spécificité de ce qui est constellé et la précision avec laquelle la constellation prend forme importent, et cette précision et cette spécificité sont ce qui compte véritablement dans la production de nouveaux sens viables. Parler de l'art de Gerard & Kelly comme autant de constellations allégoriques, c'est aussi constater que leurs travaux fonctionnent comme un ensemble de vecteurs auxquels est incorporé un sens du mouvement. Et en tant que telles, en tant que constellations, leurs œuvres n'ont pas de centre. Leur art est sans intérieur, comme les étoiles dans le ciel.

• • •

Dans la dernière partie de *Panorama*, le son du tonnerre et de la pluie annonce ce qui pourrait constituer une fin, ou un nouveau départ. Peut-être est-ce la tempête que Mémoire avait pressentie. Rappelant la séquence d'ouverture du film, la caméra descend lentement du plafond de verre de la Bourse de Commerce pour retrouver, cette fois, Avenir au milieu de la rotonde, seul. Écrasé par l'architecture grandiose, il danse tout seul en effectuant des cercles dans l'espace sous le dôme. La musique du piano délicatement obsédante et lunatique de Julius Eastman rivalise avec les bruits de la tempête et s'entend avec plus ou moins d'intensité entre les coups de tonnerre. Miraculeusement, il pleut à l'intérieur du bâtiment. La caméra suit Avenir qui regarde vers le haut, sa tête tournée vers le plafond de verre et la source de pluie. Les gouttes d'eau se font ruisseaux, aspergent son visage tandis que la danse se poursuit au gré des retours du piano rythmique d'Eastman, insistants cette fois, comme pour propulser le mouvement d'Avenir vers l'avant. La caméra est maintenant beaucoup plus proche et danse avec Avenir, attrapant au vol des plans furtifs de son visage, de son torse, de ses bras, de ses mains et de ses épaules, dont certains sont troublés par la buée sur l'objectif. Puis le noir complet, et le piano d'Eastman devient plus fort et plus ascendant, voire urgent. Le visage mouillé d'Avenir réapparaît très brièvement. Plus de danse. Il confronte le regard du spectateur. Son expression est mystérieuse, pas tout à fait vide mais pas non plus inexpressive. Y a-t-il du chagrin dans ces yeux, dans cette contenance ? Est-ce de l'inquiétude ? De la colère ? De la résignation ? De l'anticipation ? De la peur ? De la détermination ? De l'incertitude ? De l'épuisement ? Avenir disparaît, sans réponse ; et la musique d'Eastman continue de surgir, de tourner, de chercher, tandis que se déroule le générique final.

La fin de *Panorama* est une ambiguïté dérangeante. Elle n'exprime pas le sens festif ou énergisant du nouveau départ qui attend la Bourse de Commerce en tant que musée d'art contemporain. Peut-être parce que nous ne savons que trop bien que l'art n'est pas l'antithèse du commerce. Ils seront peut-être encore nombreux à persister à croire, ou à vouloir croire, que l'art occupe un domaine supérieur, non contaminé par l'argent et le mercantilisme, mais il n'y a pas de véritable séparation entre la circulation et l'accumulation du capital financier et celles du capital symbolique aujourd'hui. L'art est devenu (ou a toujours été) un instrument très sophistiqué d'échange commercial, même s'il continue d'offrir d'autres choses comme la beauté, l'élévation spirituelle et intellectuelle. Un musée au XXIe siècle ne peut donc pas être considéré comme une zone étrangère au marché puisqu'il s'agit également d'une place de marché, quand bien même d'un autre genre, engagé dans des formes et des modes d'échanges de marchandises particulièrement abstraits et spécialisés. Il n'y aura pas à proprement parler de commerce de l'art à la Bourse de Commerce, mais on peut soutenir que l'ouverture de la collection Pinault sur ce site historique représente moins le déplacement du commerce par l'art que l'expansion des devises qui traversent ses salles – du blé et du maïs d'hier à l'art contemporain aujourd'hui. Comme Avenir, et peut-être aussi Gerard & Kelly, nous attendons ce qui est à venir ici avec appréhension et optimisme.

1.
Craig Owens, « The Allegorical Impulse: Toward a Theory of Postmodernism », *October* 102 (printemps 1980), p. 84. Owens soutient cette affirmation en rapport avec la théorie de l'allégorie de Walter Benjamin telle qu'exposée par ce denier dans *Origine du drame baroque allemand* (1928). Il écrit : « L'ouvrage sur la tragédie baroque met ainsi en relief le caractère essentiellement allégorique de toute l'œuvre de Benjamin - le projet du *Livre des passages*, par exemple, où le paysage urbain devait être traité comme une sédimentation profonde de couches de sens qui seraient progressivement mises au jour. Pour Benjamin, l'*inter*prétation est un dés*inter*nement ». En mettant l'accent sur « *inter* » dans ces deux mots, le critique veut insister ici sur le sens du préfixe « entre », qui est au cœur de la compréhension de l'œuvre de Benjamin en général et de sa théorie de l'allégorie en particulier. La théorisation de l'allégorie par Owens sera abordée en détail dans cet essai dans son rapport au travail de Gerard & Kelly. (N.d.T.) Ce texte a été récemment publié en France dans une traduction de Gaëtan Thomas. Les traductions présentées ici diffèrent quelque peu de cette version et ont été conservées dans le but de préserver l'utilisation des citations faites par l'auteure. Voir Craig Owens, « La pulsion allégorique : vers une théorie du postmodernisme (première partie) », 1980, dans Craig Owens, *Le discours des autres*, tr. fr. Gaëtan Thomas, Même pas l'hiver, Paris, 2022, p. 6586.

2.
Gerard & Kelly, « Notes sur *Panorama* » (dossier d'artiste inédit, 23 octobre 2021), p. 3.
3.
Ces rôles sont respectivement interprétés par Soa de Muse, Guillaume Diop et Germain Louvet.
4.
D'abord construit pour Catherine de Médicis sous le nom Hôtel de Soisson au XVIe siècle, sa forme, son propos et son nom plus récents datent de 1889, année de l'Exposition Universelle au cours de laquelle la Bourse de Commerce a été présentée, comme la tour Eiffel, pour illustrer les progrès de la modernité française. https://www.architecturaldigest.com/story/architect-tadao-ando-transformed-paris-bourse-de-commerce.
5.
La Bourse de Commerce est le quatrième projet majeur de rénovation/refonte architecturale commandé par François Pinault et réalisé par Tadao Ando. Les trois projets précédents sont tous situés à Venise en Italie : la rénovation du Palazzo Grassi (2006), la transformation du bâtiment de la Douane de mer (Punta de la Dogana) datant du XVe siècle en musée d'art contemporain (2009), et la réhabilitation du petit théâtre (Teatrino) du Palazzo Grassi (2013). Tous jugés très réussis, ces projets urbains à grande échelle visant à ressusciter de vieux bâtiments et des espaces désaffectés illustrent le partenariat extrêmement productif entre Pinault et Ando et témoignent de l'engagement profond et de long terme de Pinault pour l'art contemporain et l'architecture.
6.
Le nom composé de l'institution constitue une déclaration de mariage entre l'État et un simple citoyen comme fondement de cette nouvelle entreprise. Pourtant, la page d'accueil du site internet de la Bourse de Commerce – Pinault Collection expose clairement le propos de cet espace, soit une vitrine pour « exposer les collections d'un collectionneur passionné et engagé ». Il faut noter que l'identité graphique de la nouvelle institution telle qu'elle est présentée sur son site internet, et probablement dans d'autres documents de communication, inscrit « Pinault Collection » en caractères gras, et un traitement graphique comparativement plus faible de « Bourse de Commerce », ce qui souligne l'importance plus grande de l'une dans le présent, tandis que l'autre s'efface dans l'histoire. Voir https://www.pinaultcollection.com/en/boursedecommerce/publics/welcome.
7.
La structure métallique actuelle de la coupole remonte à 1811, date à laquelle François-Joseph Bélanger et François Brunet remplacèrent le vieux dôme en bois par une coupole en fer et en cuivre. Cette dernière a été classée monument historique en 1986. Voir https://www.pop.culture.gouv.fr/notice/merimee/PA00085784.
8.
Gerard & Kelly, « Notes on *Panorama* », p. 4. Sur l'ouverture retardée de la Bourse de Commerce – Pinault Collection en raison du deuxième « confinement » imposé en France pendant la pandémie de Covid, voir https://www.connaissancedesarts.com/arts-expositions/report-de-louverture-de-la-bourse-de-commerce-pinault-collection-11137591/.
9.
La peinture murale a été restaurée une première fois en 1995 et certaines sections ont reçu un deuxième traitement de restauration en 2010-13 à la suite d'un incendie. Pour un compte rendu plus détaillé des travaux de restauration du panorama, voir https://www.pinaultcollection.com/en/boursedecommerce/restoration-panorama-du-commerce.
10.
Aujourd'hui souvent associé au cinéma, le terme « panorama », du grec « tout » + « vue », a été inventé par Robert Barker, un peintre anglo-irlandais qui breveta un support visuel à 360 degrés sous l'intitulé « Appareil pour exposer des images » en 1787. Ses peintures de Londres et d'Édimbourg attirèrent un large public en tant que divertissements de masse au XVIIIe siècle. Offrant une expérience panoptique immersive d'un paysage, les vues globales proposées par les panoramas sont comparables à celle dont on a pu profiter depuis le haut du World Trade Center dans le centre de Manhattan, que Michel de Certeau a analysé dans son texte, *L'invention du quotidien* (1980). Selon de Certeau, une telle vision renforce la sensation de pouvoir et de domination du regardant sur le paysage, la topographie, les incidents historiques, et même sur les personnes présentes dans l'image/vue. En tant que tel, le panorama est une forme de visualisation cohérente avec un regard colonialiste ou impérialiste dont on doit l'introduction en France à l'inventeur américain Robert Fulton. Pour une étude approfondie de l'histoire du panorama, en particulier en Angleterre, France et Allemagne, voir Stephan Oettermann, *The Panorama: History of a Mass Medium*, trad. Deborah Lucas Schneider (New York, Zone Books, 1997).
11.
Selon Alix Laveau, conservatrice à la Direction des Musées de France, « Le panorama est l'œuvre non pas d'un, mais de cinq artistes, d'où le manque de cohérence souligné par certains articles de presse. Quatre d'entre eux ont traité du commerce dans une partie du monde : Évariste-Vital Luminais a représenté l'Amérique et Désiré-François Laugée, la Russie et le Nord. L'Asie et l'Afrique ont été confiées à Georges-Victor Clairin, et, pour clore le panorama, l'Europe à Marie-Felix Hippolyte-Lucas. Entre chacune de ces quatre scènes, Alexis-Joseph Mazerolle, qui supervise l'ensemble, a réalisé dans la direction des quatre points cardinaux des allégories des continents et régions peintes par les autres artistes. Ainsi, l'Europe est-elle symbolisée par les arts et l'architecture, l'Afrique par le lion et la chasse, l'Orient et l'Asie par le narguilé et les éléphants ; le Grand Nord, enfin, par l'ours polaire. C'est donc à un voyage au long court qu'invite cette composition riche en détails. » La peinture murale est parfois appelée fresque, mais il est important de corriger cette erreur terminologique pour bien comprendre le sens de cette œuvre en termes formels, matériels et par rapport à l'histoire de l'art. Le panorama était en fait composé de lés de toiles peintes par les différents artistes hors site, puis recoupés et raccordés avant d'être fixés sur place au mur par les artistes selon la technique du marouflage, qui emploie du plomb blanc comme adhésif. Voir Guillaume Picon, entretien avec Alix Laveau, « Restauration du *panorama du commerce* », *Collection Pinault*, 11 janvier 2021, URL : https://www.pinaultcollection.com/fr/boursedecommerce/restauration-du-panorama-du-commerce.
12.
Cette brève séquence chorégraphique rappelle *Composition 1960 #10 (pour Bob Morris)* de La Monte Young, une partition basée sur un texte, « dessiner une ligne droite et la suivre. » L'adaptation la plus connue de cette partition est celle de Nam June Paik au concert Fluxus de 1962 à Wiesbaden en Allemagne, dans laquelle l'artiste trempa différentes parties de son corps, y compris sa tête, dans un récipient d'encre et dessina des lignes sur de longues feuilles de papier.
13.
(N.d.T.) *Un léopard / Une carrière / Un chef indien protège son visage / Deux enfants autochtones se tiennent la main / Maman... / Maman ?* [passe du français à l'anglais au créole]. *Deux esclaves portent un arbre / Le train / La lance / Des tonnes de coton / Des hectares de blé / Un arc et une flèche / Un navire dans les nuages / Colomb dans un cumulus castellanus / Colomb dans mon anus. A la vache ... / Des vaches, des cow-boys, un taureau / Un blanc barbu à son bureau* [puis, comme si elle se corrigeait...] */ hum. Un comptable caucasien... Je crois. La mousse recouvre des pierres / Un bateau à vapeur / Un phare / Une usine au loin... crache du jaune / Un pont / Des chevaux, des chevaux / Un singe, deux singes / Le chapeau de Napoléon. Le drapeau français / Un panier en osier / Un Chinois vend de la soie jaune / Geisha, geisha, geisha / Deux Michelangelo tatoués tirent un canoë / Le drapeau américain...* [se met à chanter « God Bless America »] */ Un cul de chérubin. Et le nom du peintre gravé dans la roche. E. Luminais*
14.
Gerard & Kelly, *Panorama*, 2021, Vidéo 4K couleur, son, 22 min., 04:45-06:28. Mémoire parle en français et en créole tout au long du film avec ponctuellement quelques mots en anglais lancés de manière stratégique.
15.
D'une certaine manière, Mémoire ressemble à ce que Walter Benjamin voyait dans l'*Angelus Novus* (1920) de Paul Klee, un petit monotype acquis par le philosophe en 1921. D'après Benjamin : « Une œuvre de Klee intitulée *Angelus Novus* montre un ange qui semble sur le point de s'éloigner de quelque chose qu'il contemple fixement. Ses yeux sont écarquillés, sa bouche est ouverte, ses ailes sont déployées. Tel doit être l'ange de l'Histoire. Son visage est tourné vers le passé. Là où nous percevons une série d'événements, il ne voit qu'une seule catastrophe dont les ruines s'empilent les unes sur les autres et sont projetées à ses pieds. L'ange voudrait rester, réveiller les morts et reconstituer ce qui a été brisé. Mais une tempête souffle du Paradis ; elle s'est prise dans ses ailes avec une telle violence que l'ange ne peut plus les refermer. La tempête le propulse irrésistiblement vers le futur auquel il tourne le dos tandis que les débris devant lui s'accumulent vers le ciel. Cette tempête est ce que nous appelons le progrès. » Walter Benjamin, « Theses on the Philosophy of History » (1940), *Illuminations*, trad. Harry Zohn (New York : Schocken Books, 1969), p. 249.
16.
Leslie Camhi, « The Bourse de Commerce – Pinault Collection, A Museum 20 years in the Making, Prepares for Its Grand Opening », *Vogue*, 20 mai 2021, https://www.vogue.com/article/bourse-de-commerce-pinault-collection-opens.
17.
Martin Bethenod, l'ancien directeur de la fondation de la Bourse de Commerce – Pinault Collection explique : « Ce moment de la réouverture de la Bourse [en 1889] coïncidait avec les débuts du

capitalisme et de la mondialisation, et sous un jour moins positif, à une période de grand colonialisme. » Il concède que le musée ne peut faire abstraction de ce fait historique. Cité dans Camhi, « La Bourse de Commerce – Pinault Collection ».

18.
Gerard & Kelly, *Panorama*, 07:05-08:15. Au début de cette séquence, Mémoire et Allégorie se déplacent et parlent tandis qu'Avenir les suit comme en écho, une ombre, imitant leurs gestes et leurs mots avec un léger décalage. Dès qu'Avenir rattrape son retard et se synchronise, tous trois évoluent et parlent à l'unisson, puis Mémoire se retire, laissant Avenir mener avec Allégorie à ses côtés.

19.
Gerard & Kelly, « Notes on *Panorama* », p. 2. Il faut noter que les artistes ne disent pas « réinventer le monde dans le présent ». L'ajout du mot « temps » – « réinventer le monde dans le *temps* présent » — évite le sentiment d'un arrêt complet dans le présent et préserve active et continue l'œuvre de réinvention pour (ré)imaginer sans arrêt le présent.

20.
Tadao Ando, « To France, the Country of Culture and Art », *Archilovers*, 13 février 2019, https://www.archilovers.com/projects/245021/bourse-de-commerce-pinault-collection.html#info.

21.
Voir Tadao Ando, cité par Camhi, « La Bourse de Commerce ».

22.
Parfois, cela comprend un sens primordial du temps avant l'histoire. Lorsque le projet d'Ando est une nouvelle construction plutôt que la rénovation d'un bâtiment historique, comme dans le cas présent, le sens du passé qui domine semble moins lié à l'histoire et plus à la nature, quelque chose de plus primitif ou primal. Son projet architectural à Naoshima au Japon, par exemple, rentre dans cette catégorie. Voir Miwon Kwon, « A Position Elsewhere: Lessons from Naoshima » in *Naoshima: Nature, Art, Architecture*, éd. Kayo Tokuda (Naoshima, Japon et Ostfildern, Allemagne: Benesse Holdings Inc., Fondation du musée d'art Naoshima Fukutake et Hatje Cantz Verlag, 2010).

23.
À l'époque de la réalisation du « Panorama du Commerce », l'esclavage est légalement aboli en France (1848) et aux États-Unis (1865), quoique toujours pratiqué dans la réalité. Mais compte tenu du fait que cette peinture murale n'est pas strictement une peinture historique représentant des évènements ou des personnages spécifiques, les figures représentées dans cette scène comme dans le reste du panorama sont allégoriques et servent d'emblèmes.

24.
La référence la plus évidente ici est le travail de la théoricienne du cinéma féministe Laura Mulvey et en particulier son essai très influent « Visual Pleasure and Narrative Cinema », publié en 1975 dans la revue britannique *Screen*. Son analyse de la construction cinématique du regard et de sa relation avec l'organisation du pouvoir entre masculin et féminin, regardant et regardé, avec relations et sans relations, sujet et objet, possessif et possédé, etc. a eu un impact majeur sur le développement non seulement de la théorie du cinéma, mais aussi sur celui des études féministes, de l'histoire de l'art et des études culturelles dans les années 1980 et au-delà.

25.
Owens, « The Allegorical Impulse », p. 69. L'accentuation de « lu à travers » est dans l'original.

26.
Owens, « The Allegorical Impulse », p. 68.

27.
Owens, « The Allegorical Impulse », p. 69.

28.
Selon Owens, « L'histoire de la peinture moderniste débute avec Manet et non avec Courbet, qui persista à peindre de « vraies allégories ». Même les plus favorables des contemporains de Courbet (Proudhon et Champfleury) restaient perplexes face à son penchant pour l'allégorie ; on était un réaliste *ou* un allégoriste, insistaient-ils, signifiant ainsi que l'on était soit moderniste, soit historiciste. [...] De sorte que lorsque Courbet tenta de sauver l'allégorie pour la modernité, la ligne qui les séparait avait été clairement tracée, et l'allégorie, conçue comme antithétique au credo moderniste *Il faut être de son temps*, fut condamnée, tout comme la peinture historique, à une existence historique purement marginale. », Owens, « The Allegorical impulse », p. 76-77.

29.
Owens, « The Allegorical Impulse », p. 75.

30.
Pour l'auteur de cet essai, le terme « hybride » ne semble pas tout à fait juste pour décrire le travail de Gerard & Kelly puisque les artistes semblent conserver un sentiment de multiplicité (des catégories) plutôt que de réaliser une nouvelle synthèse dans leur pratique. *Panorama* est une accumulation de danse, *et* d'un film, *et* d'un essai ; pas nécessairement leur fusion.

31.
Owens, « The Allegorical Impulse », p. 74-75.

32.
Owens, « The Allegorical Impulse », p. 71.

33.
Avec Douglas Crimp, Owens est l'un des principaux penseurs qui très tôt ont affirmé les termes d'*in situ* [*site specific*] comme pratique postmoderne. Un autre texte important à ce sujet est celui de Rosalind Krauss, « Sculpture in the Expanded Field », *Octobre* 8 (printemps 1979) : 30-44. (N.d.T.) Voir Rosalind Krauss, *L'origine de l'avant-garde et autres mythes modernistes*, tr. fr. Jean-Pierre Criqui, Macula, Paris, 1993. Sur le développement et l'élaboration de l'art *in situ* dans les années 1990, voir Miwon Kwon, *One Place After Another: Site-specific Art and Locational Identity* (Cambridge, MA : MIT Press, 2002).

34.
Owens, « The Allegorical Impulse », p. 71.

35.
Owens « The Allegorical Impulse », p. 71. La théorisation par Smithson du *site/non-site* s'accorde avec cette compréhension de la relation entre l'œuvre et le site comme dialectique. Owens conclut son essai par un retour à Smithson et au texte important de l'artiste, « A Sedimentation of the Mind » (1968).

36.
L'opération de doublement dans *Spiral Jetty* est en fait multiple : en tant que travail de terrassement, *Spiral Jetty* reproduit le site sous une nouvelle forme sculpturale ; elle est aussi répliquée dans un double filmique (aussi appelé *Spiral Jetty*) ainsi que dans un texte (intitulé *Spiral Jetty*). Le monde visuel et le monde verbal convergent décidément dans l'art de Smithson.

37.
Owens, « The Allegorical Impulse », p. 71.

38.
Owens, « The Allegorical Impulse », p. 70.

39.
Owens, « The Allegorical Impulse », p. 78.

40.
À l'image de Walter Benjamin, Owens soutenait que Baudelaire souhaitait protéger ou revendiquer l'allégorie pour la modernité. Le critique souligna que les principaux écrits du poète sont fondés sur « un socle théorique d'une fusion entre présent et passé », une idée dont il a été établi qu'elle est au cœur du travail de Gerard & Kelly. Owens poursuit en disant que pour Baudelaire la modernité se définit comme « le transitoire, le fugace, le contingent » mais ceci n'est que « la moitié de l'art [moderne], l'autre étant l'éternel et l'immuable ». Owens poursuit : « Si l'artiste moderne a été exhorté à se concentrer sur l'éphémère, c'était bien pour sa qualité intrinsèque, c'est-à-dire par crainte d'une disparition sans trace. Baudelaire concevait l'art moderne au moins en partie comme le sauvetage de la modernité pour l'éternité ». Selon Owens, Walter Benjamin reconnaissait cette dimension allégorique de la pensée de Baudelaire et estimait qu'elle faisait écho à l'immense étude de Maxime Du Camp de la vie quotidienne de Paris, *Paris ses organes, ses fonctions et sa vie dans la seconde moitié du XIX*e *siècle* (1869-1875). Incidemment, Du Camp est mieux connu aujourd'hui pour ses photographies de voyages en Afrique, au Moyen-Orient et en Orient, dont beaucoup sont des images de ruines. Pour plus de détails sur les subtilités de l'argumentation d'Owens sur Baudelaire, voir Owens, « The Allegorical Impulse », p. 77-78.

41.
Voir note 15 sur la figuration de cette tendance chez Paul Klee dans son *Angelus Novus* (1920), selon l'interprétation qui en est faite par Walter Benjamin.

42.
Cette sensibilité aux ruines dont Owens traite dans son essai peut ne pas être parfaitement en phase avec l'usage qu'en font Gerard & Kelly, puisque le critique affirmait que la volonté de préserver les traces de quelque chose de mort ou de mourant constituait une caractéristique essentielle de l'allégorie. Ainsi, l'intérêt de Gerard & Kelly pour les ruines n'est-il pas motivé par la préservation. Il ne reflète pas un désir fétichiste de figer les vestiges du passé de manière à les voir exister en spécimens morts pour le présent et l'avenir. En d'autres termes, leur engagement avec les ruines n'est pas motivé par l'éthos de celui ou celle qui préserve ou conserve un art du passé conceptuellement maintenu comme une entité distante, séparée et à distance du présent. Il peut également différer de la forme de fascination pour les ruines qui alimente le modèle allégorique posé par Owens.

43.
Gerard & Kelly, « Notes on *Panorama* », p. 4.

44.
Owens, « The Allegorical Impulse », p. 77.

45.
La notion de « ruines du modernisme » apparaît dans plusieurs écrits inédits et programmes dans les archives de Gerard & Kelly. Elle apparaît également dans une série de documents de communication autour de la série *Modern Living*. Voir par exemple https://pioneerworks.org/exhibitions/gerard-kelly et https://www.gsd.harvard.edu/event/gerard-and-kelly-on-modern-living/.
46.
Selon les artistes, la série est structurée en chapitres et se poursuit. Les projets achevés dans les quatre bâtiments mentionnés constituent les quatre premiers chapitres de *Modern Living*. Un cinquième chapitre est prévu pour la Villa E-1027 conçue par Eileen Gray (1929) à Roquebrune-Cap-Martin en France.
47.
Depuis 1994, la Schindler House abrite le Centre MAK pour l'art et l'architecture, une organisation artistique à but non lucratif et un satellite du Musée des arts appliqués de Vienne. Pour toute information générale sur l'histoire et les programmes du centre, voir https://www.makcenter.org/.
48.
Pour un résumé incisif de l'histoire de la Schindler House et de la performance de Gerard & Kelly produite dans ses murs en 2016, voir Mimi Cheng : « Modern Lives, Modern Loves: Gerard & Kelly's *Schindler/Glass* », in *Avery Revue* 33 (septembre 2018), http://averyreview.com/issues/33/modern-lives-modern-loves.
49.
Il convient de rappeler que la Glass House a été conçue et construite vingt ans avant la rébellion de Stonewall avant que ne s'opère un appel plus large en faveur des droits civils des homosexuels. Elle a aussi été conçue et construite en même temps que la Brick House – les deux structures ayant été élaborées comme une seule composition. Les deux bâtiments ne sont pas seulement situés l'un à proximité de l'autre sur la même propriété de vingt hectares, ils sont aussi reliés par une cour verdoyante. Si la Glass House est toute lumière et transparence, à tel point qu'elle semble parfois disparaître dans le paysage, la Brick House n'est qu'enceinte et confinement, avec une présence obstinée. On pourrait soutenir que les deux bâtiments fonctionnent comme un miroir l'un de l'autre, une expérimentation sur la coordination des opposés ainsi que, peut-être, un essai architectural sur le couple. Au sujet de la relation entre l'identité homosexuelle de Johnson et l'interprétation de la Glass House en tant qu'espace queer, voir https://theglasshouse.org/whats-on/the-glass-house-as-queer-space/.
50.
Gerard & Kelly, *Schindler/Glass*, 2017, Vidéo HD, deux canaux, couleur, son, 35 min., 00:24-01:15.
51.
D'autres œuvres performatives de Gerard & Kelly, telles que *Timelining* (2014) et *Clockwork* (2018), impliquent aussi des interprètes marquant vocalement le temps par le comptage comme structure pour générer et séquencer le mouvement. Les danseurs deviennent leurs propres horloges, intégrant des fragments de leur propres souvenirs personnels comme base matérielle de leurs performances. Certains aspects de *Timelining* et de *Clockwork* du même genre peuvent se retrouver dans des séquences de *Schindler/Glass*. En outre, et bien que d'une manière non explicite, les œuvres de Félix González-Torres, surtout celles qui manifestent le passage simultané du temps et des corps, ainsi que ses profondes réflexions sur le couple, parfaitement figurés par les horloges jumelles mourantes de *Untitled (Perfect Lovers)* (1991), par exemple, sont des références essentielles dans la pratique de Gerard & Kelly. La richesse de ce rapport devra attendre l'occasion d'une réflexion approfondie qui pourra faire l'objet d'un tout autre essai.
52.
Une partie de la chorégraphie de ce dernier segment à la Glass House incorpore le fantôme d'un salut nazi, invoquant l'implication controversée de Philip Johnson dans le nazisme dans ses jeunes années, ce qui a hanté sa carrière par ailleurs célébrée d'architecte. La musique aux airs d'hymne que les danseurs fredonnent à l'unisson est également liée à cette histoire. Selon Gerard & Kelly, cet hymne est leur transcription pour voix du troisième mouvement de la Symphonie en trois mouvements d'Igor Stravinsky (achevée en 1945 et créée en 1946 par l'Orchestre philharmonique de New York), à propos de laquelle le compositeur confia qu'elle lui avait été inspirée par ses souvenirs de soldats allemands marchant au pas de l'oie. Fait intéressant, George Balanchine a chorégraphié un ballet sur cette composition en 1972 pour le New York City Ballet, dont la résidence est un autre bâtiment conçu par Johnson, le New York State Theater (renommé en 2008 David H. Koch Theater) et où Ryan Kelly s'est produit lorsqu'il était membre de la compagnie au début des années 2000. Ancré profondément dans la réflexion critique de Gerard & Kelly autour du propos politique de Johnson dans *Schindler/Glass* se trouve un hommage subtil à sa conception architecturale pour le New York State Theater, qui place la Glass House dans une constellation différente mais connexe d'histoires personnelles et publiques. (Ryan Kelly, courriel à l'auteure, 30 août 2022).
53.
La compositrice pour la partie Glass House de *Schindler/Glass* est la regrettée productrice de musique SOPHIE. La bande son de la partie Schindler House du film est assurée par le duo de musiciens expérimentaux Lucky Dragons, basé à Los Angeles.
54.
Trisha Brown est à juste titre considérée comme une figure exemplaire des expérimentations artistiques multidisciplinaires ou intermédia de l'après-guerre. Plus récemment, de nombreux chercheurs dans le domaine de l'histoire de l'art ont commencé à accorder une plus grande attention à son importante contribution au développement de l'art contemporain (au-delà de la danse). En sortant la danse de la scène et du théâtre pour l'entrainer sur le terrain urbain du centre-ville de Manhattan, *Roof Piece* (1971) présentait les danseurs sur différents toits de lofts dans et autour des rues Wooster et Lafayette à SoHo ; chaque danseur imitait le mouvement d'un autre danseur sur un autre toit. L'œuvre a été reprise ces dernières années sur les toits de différentes villes. Pour une réflexion sur les questions soulevées par la reconstitution de cette œuvre spécifique au site, voir l'essai d'Amanda Jane Graham, « Out of Site: Trisha Brown's 'Roof Piece' », in *Danse Chronicle*, vol. 36, no 1 (2013) : p. 56-76. Il est important de noter que si les récentes reprises de cette œuvre tentent d'en affirmer l'authenticité et l'originalité en tant qu'œuvre d'art singulière créée par une autrice, Trisha Brown, l'hommage/imitation de Gerard & Kelly à la Schindler House opère plutôt un doublage et une dispersion allégoriques de celle-ci.
55.
Ce relais et ce processus de transmission, qui comprend non seulement l'observation et l'imitation mais aussi l'écoute et la réplication, structure une œuvre antérieure de Gerard & Kelly intitulée *Reusable Parts/Endless Love* (2011).
56.
(N.d.T.) *Ring Around the Rosie* est une comptine anglo-saxonne qui accompagne une ronde dans laquelle les enfants tombent au sol après avoir tourné en rond en se tenant par la main. Elle ferait référence à l'épidémie de peste bubonique qui s'est abattue sur la Grande Bretagne au XVIIe siècle, entraînant la mort de millions de personnes « tombées » sous l'effet des fortes fièvres.
57.
Comme Trisha Brown, Simone Forti est une figure centrale de l'art d'après-guerre, du minimalisme en particulier, dont l'influence et les contributions restent peu reconnues et insuffisamment étudiées. Son statut de danseuse et chorégraphe et son penchant pour le travail à contre-courant de la danse et de l'art de son temps ainsi que du marché l'ont mise en marge de l'histoire de l'art (qui continue d'être allergique à ce qu'elle juge comme « théâtral »). Fort heureusement, des recherches sont entreprises par la jeune génération, en particulier celles de Megan Metcalf sur Forti qui sont particulièrement précieuses. Voir « Making the Museum Dance: *Huddle* de Simone Forti (1961) and its Acquisition by the Museum of Modern Art », in *Dance Chronicle*, Vol. 45 (2022), p. 30-56.
58.
Pour une description détaillée de ce travail en relation avec l'histoire et l'historiographie de la Farnsworth House ainsi que du processus de travail de Gerard & Kelly dans la création de l'œuvre, voir Nora Wendl, « I remember: On Modern Living », in *Ventriquolism, Performance and Contemporary Art*, éds Jennie Hirsch et Isabelle Loring Wallace (Abingdon, RU ; New York, NY : Routledge, à paraître).
59.
La performance à la Villa Savoye était inscrite au programme du Festival d'Automne à Paris et fut présentée au public les 28 et 29 septembre et les 5 et 6 octobre 2019. D'après le programme de l'événement, « L'œuvre évoque la rencontre entre l'architecte [Le Corbusier] et l'interprète américaine Joséphine Baker qui eut lieu lors d'un voyage transatlantique en 1929 au moment où il concevait la maison. ». Voir aussi https://www.festival-automne.com/en/edition-2019/gerard-kelly-modern-living.

Là où la subjectivité vacille

Lou Forster en conversation avec Gerard & Kelly

Réalisé le 20 janvier 2021 et le 18 mai 2022, chez l'auteur à Paris et dans le studio de Gerard & Kelly à Aubervilliers, France, cet entretien aborde la conception de l'exposition *Ruines* et les œuvres qui la compose. La discussion se développe sur fond d'une expérience partagée puisque l'auteur a également interprété leur performance *Timelining* au côté de la danseuse et chorégraphe Lenio Kaklea de 2014 à 2017. Une place significative est donc accordée au rôle que les artistes donnent à leur collaboration avec des interprètes, et la manière dont leurs œuvres (performances ou films) exposent le récit d'une expérience de vie.

Lou Forster
Comment avez-vous abordé l'exposition à Carré d'Art ? S'agit-il d'une rétrospective de votre travail initié il y a bientôt 20 ans ?
Ryan Kelly
Lorsque nous sommes arrivés à Nîmes, j'ai été impressionné par ce site post-moderne qui rassemble sur la même place ce temple romain qu'est la Maison Carrée, vieille de deux mille ans, et Carré d'Art, cette « *glass box* » de l'architecte Norman Foster, vieille de trente ans. C'est une vue déconcertante, parce que l'architecture du musée est à la fois un palimpseste et une ruine. J'ai l'impression que pour penser l'exposition, nous revenons sans cesse à cette vue qui me fait penser à ce que Craig Owens et Douglas Crimp ont écrit sur le musée[1]. De ce fait, les archives, l'histoire, les formes abstraites, la temporalité, le récit sont autant de sujets qui flottent sur l'exposition.
Brennan Gerard
Je ne dirais pas qu'il s'agit d'une rétrospective, mais d'un aperçu de notre travail sur un peu plus d'une décennie. L'exposition explore des enjeux de relations et d'intimité à travers la sculpture, le film et l'installation. Quant à notre pratique performative, elle se trouve repoussée à la toute fin de l'exposition. Bien que composée d'œuvres autonomes, il s'agit bel et bien d'une exposition *in situ*. Qu'est-ce que ce site conçu par Norman Foster ? Une architecture fidèle au canon moderniste dans laquelle l'utilisation du verre est dominante. Notre projet pour ce musée est lié à ce site de manière discursive, mais aussi phénoménologique. La première chose que les visiteurs et les visiteuses verront en montant les escaliers, c'est l'installation *Relay* (2018), une œuvre en vinyle multicolore appliqué sur les fenêtres au dernier étage de Carré d'Art, d'où l'on aperçoit la vieille ville. Cette œuvre change constamment à cause de la lumière qui passe à travers, elle possède une dimension performative. Elle est la trace d'une pièce réalisée en 2016 dans le cadre du projet *Modern Living*. Neuf danseurs transmettaient un message gestuel à travers une architecture et un site. L'ordre des couleurs est celui des costumes monochromes que portaient les danseurs et les danseuses. *Relay* est le diagramme en mouvement de cette pièce qui s'avère, finalement, plus proche de la performance qu'aucune documentation ne pourrait jamais l'être.

Modern Living

LF
Le projet *Modern Living* a été développé en deux phases. De 2016 à 2018, vous avez travaillé aux États-Unis dans trois maisons emblématiques d'architectes modernistes, la Schindler House (1922) de Rudolf Schindler et les deux Glass Houses de Philip Johnson et Ludwig Mies van der Rohe, construites respectivement en 1949 et 1951. Depuis 2018, votre activité s'est déplacée en France, où vous vous êtes intéressé à plusieurs habitations de Le Corbusier, son Appartement-Atelier à Paris (1934), la Villa Savoye à Poissy (1931), et la Cité Radieuse à Marseille (1952). Pourriez-vous parler de la genèse de ce projet ?
BG
Il me semble que *Modern Living* est une extension de nos projets précédents, *Timelining* (2014) et *Reusable Parts/ Endless Love* (2011), dans lesquels nous traitions de la question du couple. Aborder la maison était une suite logique. Cela correspondait à un moment où nous étions nous-mêmes à la recherche d'un lieu où habiter. Nous avons réalisé à quel point l'architecture était structurée de manière hétéronormative et ne pouvait accueillir la manière dont nous vivons et travaillons ensemble. C'est à peu près à ce moment-là que nous avons découvert la Schindler House à Los Angeles. Elle avait été construite au cours des années 1920 pour deux jeunes couples qui avaient décidé de vivre dans ce qui s'apparentait à une commune. Chaque membre y possédait un espace propre où il ou elle travaillait, tandis que les tâches domestiques étaient réparties de manière égalitaire. Cette manière de vivre qui résonnait si fortement avec nos propres aspirations nous a poussés à nous intéresser à d'autres maisons, et d'autres expérimentations modernistes où les architectes cherchent des réponses formelles (les murs en verre, le plan libre) pour rendre possible nos relations les plus intimes.
RK
Le *design* de l'espace influence notre manière de vivre avec les autres. Dans des espaces proto-*queer* comme la Schindler House la reproduction n'est plus au centre de l'espace domestique, et la relation entre l'intérieur et l'extérieur se trouve redessinée. À partir des années 1990, les études *queers* se sont principalement intéressées à l'espace public : boîtes de nuit, bars gays, rues, docks, toilettes publiques, etc. Mais l'espace domestique se trouvait décrit, le plus souvent, de manière négative comme un placard[2]. Il nous a semblé que des formes moins normatives de sexualité transforment aussi la maison, et qu'il fallait revendiquer l'espace

domestique comme un lieu de production de subjectivités *queers*, et tracer une généalogie de ces autres manières d'habiter.

LF

Bien que vous ayez recours à une variété de médiums (films, sculptures, performances), le principal outil d'investigation pour *Modern Living* est la danse, en particulier, une partition intitulée « *Clock* » qui vous permet de produire des matériaux chorégraphiques qui croisent l'appréhension de l'espace et du temps. Qu'est-ce que cette « Montre » [*clock*]? Et en quoi permet-elle d'enquêter sur la manière dont ces architectes pensent l'espace domestique ?

RK

Au moment où nous commencions *Modern Living*, nous utilisions une partition que nous appelions une « Montre » pour travailler quotidiennement dans le studio. Elle associe des gestes à la position des chiffres sur le cadran d'une horloge (12 devant vous, 6 derrière, etc.). Le changement d'appui produit ainsi une oscillation régulière du corps qui devient la signature temporelle de chaque performeur. Si je devais définir ce qu'est une « Montre », je dirais que c'est « une machine à habiter », un véhicule pour voyager dans le temps, une manière d'organiser le temps et l'espace, de manipuler le vide et la banalité du studio, de danser dans l'espace restreint de l'habitat domestique, une manière d'induire du mouvement, une interface rythmique entre soi et les autres. En travaillant dans la Schindler House, nous avons dû créer rapidement des matériaux chorégraphiques adaptés à l'échelle de ces pièces pour les danseurs du L.A Dance Project. Cet outil s'est alors imposé à nous.

BG

Le performer ou la performeuse qui interprète une « Montre » associe des souvenirs personnels aux heures de la journée. Ce processus de remémoration a une dimension analytique, il met en jeu ou en représentation la formation du sujet qui l'énonce et qui danse : d'où je viens, quels sont les évènements qui m'ont construit. Cette tâche impose d'être présent ici et maintenant, ce que rendent difficile au quotidien les dispositifs de télécommunication qui traversent l'espace domestique. Une partie du film *Schindler/ Glass* (2017) repose sur les matériaux chorégraphiques créés à travers ce processus.

RK

À partir de 2018, ce qui était une pratique de studio est devenue une performance autonome intitulée *Clockwork*. Cette pièce repose sur une partition, elle est réitérable, vendue en édition limitée, et peut se passer de nous pour exister. Elle a été formalisée lors de l'exposition éponyme à Pioneer Works, New York, en 2018.

BG

Une des influences importantes pour *Clockwork* est la pièce de Félix González-Torres, *Untitled (Perfect Lovers)* (1991). Deux horloges identiques qui, au cours du temps, se désynchronisent. Elle schématise un type de relation, et fonctionne comme un protocole : vous pouvez acheter ces horloges n'importe où. Cela nous intéressait d'importer cette manière de travailler dans le champ de la performance.

RK

Clockwork et *Timelining*, une autre performance protocolaire, ont été développées à la même époque, entre 2010 et 2013, quand nous étions en troisième cycle à l'Université de Californie, Los Angeles. Une première esquisse de ces pièces est un objet étrange intitulé *Recto Verso*, dans lequel nous dessinions des cercles au sol. On en trouve encore quelques traces sur internet. Il s'agissait d'une forme rudimentaire de « Montre » qui donne, bien plus tard en 2018, *Clockwork*. Il nous a presque fallu une dizaine d'années pour métaboliser ce qui était une pratique de studio et en faire une œuvre.

BG

Il est très compliqué de créer un outil chorégraphique qui permet de générer des mouvements qui ne soient ni expressionnistes, ni dépendants de votre état d'esprit du moment, ni liés à des compétences ou des techniques particulières. Cette recherche correspond à une période durant laquelle nous avons travaillé avec Simone Forti, et une génération d'artistes qui créaient des outils pour générer des œuvres à partir de leurs corps et de l'espace. Mais cet héritage de Simone Forti, Yvonne Rainer ou Yoko Ono, n'est pas seulement formel, il correspond aussi à une manière de vivre. Par exemple, les *Dance Constructions* (1961) de Forti étaient performées dans le loft dans lequel Ono habitait. Cette interpénétration du public et du privé était constitutive de leur manière de faire. En regard des années 1960, je pense que notre contribution consiste à montrer en quoi ces intersections propres à certaines pratiques chorégraphiques sont un lieu où se produisent des subjectivités *queers*.

LF

Modern Living vous a donné l'opportunité de réaliser votre premier film *Schindler/Glass*. Pourriez-vous revenir sur cette articulation avec la performance *live* ?

RK

Il est très rapidement devenu évident que les évènements que nous réalisions dans ces maisons d'architectes étaient uniques. Ils ne pourraient, probablement, pas être refaits ailleurs ni transposés. L'installation permet de faire circuler ces pièces, au moins, à un certain niveau. Nous n'avons jamais été intéressés par la documentation, même pour d'autres projets. Il nous a donc semblé intéressant de faire se rejoindre deux lieux, la Schindler House et la Glass House, dans l'espace virtuel du film.

BG

Nous avons d'abord envisagé des installations multicanaux qui reproduiraient l'expérience du *live*, mais comme nous avions déjà réalisé les performances, il nous a semblé plus intéressant d'explorer l'espace filmique.

Vers la fiction

LF

En termes de genre, *Schindler/Glass* se trouve à l'intersection du film d'architecture et du film de danse. Avec *Bright Hours* (2022), vous créez une fiction, la relation amoureuse de Le Corbusier et de Joséphine Baker, dont on ne connaît pas les détails bien qu'elle ait été partiellement attestée.

RK

Cette évolution me semble liée aux matériaux avec lesquels nous travaillons. Notre décision d'écrire une fiction n'est pas motivée par une fidélité à un genre, mais par l'espace discursif dans lequel nous nous plaçons. Sur les questions des constructions raciales et coloniales, nous nous trouvons du côté des privilégiés, ce qui n'était pas le cas pour la sexualité. Nous avons donc besoin d'une forme de polyphonie que seul le récit semble pouvoir nous donner. Par ailleurs, l'histoire que nous racontons, la rencontre de Joséphine Baker et de Le Corbusier, a été très peu documentée[3]. On se trouve donc contraint de devoir combler ces lacunes. Qu'est-ce qui se serait passé si Le Corbusier et Joséphine Baker avaient eu une relation amoureuse lors de leur traversée de l'Atlantique ? Que cette aventure eût transformé la vision qu'avait Le Corbusier de l'architecture ? Qu'elle permît de comprendre que Joséphine Baker est l'une des architectes de la modernité ? Et que cette fiction fasse des danseuses, des artistes populaires, des femmes et des personnes de couleur, des actrices à part entière de l'histoire de l'art. Ce récit spéculatif propose une vision plurielle de la modernité. La thèse sous-jacente est que Joséphine Baker est une moderniste. Si l'on prend ce paradigme qu'est la mécanisation, le corps dansant particulier de Joséphine Baker peut être qualifié de machine à danser [*dancing machine*]. Baker coupe et juxtapose les matériaux chorégraphiques d'une manière artificielle, comme dans le montage d'un film. Elle danse un peu de Martha Graham, place à côté son interprétation d'une danse afro-caribéenne, de la danse jazz et une bribe de cabaret parisien. Elle travaille comme Picasso avec le collage. C'est à travers cette manière de danser et de chorégraphier que nous avons commencé à considérer Baker comme une moderniste. C'est également comme cela que nous avons travaillé avec Emara Neymour-Jackson qui interprète ce rôle.

BG

Au cours du tournage avec Emara et Jeanne Balibar qui interprète Le Corbusier, nous avons compris à quel point jouer ou danser pour la caméra est un processus mécanique. Vous avez des marques, vos déplacements sont millimétrés, chaque mouvement de tête est capturé. Le plateau de tournage est une machine qui se met en marche, le défi consistant alors à retrouver cette image subjective qui échappe au contrôle de l'acteur et du réalisateur. Il faut que quelque chose se passe au moment du tournage, à un niveau conscient ou inconscient.

LF

Dans *Bright Hours,* vous associez la rencontre de Le Corbusier et de Baker à une transformation de son approche architecturale. Si dans les années 1920, il est un adapte de la chaux vive, il développe à partir de 1931 une architecture polychrome. *Bright Hours* suggère que la découverte de la couleur s'opère à travers la rencontre avec Baker et qu'elle n'est pas uniquement un enjeu architectural.

RK

Nous sommes en mesure de faire cette spéculation grâce à un tournant opéré dans le champ de la critique culturelle au cours des dix dernières années. Le tabou que constituait l'intimité a été dépassé, ce qui permet une compréhension renouvelée des relations qui structurent la production culturelle.

Un dispositif de cadrage

LF

Dans votre travail, vous abordez l'architecture comme un dispositif de cadrage. Cette question apparaît dans *Panorama* (2021), un film qui tourne autour du « Panorama du Commerce », la peinture monumentale du bâtiment de la Bourse de Commerce, aujourd'hui Pinault Collection, réalisée entre 1886 et 1889.

BG

À travers *Bright Hours* et *Panorama,* nous essayons d'insuffler un peu de dialectique dans l'expérience de l'architecture. Aujourd'hui, les architectes travaillent essentiellement à l'ordinateur avec des images numériques. Quand nous avons enseigné à la Graduate School of Design d'Harvard, nous avons initié les étudiants et les étudiantes à des pratiques de mouvement afin qu'ils et elles puissent incorporer une certaine perception de l'espace[4]. À l'inverse, notre expérience de l'architecture de Le Corbusier nous a amenés à relativiser une partie du discours critique qui fait de ses constructions des dispositifs optiques. Je suis très sensible à la manière dont son approche est liée au corps et pensée à une échelle humaine.

RK

Une chose qui nous a impressionnés en visitant la Bourse de Commerce pour la première fois, alors que l'intervention de Tadao Ando était en cours de réalisation, c'est que le panorama est la seule œuvre permanente. Cette peinture monumentale a été restaurée à cette occasion. Ce choix est étonnant. Elle donne une représentation stéréotypée des sujets coloniaux et c'est cette histoire de la violence faite au nom d'un État raciste qui occupe une place centrale dans le musée. Ce panorama est aussi un dispositif de cadrage du bâtiment, ce qu'Ando a parfaitement compris avec son cylindre de béton. Dans le film, nous ne faisons que reprendre les repères de ce cadrage. Nous avons investi l'espace central avec le poids de sa coupole. Mais nous avons aussi utilisé l'espace périphérique dans l'ombre du dôme. C'est dans cet espace marginal que se dit sur un mode ironique quelque chose de l'ordre de la vérité : l'histoire croisée de la violence et du commerce.

BG

Le panorama de la Bourse est conçu pour mettre le voyeur au centre de l'espace. Le voyeur dit « universel » est cet homme blanc européen hétéronormatif qui possède un certain capital. Ce qui encadre ce centre, ce sont tous ces personnages représentés dans le tableau. Dans notre film, cette peinture est regardée depuis la marge. Le travail de Douglas Crimp, Craig Owens ou Mary Kelly sur ce dispositif qu'est le cadre ont structuré notre approche, même si dans le film nous le faisons avec une dose de *camp*[5]. Mais *Panorama* possède également une dimension réparatrice. Elle s'incarne à travers les trois personnages, Mémoire, Allégorie et Avenir et leurs interprètes Soa de Muse, Germain Louvet et Guillaume Diop, dont les relations ne sont pas structurées par la violence, mais par une sorte de convivialité, de plaisir, d'intimé, mais aussi de colère dirigée contre la position qui leur est assignée par le panorama. Ce film est moins un travail de critique institutionnelle qu'une critique discursive contre les institutions de l'hétéronormativité, du capitalisme et du colonialisme.

LF

Je suis heureux que vous mentionniez les interprètes, car, d'une certaine manière, le film opère un glissement entre la forme de représentation panoramique vers celle du portrait. Il pourrait être regardé comme le portrait de trois danseurs.

BG

Je pense que le portrait est une catégorie intéressante. *Lives of Performers* (1972) d'Yvonne Rainer n'est certes par une référence immédiate, mais elle fait sens pour nous dans la manière dont le sujet de Rainer est toujours d'abord l'artiste, le performer. *Panorama* consiste à créer un espace dans lequel la subjectivité de l'artiste vacille devant l'œil du spectateur ou de la spectatrice.

Dance Constructions

LF

Vous avez évoqué les *Dance Constructions* de Simone Forti. Parmi les œuvres performatives que vous avez créées, *State of* (2017-2019) se rapporte le plus directement à cette définition d'une pièce de danse agencée ou structurée par un plan incliné, un poteau, un danseur et un « costume-drapeau ».

BG

Ces références à l'histoire de l'art sont très personnelles pour nous, puisque nous avons travaillé et côtoyé Simone et Yvonne. En créant *State Of* nous n'y avons pas pensé, probablement parce qu'elles nous ont transmis des manières de faire qui sont devenues ataviques. On peut voir *State of* comme un croisement de *Trio A With Flags* (1970) de Rainer et *Slant Board* (1961) de Forti. En travaillant avec Forty Smooth, l'un des pionniers de la *pole dance* dans le métro de New York, nous avons appris qu'il existait un mouvement appelé le *flag* [drapeau] qui consiste à mettre le corps à l'horizontale. Comment un corps se place-t-il perpendiculairement à un poteau ? Cette question physique, sculpturale et chorégraphique a guidé notre travail. Et puis, évidemment, il y a eu la décision d'incorporer le drapeau américain : qui peut représenter les États-Unis, et qui est représenté par l'hymne national ?

RK

D'une manière surprenante *State of* se rapporte aussi à l'architecture spécifique de Carré d'art et de la Maison Carrée. En examinant l'histoire de ce temple romain, nous avons découvert qu'il avait fasciné Thomas Jefferson. Il a demandé à un architecte d'en faire une maquette et de l'envoyer en Amérique. Il a ensuite utilisé ce modèle pour concevoir le Capitole de l'État de Virginie à Richmond. Il n'y a que deux maisons d'État sur les cinquante que comptent les États-Unis basées sur un modèle antique. Soixante-dix ans après sa construction pendant la guerre de Sécession, elle est devenue le siège de la Confédération pendant les dernières années de la guerre. La barbarie du Sud américain et sa défense de l'institution de l'esclavage ont utilisé très consciemment cette représentation de la raison à la base des Lumières.

Lire et écrire

LF

L'écriture et la lecture jouent un rôle important dans votre pratique artistique. Vous écrivez des partitions qui, dans *Timelining* ou *Clockwork*, amènent les interprètes à produire eux-mêmes des textes. Vous écrivez les scénarios des films que vous réalisez. Vous créez aussi des sculptures comme la série des *Transcripts* (2014) qui impliquent une certaine relation à la lecture pour le visiteur.

BG

L'écriture comme le dessin sont des pratiques parallèles à celle du film et de la performance. Chaque fois que nous travaillons avec ces médiums, nous avons des contraintes de temps et d'argent. Nous devons aussi gérer cette matérialité périssable du corps et de la voix, alors que dans l'écriture, il existe une forme de liberté. L'exposition permet à ces pratiques multiples d'exister dans leurs différents états. Les *Transcripts* sont des sculptures composées de deux pièces de cuivre transcrivant en braille un fragment de nos chronologies, telles qu'elles sont énoncées dans la performance *Timelining*. Pour lire ces œuvres, il est nécessaire de s'en approcher pour les toucher. Le cuivre est un matériau qui indexe les empreintes digitales. Ainsi, chaque lecture de l'œuvre laisse une trace de lecture.

RK

Transcripts renvoie aussi à notre relation comme la source de cette exposition. Elles permettent de mesurer le temps écoulé depuis 2014. Elles inscrivent notre histoire dans l'Histoire au côté de la Schindler House, du colonialisme français, de la Maison Carrée, de la guerre civile américaine. Ce qui se trouve à l'intérieur de ces fragments, ce sont aussi des citations, des évènements publics et privés qui peuvent structurer la relation des visiteurs à l'exposition, à moi, à nous. Certains éléments des transcriptions vont correspondre à l'histoire particulière de chaque spectateur et spectatrice, et d'autres vont différer. Cette œuvre fonctionne comme une clé permettant de se positionner dans cette ruine, dans cette archive postmoderne qu'est l'exposition. Lou, tu as toi-même performé *Timelining* avec Lenio Kaklea. Quelle a été ton expérience de la pièce ?

LF

Je me souviens d'être impressionné par l'ensemble des techniques d'écriture que vous aviez partagées avec nous pour que nous produisions nos chronologies. C'est quelque chose qui a probablement à voir avec votre expérience de chorégraphes qui consiste à placer les interprètes dans un processus de production à partir d'eux-mêmes. Dans ma formation d'historien de l'art, on apprend d'abord à écrire à partir de l'extérieur ce qui n'empêche pas des formes de réflexivité. En travaillant avec vous, j'ai expérimenté le mouvement inverse.

BG

Je pense que nous essayons tous les deux d'insister sur l'écriture en tant que pratique physique et subjective. Cela nous ramène à ta première question sur l'exposition dans laquelle nous abordons le fait de lire ou de regarder comme une expérience incorporée.

1.
Voir Craig Owens, « La pulsion allégorique vers une théorie du postmodernisme (première et deuxième partie) », 1980, dans Craig Owens, *Le discours des autres*, tr. fr. Gaëtan Thomas, Même pas l'hiver, Paris, 2022 et Douglas Crimp, *On The Museum's Ruins*, MIT Press, Cambridge, 1993.

2.
Il faudrait, toutefois, mentionner quelques exceptions tels que Beatriz Colomina, *Sexuality and Space*, Princeton Architectural Press, Princeton, 1992 ; Aaron Betsky, *Building Sex: Men, Women, Architecture, and the Construction of Sexuality*, William Morrow, New York, 1995 ; Joel Sanders, *Stud: Architectures of Masculinity*, Taylor & Francis, Londres, 1996 ; Aaron Betsky, *Queer space: architecture and same-sex desire*, HarperCollins, New York, 1997 ; Paul B. Preciado, *Pornotopie : "PlayBoy" et l'invention de la sexualité multimédia*, trad. de l'espagnol par Serge Mestre et Paul B. Preciado, Paris, Climats, 2011 ; et Mario Gooden, *Dark Space: Architecture, Representation, Black Identity*, Columbia Books on Architecture and the City, Bethesda, 2016.

3.
Le récit que fait Anne Anlin Cheng de cette rencontre a été une source d'inspiration importante. Voir Anne Anlin Cheng, *Second Skin : Josephine Baker & the Modern Surface*, Oxford University Press, New York, 2010, p. 90-99.

4.
Pour un compte-rendu de cet atelier codirigé avec l'architecte Andrew James Holder, voir Vrinda Kanvinde, « The Queer Home : Combining Architecture with Movement to Speculate on the Future of Housing », Harvard University Graduate School of Desing, 20 mai 2002, URL : https://www.gsd.harvard.edu/2022/05/the-queer-home-combining-architecture-with-movement-based-practice-to-speculate-on-the-future-of-housing/ (consulté le 9 août 2022).

5.
Craig Owens traduit en anglais le texte de Jacques Derrida, « *Parergon* » in *La vérité en peinture*, Éditions Flammarion, Paris, 1978. Cette référence joue un rôle important dans le développement de sa propre réflexion sur le cadre. Voir Craig Owens, *Beyond Recognition. Representation, Power and Culture*, University of California Press, Berkeley, 1994, partielle traduit dans Craig Owens, *Le discours des autres*, op. cit. Cette réflexion influence Douglas Crimp pour son exposition *Pictures* présentée en 1977 à Artists Space, New York. Il en rend compte dans *Before Pictures*, University of Chicago Press, Chicago, 2016. Enfin, cette question est également travaillée par l'artiste Mary Kelly avec qui Gerard & Kelly étudient dans l'*Interdisciplinary Studio* de l'université de Califonie à Los Angeles. Voir le recueil de ses textes, in Mary Kelly, *Imaging Desire*, MIT Press, Cambridge, 1996.

Cover Gerard & Kelly, *Facades I*, 2022. Silkscreen on rag paper, 35.5 × 51 cm.

p. 7 Gerard & Kelly, *Modern Living*, 2017. Performance view: Farnsworth House, Plano, Illinois, with Julia Eichten. Photo: Robert Hickerson.

p. 8–9 Gerard & Kelly, *Modern Living*, 2019. Performance view: Villa Savoye, Poissy, with Matthieu Barbin, Julia Eichten, Damontae Hack, Kehari Hutchinson, Emara Neymour-Jackson, Jasmine Sugar. Photo: Martin Argyroglo.

p. 12 Gerard & Kelly, *Panorama*, 2021. 4K video, color, sound, 22 min.

p. 14 Gerard & Kelly, *Panorama*, 2021. 4K video, color, sound, 22 min. With Germain Louvet, Soa de Muse, Guillaume Diop.

p. 16 Tadao Ando, cutaway model for the Bourse de Commerce – Pinault Collection, Paris. © Tadao Ando Architect & Associates, Niney et Marca Architectes, agence Pierre-Antoine Gatier.

p. 16 Tadao Ando, view of the rotunda of Bourse de Commerce – Pinault Collection, Paris, 2021. © Tadao Ando Architect & Associates, Niney et Marca Architectes, agence Pierre-Antoine Gatier. Photo: Marc Domage.

p. 17 Évariste-Vital Luminais, detail of North America section of "Panorama du Commerce," 1889.

p. 19 Gerard & Kelly, *Panorama*, 2021. 4K video, color, sound, 22 min.

p. 21 Robert Smithson, *Spiral Jetty* (still), 1970. 16mm film, color, sound, 35 min. Distributed by Electronic Arts Intermix, New York. © 2022 Holt / Smithson Foundation and Dia Art Foundation / ADAGP, Paris.

p. 23 Gerard & Kelly, *Schindler/Glass*, 2017. HD video on two channels, color, sound, 35 min. Installation view: Seattle Art Fair, 2017, with Anthony Bryant, Nathan Makolandra.

p. 24 Gerard & Kelly, *Schindler/Glass*, 2017. HD video on two channels, color, sound, 35 min. With Lilja Ruriksdottir.

p. 25 Gerard & Kelly, *Schindler/Glass*, 2017. HD video on two channels, color, sound, 35 min. With Morgan Lugo, Anthony Bryant.

p. 26–27 Gerard & Kelly, *Schindler/Glass*, 2017. HD video on two channels, color, sound, 35 min.

p. 28 Trisha Brown, *Roof Piece*, 1973. Performance view: New York. Photo: Peter Moore. © Northwestern University. Courtesy of Paula Cooper Gallery.

p. 29 Simone Forti, *Huddle*, 1961. Performance view: Loeb Student Center, New York University, New York, May 4, 1969. Photo: Peter Moore. © Northwestern University. Courtesy of Paula Cooper Gallery.

p. 30 Gerard & Kelly, *Schindler/Glass*, 2017. HD video on two channels, color, sound, 35 min.

p. 31 Gerard & Kelly, *Bright Hours*, 2022. 4K Video, color, sound, 25 min. With Emara Neymour-Jackson, Jeanne Balibar.

p. 33 Gerard & Kelly, *Panorama*, 2021. 4K video, color, sound, 22 min. With Guillaume Diop.

p. 34–35 Gerard & Kelly, *Modern Living*, 2016. Performance view: MAK Center for Art and Architecture at the Schindler House, West Hollywood, California, with Julia Eichten, Rachelle Rafailedes.

p. 37 View of the Maison Carrée and Carré d'Art, Nîmes. Photo: Morris-Gilbert Soar.

p. 38 Gerard & Kelly, *Modern Living*, 2016. Performance view: MAK Center for Art and Architecture at the Schindler House, West Hollywood, California, with Robbie Moore, Morgan Lugo.
p. 39 Gerard & Kelly, *Score Drawing SH.3*, 2018. Silkscreen and letterpress on rag paper, 14 × 18 in.
p. 40 Gerard & Kelly, *Clockwork*, 2019. Performance view: Le Corbusier's Apartment-Studio, Paris, with Julian Eichten.
p. 42 Gerard & Kelly, *Bright Hours*, 2022. 4K Video, color, sound, 25 min. With Jeanne Balibar, Emara Neymour-Jackson.
p. 44–45 Gerard & Kelly, *Panorama*, 2021. 4K video, color, sound, 22 min. With Germain Louvet, Guillaume Diop.
p. 46 Gerard & Kelly, *Bright Hours*, 2022. 4K Video, color, sound, 25 min.
p. 47 Gerard & Kelly, *State of*, 2019. Performance view: MAAT Museum of Art, Architecture and Technology, Lisbon, with Ryan Kelly, Forty Smooth, Quenton Stuckey. Photo: Bruno Simão.
p. 48 Gerard & Kelly, *Transcript 2 (Shock and Awe in front of I met you / I met you in front of moved to NYC / moved to NYC in front of graduated college / graduated college in front of stolen election / stolen election in front of my uncle died / my uncle died in front of boyfriend's lisp / boyfriend's lisp in front of Newports // Weapons of Mass Destruction in front of I met you / I met you in front of first cigarette / first cigarette in front of Chevy Cavalier / Chevy Cavalier in front of aware of AIDS / aware of AIDS in front of Haley's Comet / Haley's Comet in front of)*, 2014. Polished copper embossed with Braille. Two parts: 95 × 22 × 1⁄16 in. each. Installation view: *Storylines: Contemporary Art at the Guggenheim*, Solomon R. Guggenheim Museum, New York, June 5–September 9, 2015. Photo: Kristopher McKay.
p. 50 Gerard & Kelly, *Modern Living*, 2016. Performance view: The Glass House, New Canaan, Connecticut, with Rachelle Rafailedes. Photo: Evan Whale.
p. 51 Gerard & Kelly, *Modern Living*, 2019. Performance view: Villa Savoye, Poissy, with Kehari Hutchinson. Photo: Martin Argyroglo.
p. 65 Glenn Ligon, *Double America*, 2012. Neon and paint, 91.4 × 340.8 cm. Courtesy of the artist; Hauser & Wirth, New York; Regen Projects, Los Angeles; Thomas Dane Gallery, London; Chantal Crousel, Paris.

Gerard & Kelly

American artists based in Paris, Gerard & Kelly (Brennan Gerard and Ryan Kelly) have collaborated for nearly two decades on performance, video, and installation, among other formats. Having collectively studied ballet, visual art, literature, and gender studies, Gerard & Kelly use conceptual strategies within art and dance to look at broader themes of memory, history, sexuality, and identity. Their questions are often set against a particular architectural space, pushing the related sociocultural and political precedents of the site into an open engagement with the artists' work.

Brennan Gerard was born in Ohio in 1978, and Ryan Kelly was born in Pennsylvania in 1979. They were Van Lier Fellows of the Whitney Museum Independent Study Program and graduated with MFAs from the Interdisciplinary Studio at the University of California, Los Angeles (UCLA) in 2013. Solo exhibitions and performances of their work have been held at MAMCO, Geneva (2020), MOCA, Los Angeles (2020), Festival d'Automne, Paris (2017 & 2019), The Getty Museum, Los Angeles (2019), Pioneer Works, New York (2018), Centre Pompidou, Paris (2017), Palais de Tokyo, Paris (2016), New Museum, New York (2015), and The Kitchen, New York (2014). Their work has been included in group exhibitions at the FRAC Franche-Comté, Besancon (2022), Chicago Architecture Biennial (2017), Solomon R. Guggenheim Museum, New York (2015), and Hammer Museum, Los Angeles (2014), among others. Their work is included in the collections of Solomon R. Guggenheim Museum, New York; Hammer Museum, Los Angeles; LACMA Los Angeles County Museum of Art; FRAC Franche-Comté, Besançon; and Carré d'Art–Musée d'art contemporain, Nîmes.

Ruins at Carré d'Art marks the duo's first museum survey exhibition.

Américains basés à Paris, Gerard & Kelly (Brennan Gerard et Ryan Kelly) collaborent depuis 2003 sur la performance, la vidéo et l'installation, entre autres formats. Ayant étudié les arts visuels, la littérature et les études de genre, Gerard et Kelly utilisent des stratégies conceptuelles dans l'art et la danse pour aborder des thèmes plus larges comme la mémoire, l'histoire, la sexualité et l'identité. Leurs reflexions s'inscrivent souvent dans un espace architectural particulier, engageant les antécédents socioculturels et politiques du site dans leur travail.

Brennan Gerard est né dans l'Ohio en 1978, et Ryan Kelly est né en Pennsylvanie en 1979. Lauréats du Whitney Museum Independent Study Program à New-York, ils sont diplômés de l'Interdisciplinary Studio de l'université de Californie à Los Angeles (UCLA). Leur travail a fait l'objet d'expositions personnelles et leurs performances ont notamment été présentées au MAMCO Genève (2020), au MOCA, Los Angeles (2020), au Festival d'Automne, Paris (2017 et 2019), au Getty Museum, Los Angeles (2019), à Pioneer Works, New York (2018), au Centre Pompidou, Paris (2017), au Palais de Tokyo, Paris (2016), au New Museum, New York (2015) et à The Kitchen, New York (2014). Ils ont également participé à des expositions collectives, notamment au FRAC Franche-Comté, Besançon (2022), à la Chicago Architecture Biennial (2017), au Solomon R. Guggenheim Museum, New York (2015), et au Hammer Museum, Los Angeles (2014). Leurs œuvres sont présentes dans les collections des musées Solomon R. Guggenheim de New York, Hammer à Los Angeles, LACMA Los Angeles County Museum of Art, FRAC Franche-Comté et Carré d'Art.

Ruines à Carré d'Art est leur première exposition personnelle dans une institution européenne.

Miwon Kwon

Miwon Kwon is Professor and The Walter Hopps Chair in Modern and Contemporary Art at University of California, Los Angeles (UCLA). Her research and writings have engaged several disciplines including contemporary art, architecture, public art, and urban studies. She is the author of *One Place After Another: Site-Specific Art and Locational Identity* (MIT Press, 2002) in addition to lengthy essays on the work of many contemporary artists, including Francis Alÿs, Michael Asher, Nairy Baghramian, Cai Guo-Qiang, Jimmie Durham, Félix González-Torres, Barbara Kruger, Christian Marclay, Ana Mendieta, Josiah McElheny, Christian Philipp Müller, Gabriel Orozco, Jorge Pardo, Oscar Tuazon, and Do Ho Suh, among others. In 2012, she co-organized a major historical exhibition entitled *Ends of the Earth: Land Art to 1974* with co-curator Philipp Kaiser, which was presented at the Museum of Contemporary Art in Los Angeles in 2012 and traveled to the Haus der Kunst in Munich. The catalogue for the exhibition (published by Prestel) received the 2013 Alfred H. Barr Jr. Award from the College Art Association for the most distinguished catalogue in the history of art, published in the English language under the auspices of a museum, library, or collection.

Miwon Kwon est professeure et titulaire de la chaire Walter Hopps d'art moderne et contemporain à l'université de Californie à Los Angeles (UCLA). Ses recherches et ses écrits ont concerné plusieurs disciplines, notamment l'art contemporain, l'architecture, l'art public et les études urbaines. Elle est l'auteure de *One Place After Another : Site-Specific Art and Locational Identity* (MIT Press, 2002) ainsi que de longs essais sur le travail de nombreux artistes contemporains, dont Francis Alÿs, Michael Asher, Nairy Baghramian, Cai Guo-Qiang, Jimmie Durham, Félix González-Torres, Barbara Kruger, Christian Marclay, Ana Mendieta, Josiah McElheny, Christian Philipp Müller, Gabriel Orozco, Jorge Pardo, Oscar Tuazon et Do Ho Suh, entre autres. En 2012, elle a co-organisé une grande exposition historique intitulée *Ends of the Earth : Land Art to 1974* avec le co-commissaire Philipp Kaiser, qui a été présentée au Museum of Contemporary Art de Los Angeles en 2012 et a voyagé jusqu'à la Haus der Kunst de Munich. Le catalogue de l'exposition (publié par Prestel) a reçu le prix Alfred H. Barr Jr. 2013 de la College Art Association pour le catalogue le plus prestigieux en histoire de l'art, publié en langue anglaise sous les auspices d'un musée, d'une bibliothèque ou d'une collection.

Lou Forster

Curator and art historian Lou Forster works at the intersection of dance, humanities and visual arts. Between 2010 and 2013, he joined the editorial board of *Art 21*. Following this first experience as an art critic, he wanted to deepen his knowledge about choreographic practices and diversify the ways to account for it. During these early years, he also developed his work as a curator. He assisted Pierre Bal-Blanc for *The Living Currency* and participated in documenta 14 as a curatorial assistant. In 2014, he began an ambitious project on the choreographer Lucinda Childs. He curated the first retrospective exhibition about her work, *Lucinda Childs, Nothing Personal (1963–1989)*, at the CND Centre national de la danse and Thaddaeus Ropac Gallery in the framework of the Festival d'Automne, Paris. He is currently writing his dissertation at the École des Hautes Études en Sciences Sociales, a historical anthropology of Childs' dance company focused on the crafts and techniques employed to embody minimalism. Parallel to his individual research, he founded abd with choreographer Lenio Kaklea in 2010 to develop projects that explore the intersection of dance, research, and critical theory.

Historien de l'art et commissaire d'exposition, Lou Forster travaille à l'intersection des sciences humaines, de la danse et des arts visuels. Entre 2010 et 2013, il participe au comité éditorial de la revue *Art 21*. Cette première expérience le pousse à approfondir sa connaissance des formes et des pratiques artistiques et à réfléchir à une variété de formats pour en rendre compte. En parallèle, il développe une pratique curatoriale. Il assiste Pierre Bal-Blanc pour *La Monnaie Vivante* et travaille pour la documenta 14 en tant qu'assistant-curateur. À partir de 2014, il lance un ambitieux projet autour de la chorégraphe Lucinda Childs qui prend la forme d'une exposition monographique, *Lucinda Childs, Nothing Personal (1963–1989)*, présenté au Centre national de la danse et à la Galerie Thaddaeus Ropac dans le cadre du Festival d'Automne à Paris. Il écrit actuellement un doctorat à l'École des Hautes Études en Sciences Sociales où il déploie une anthropologie historique de la compagnie, attentive aux techniques et aux savoir-faire permettant l'incorporation du minimalisme. Il a fondé en 2010 avec la chorégraphe Lenio Kaklea, abd, une plateforme qui développe des projets à l'intersection entre danse et théorie critique.

This book is published on the occasion of the exhibition /
Ce livre est publié à l'occasion de l'exposition

Gerard & Kelly: *Ruins*

Carré d'Art–Musée d'art contemporain
October 14, 2022–March 26, 2023 /
14 octobre 2022 - 26 mars 2023

Carré d'Art–Musée d'art contemporain
Place de la Maison Carrée
30000 Nîmes, France
+33 (0)4 66 76 35 70
info@carreartmusee.com
www.carreartmusee.com

Exhibition / Exposition

Director / Directeur
Jean-Marc Prevost

Deputy Director / Directrice-adjointe
Delphine Verrières-Gaultier

Administration / Administration
Claire Magnier

Registrar / Régie des œuvres
Béatrice Paquereau

Technical Production / Réalisation technique
Mathieu Sabatier, Patrice Higuinen

Installation Team / Équipe de montage
Sidonie Lelièvre, Mathieu Mortier, Léo Schweiger

Cultural Department / Service culturel
Fabien Garcin

Secretariat / Secretariat
Vivette Durand

Documentation / Centre de documentation
Emmanuella Stauron

Exhibition Design / Conception de l'exposition
Gerard & Kelly in collaboration with Simon de Dreuille /
Gerard & Kelly en collaboration avec Simon de Dreuille

Video Projection / Projection vidéo
A.J. Chami

Graphic Design / Graphisme
Clément Witbaut

Gerard & Kelly Studio Manager / Responsable du studio
Vincent Brou

Exhibition furniture graciously provided by /
Mobilier de l'exposition généreusement fourni par
Cassina
ClassiCon
Domus

This exhibition was made possible thanks to /
Cette exposition a été réalisée grâce à
Municipality of Nîmes / Ville de Nîmes
Région Occitanie. Pyrénées – Méditerranée
Direction régionale des Affaires Culturelles

Catalog / Catalogue

Publishing Editor / Editeur de publication
Ilaria Bombelli, Mousse

Copyediting / Suivi éditorial
Delphine Verrières-Gaultier

Translation / Traduction
Macklin Kowal, Frédérique Destribats

Graphic Design / Conception graphique
Marcello Biffi, Mousse

Special thanks / Remerciements
Danielle Berger Fortier, Tristan Pierard

Carré d'Art
Musée d'art contemporain de Nîmes

NÎMES

La Région Occitanie Pyrénées · Méditerranée

PRÉFET DE LA RÉGION OCCITANIE
Liberté
Égalité
Fraternité

Published and distributed by / Publié et distribué par
Mousse Publishing - Contrappunto s.r.l.
Via Decembrio 28
20137, Milan–Italy

First edition / Première édition
2022

Printing and Binding / Impression et façonnage
Artigiana Grafica, Italy / Italie

Available through / Disponible auprès de
Mousse Publishing, Milan
(moussemagazine.it)
DAP | Distributed Art Publishers, New York
(artbook.com)
Vice Versa Distribution, Berlin
(viceversaartbooks.com)
Les presses du réel, Dijon
(lepressesdureel.com)
Antenne Books, London / Londres
(antennebooks.com)

ISBN 978-88-6749-540-5
EUR 27 / USD 30